Harilal Gandhi

Gandhi Studies

The life and thought of Mahatma Gandhi are intertwined and inseparable. His politics was imbued with his spiritual experiments and his spirituality was tempered by his vision of a non-violent society, and his constructive work was integral to his politics. The unique practices of Gandhi, his control of palate, his fasts, his spinning, his silence and his prayers were as much a part of his politics as of his spiritual life. These practices and experiments were sustained and nurtured by the ashrams that he founded. The ashram community through its own practices affirmed, modified and validated Gandhi's ideals and practices.

Gandhi Studies aspires to examine and elucidate the relationship between life and thought, between experiment and practice, and between Gandhi and the institutions he founded and the experiments he inspired. Biographical studies of Gandhi and his associates, histories of institutions and ideas, along with translations of scholarly and memoir literature from various Indian languages would form part of this endeavour. This series is committed to no one fixed way of understanding Gandhi; it hopes like Gandhi himself to be deeply dialogic.

In the series

Harilal Gandhi: A Life, C.B. Dalal (Trans. Tridip Suhrud)
In the Tracks of the Mahatma: The Making of a Documentary, A.K. Chettiar (Ed. A.R. Venkatachalapathy; Trans. S. Thillainayagam)

Forthcoming titles

My Life is My Message: A Biography of Mahatma Gandhi, Narayan Desai, 4 volumes (Trans. Tridip Suhrud)
Non-violent Relationality: Rethinking Gandhi in the World, (Ed. Debjani Ganguly and John Docker)

Harilal Gandhi

A Life

CHANDULAL BHAGUBHAI DALAL

Edited and translated
from the Gujarati
by
TRIDIP SUHRUD

Orient Longman

ORIENT LONGMAN PRIVATE LIMITED

Registered Office
3-6-752 Himayatnagar, Hyderabad 500 029 (A.P.), India
Email: cogeneral@orientlongman.com

Other Offices
Bangalore / Bhopal / Bhubaneshwar / Chennai
Ernakulam / Guwahati / Hyderabad / Jaipur / Kolkata
Lucknow / Mumbai / New Delhi / Patna / Pune

First published 2007
This paperback edition 2007

The Gujarati original of *Harilal Gandhi* was published by the Sabarmati Ashram Preservation and Memorial Trust, Ahmedabad, in 1977.

ISBN 13: 978-81-250-3379-0
ISBN 10: 81-250-3379-3

Typeset by
Universal Print Systems Limited
Chennai 600 008

Printed in India at
Chaman Enterprises
Delhi

Published by
Orient Longman Private Limited
1/24 Asaf Ali Road
New Delhi 110 002
e-mail: delgeneral@orientlongman.com

Contents

Acknowledgements

I am indebted to Shri Kashyap Dalal and his family. They gave me the permission to translate their father's work. I am especially grateful to Kashyapbhai. He shared Chandulal Dalal's research notes with me and gave me the notes that Chandulal Dalal had made on the first Gujarati edition of the book; the changes that the author had wished to incorporate in the future editions of the book have been incorporated in the present translation.

The Sabarmati Ashram Preservation and Memorial Trust, Ahmedabad, the publisher of the Gujarati edition, enthusiastically supported the work, providing unfettered access to the archives and the library. My special thanks to Amrutbhai Modi, secretary of the Trust and the director of the Gandhi Smarak Sangrahalaya. I thank Kinnari, Viral, Durgeshbhai and all my other associates at the Ashram for making me a part of it.

I am deeply indebted to Neelam Parikh. She allowed me to translate and publish a large number of letters written by Gandhiji and Harilal that were first published in her biography of Harilal, *Gandhiji nu Khovayelu Dhan: Harilal Gandhi*.

Navjivan Trust and Shri Jitendrabhai Desai granted me the permission to quote from Gandhiji's writings and to publish Gandhiji's letters to Harilal from the *Collected Works of Mahatma Gandhi*. I thank them; they have, as always, been very generous.

Dr. Peter Heehs responded to my request for copies of Harilal's correspondence with Sri Aurobindo and the Mother like a true scholar and ashramite. I am grateful to him and the trustees of the archives of Sri Aurobindo Ashram, Pondicherry, for making available three letters.

I thank Dr. T.S. Kumbar and the staff of the DA-IICT library who have always been very supportive of the requests made to them. I also thank Ranjit Chauhan for administrative support.

I read some parts of this translation at the seminar on "Gandhi, Non-violence and Modernity", organised by the Humanities Research Centre, Australian National University. I am grateful to Dr. Debjani Ganguli and Dr. John Docker for making the presentation possible. I thank Prof. Thomas Weber, Prof. Dipesh Chakraborty, Dr. Jim Masselos, Prof. Makarand Paranjape and Prof. Charles Disalvo for their encouragement. I thank Ajay Skaria and Leela Gandhi for the warmth and compassionate understanding—I am ever so grateful.

Conversations with Suresh Sharma during the last decade have deepened my understanding of Gandhiji. Working with Suresh Sahib on the critical edition of Gandhiji's *Hind Swaraj* has made me sensitive to questions of language, textual fidelity and interpretation of the scholarship surrounding Gandhiji. I am deeply grateful for this relationship. I thank Ganesh Devy for revalidating the intellectual worth of translation.

Shiv Visvanathan never failed to playfully remind me that Harilal was a part of me. I thank him for the affection. I thank Binita Desai, Punam Zutshi and Amit Bhatt for their friendship. Special thanks to Bini for the cover and the layout of this book.

I thank Vidya Rao and Hemlata Shankar at Orient Longman who encouraged the publication of this translation. I thank R. Sivapriya, my editor at Orient Longman, who entered the text with empathy and care.

I thank my family – Suhrud, Megha and Katyayani – for being so wonderful.

Shri Ramchandra Gandhi, my pranam to you.

This translation is in memory of my friend and mother, Taralika.

Tridip Suhrud
March 2006
Ahmedabad

Foreword to Translation

Less than twenty years younger than his father, a satyagrahi in South Africa at the age of fifteen, devoted to his mother and brothers throughout his life, Harilal Gandhi was yet a fierce critic of his father.

Harilal could not understand Bapu's conviction that one should love other people's children as much as one's own; more, if their need was greater. Like Nathuram Godse could not understand Gandhi's special concern for vulnerable Muslim minorities in India after partition. Harilal, of course, did not ever want to kill his father. But the comparison is instructive.

The education that Gandhi's ashramas provided was one of India's greatest experiments with truth. No caste restrictions, obligatory manual labour, no gender discrimination, the development of religious tolerance—all that the great ashramas of antiquity lacked. The uniqueness of this experiment seems to me to have hardened Bapu against the good that conventional education could provide, and Harilal was too dazzled by modern education and lifestyles (as his father had been for a while) to take seriously the alternative education that Bapu was experimenting with.

A clash of fundamentalisms seems to me to characterise the conflict between father and son regarding many matters.

Harilal gave himself up to alcohol, even as Gandhi gave himself upto Ramanama. The son suffered privations, the father won martyrdom and, possibly, moksha.

There are greater similarities between them than we would care to notice.

On one point Bapu seems to me to be theologically wrong. He thought that his own carnal nature as a youth was punished by God in the form of a bad son. Surely God must have more things to do than punish fathers with recalcitrant sons!

Harilal's rebelliousness must have tempered Bapu's ego by the realisation that he could not control everything.

Harilal's role in the spiritual growth of Gandhi cannot be overestimated.

Nor can one withhold criticism of Harilal's moral failures.

I had the privilege as a child to see Harilal Kaka during his visit to my father's home in Delhi, and observe the great affection that my father, Devadas, Gandhiji's youngest son, had for his older brother.

I am myself an old man now. It seems to me that in Gandhiji's life Harilal was a morally non-conformist angel whose alcoholic stupor indicated, by way of caricature, the complete renunciation of ego which is the svaraj of moksha.

Some of the rambling wisdom of Gandhiji's addresses after prayer meetings in Delhi towards the end of his life is suggestive of an inebriation which is greater than the sanity and worldly wisdom of teetotallers, and enables me to see Harilal Kaka's self-destructive alcoholism with more compassion.

May this English translation of Shri Chandulal Bhagubhai Dalal's Gujarati biography of Harilal Gandhi by Shri Tridip Suhrud urge us to think beyond the clash between son and father, and see a deeper mystery which united them.

Ramchandra Gandhi
December 2004
New Delhi

Introduction to Translation

In October 2003, I began translating Narayan Desai's biography of Gandhiji from Gujarati into English. I saw the translation of this four-volume, 2200-page biography as an attempt to comprehend and be close to a life and a time whose absence I felt most acutely after the communal violence of 2002. Narayan Desai's life has been illuminated by Gandhiji, Vinoba Bhave and Jayprakash Narayan. He was to be the medium of my apprenticeship to the life and thought of Gandhiji.

And almost unknowingly, but with persistence, Harilal Gandhi – Kasturba and Gandhiji's eldest son – began to creep into my conscience. When I re-read Chandulal Bhagubhai Dalal's biography of Harilal, I was struck that it was published in 1977 by the Sabarmati Ashram Preservation and Memorial Trust, Ahmedabad.

Gandhiji had founded his ashram in 1915 with the objective that its members should qualify themselves for, and make a constant endeavour towards, the service of the country, not inconsistent with universal good. Harilal's rebellion was in some measure against the ideals and observances of the Phoenix Settlement and its community, where the idea of the ashram was first experimented. What did this publication signify? To me, it was an act of recognition. Recognition of a life that had been lived in the shadows. It was an attempt to bring that life to light.

I began to translate Chandulal Dalal's life of Harilal Gandhi in November 2003. But this was a surreptitious act. During the day I translated the life of Gandhiji; something that I was willing to acknowledge and be proud of. But at night, in the basement of my house, on a table that was not mine, I translated Harilalbhai's life. I wanted to keep the two worlds – of day and night, of light and darkness, of work and home – spaces apart. Somehow, I feared that Harilal would creep into my reading of Gandhiji, that he would cause disturbance in the process of my immersion. I feared his power to contaminate and to corrupt. And yet, I would not stop translating.

Chandulal Bhagubhai Dalal is part of a long Gujarati intellectual tradition of writing on Gandhiji's life and thought. Kishorlal Mashruwala, Swami Anand, Kaka Saheb Kalelkar, Narhari Parikh, Ravjibhai Patel and Prabhudas Gandhi wrote philosophical and biographical works of great merit in Gujarati. Of course, the greatest chronicler of Gandhiji was Mahadev Desai. The twenty-three volumes of published diaries bear testimony to Mahadevbhai's sadhana. His sadhana was to witness and capture the multilayered unfolding of Truth. This tradition, in some ways, has culminated in Narayan Desai's biography of Gandhiji, *Maru Jivan ej Mari Vani.*

Chandulal Dalal is part of that intellectual tradition, but he differs from the others in one crucial aspect. He was not an associate of Gandhiji. He was not an ashramite. But this in no way diminished his quest to comprehend and chronicle the life of Gandhiji. This quest took many forms. Chandulal Dalal read and classified over 34,000 letters, articles, essays and manuscripts that today form the archives of the Sabarmati Ashram Preservation and Memorial Trust. That the archive is today one of the finest and most detailed repositories of Gandhiji's life and thought is to a large measure due to the rigorous, meticulous and patient scholarship of Chandulal Dalal.

His intimate knowledge of Gandhiji's letters and papers led him to write what perhaps is the only detailed, exhaustive history of the satyagraha in South Africa to be found in any Indian language. His five-volume study published in 1957–58, *Gandhiji ni Dakshin Africa ni Ladat,* remains a definitive work about the struggle of the Indian people in South Africa under Gandhiji's leadership.

Chandulal Dalal had a quality that defined scholarship in an earlier era. He had the ability to work patiently for years, pursuing an idea, a question, a thought; unmindful of the obscurity that such enquiries tend to invite. He wished to compile an account of Gandhiji's life, providing details of his movements, travels, meetings, significant letters received and sent, and personal observances such as a fast or a vow of silence. His aspiration was to do such a compilation for every day of Gandhiji's life. The result was a two-part detailed chronology of Gandhiji's life. The first part covers the period from 2 October 1869 to 9 January 1915. The years in Kathiawad, his life as a student in England, and from 24 May 1892, his life in South Africa, constituted a period of relative obscurity. Chandulal, who was an auditor by profession, informs us that he has been able to get exact details of Gandhiji's movements for 4810 days out of the total 16,434 days of this period. The second part of the chronology covers Gandhiji's life from 9 January 1915, the day he arrived in India, to 30 January 1948, the day of his assassination. Chandulal Dalal's chronology has the exact account of 11,739 days out of the total 12,075 days; of the remaining days, he has sufficient documentary proof for 124 days, and he is regretfully forced to make conjecture for about two hundred and twelve days of Gandhiji's life. This monumental chronology lists even the modes of transport used by Gandhiji and also over two thousand places that he visited during this period. Even a casual reader would be struck by Chandulal Dalal's absolute fidelity to facts and documentary evidence. It is a tradition of scholarship which makes no statement that cannot be substantiated by documentary proof. It is deeply interpretative and hermeneutic because it is rooted in evidence.

Chandulal Dalal's life of Harilal Gandhi is one of the finest outcomes of such scholarship. Its impulse is so very deeply Gandhian. It is moved by an acute desire to undo a wrong, to rescue a life from a world of perpetual rumours, shadows and darkness. It is an act of compassion. And because it is fundamentally part of the Gandhian intellectual tradition, it wants to speak the truth. A reader at once recognises that Chandulal Dalal's narrative is documentary in style. His writing is based on documents. His sentences are short, pithy and accurate. His language is unambiguous. His prose is sparse, unadorned. He is empathetic; compassionate towards all—Harilal, Gandhiji, Kasturba and other members of the Gandhi family. He is compassionate towards all, but his commitment is only to truth. At no point in the biography is he tempted to make a conjecture, offer a hypothesis, or make a psychological observation not rooted in evidence.

Chandulal Dalal's task was not easy. Harilal, despite his public and acrimonious fallout with his father and his followers, lived an obscure life. After the death of his wife Chanchalbehn, he roamed the country. As Devdas Gandhi has observed, his travels by train across the country rivalled that of their father. He wrote few letters. He wrote to his father, occasionally to his brothers and more regularly to his sister-in-law. Very few of these letters survive. Gandhiji and his associates preserved almost every scrap of correspondence. The hundred volumes of the *Collected Works of Mahatma Gandhi* bear testimony to the acute archival sense that Gandhiji and his associates possessed.

But Gandhiji asked that the letters of Harilal be destroyed. There are two instances to substantiate this claim. On 27 April 1932, Gandhiji wrote to Harilal from the prison: "And hence, contrary to my usual practice, I am preserving your letter so that, when you have awakened, you may see the insolence of your letter and weep over it and laugh at your folly."[1] Some years later, in a letter to Devdas Gandhi, Gandhiji refers to Harilal's public statement that he was seriously thinking of adopting Hinduism again. Gandhiji mentions the tearing of Harilal's letter to pieces: "After I had torn up the letter it occurred to me that probably you had not come across it, so I decided to send you the pieces."[2]

What does this act of destruction imply? Clearly it was not an attempt to hide a deeply troubling relationship. Gandhiji had on various occasions publicly acknowledged the differences that separated Harilal and him. He had more than once publicly declined to take responsibility for Harilal's financial dealings. Harilal, Gandhiji, and even Kasturba, had at different times written public letters explaining their conduct towards each other. Therefore, it was not an attempt to hide the troubled relationship that prompted the destruction of the letters.

It is tempting to provide a hurried psychoanalytic conclusion. Harilal, as Gandhiji was often given to saying, was a product of his passionate self. He saw Harilal's debauched conduct a divinely ordained punishment for his own intensely sexually charged conduct towards Kasturba. By destroying Harilal's letters, Gandhiji was in fact denying a part of his own self—a part

---

1. "Fragment of a Letter to Harilal Gandhi, April 27, 1932", *The Collected Works of Mahatma Gandhi (CMWG)*, vol. 49, p. 375.
2. "Letter to Devdas Gandhi, November 12, 1936", *CMWG*, vol. 64, p. 23–24.

that troubled him. I am ill equipped to offer such a hypothesis and, more significantly, ill at ease with such an explanation.

The other equally significant absence – of Harilal Gandhi – is in the diaries of Mahadev Desai. Modern India has rarely seen a witness, a chronicler and a bearer of truth comparable to Mahadevbhai. His diaries begin from the day he joined Gandhiji, and he maintained them till a day before his death in the Agakhan Palace Prison on 15 August 1942. He maintained detailed accounts of each day he spent with Gandhiji. That is, on the days during which he was not with Gandhiji, either because they were imprisoned in different jails or travelling to different destinations, Mahadevbhai did not write his diary. Otherwise his diaries are records, often verbatim, of letters received, Gandhiji's responses to them, including discussions about his responses in the secretariat, the interviews that Gandhiji granted, the discussions that he had with visitors, including conversations that the ashram children had with him. The diaries contain the details of conversations that Gandhiji had with his closest associates and the debates of the Congress. The diaries even record the leisurely life – experienced as inmates in various prisons – of reading, writing and long conversations.

These extraordinary diaries are almost entirely silent about Harilal. The diaries do not record even the days that Harilal spent at the ashram. And this was no routine or everyday occurrence. Often, Harilal's visits to the ashram were preceded by a long exchange of letters. The visits required exceptional concessions, such as allowing him to smoke in the ashram surroundings. Mahadevbhai remains silent about these as well. A statistical look at the diaries is also revealing. Mahadevbhai's published dairies cover twenty-three volumes that run into 9706 printed pages. In all these pages, there are only thirty instances where Harilal's name has been mentioned. Often, these are records of Gandhiji's letters to Harilal or to other members of the family concerning Harilal's conduct. Fifteen volumes have not even one instance of Harilal's name being recorded in the diaries. This silence is extraordinary.

It remains puzzling. No relationship of Gandhiji's is so systematically blacked out. We must try and provide a hypothesis, however tentative.

Gandhiji's notion of the personal and the private was wonderfully public. He acknowledged his passions, pathos, sorrows and joys, and his deep and abiding communion with Satya Narayan, the God of Truth, publicly through his letters and in his journals. The open architecture of the houses he lived in – Hriday Kunj at Sabarmati and Bapu Kuti at Wardha – bear testimony to this transparency. Simultaneously, Gandhiji had an intensely personal and guarded sense of his inner space—a space that was not open to violation, a space that manifested itself through what he called the inner voice.

Gandhiji was equally protective and nurturing of the private world of others, including members of his family. Only those parts of the private world of others were made public, which dealt with an individual's quest to be a satyagrahi. It was part of satyagrahi sadhana to reflect with others on the inner processes about satyagrahi observances. Harilal was neither an ashramite nor a satyagrahi after he left his father's house in 1911. There was something deeply personal and intensely private in Harilal's encounters with his father and his family. We get a glimpse of Harilal's grief in the letters that he wrote to Balibehn, his sister-in-law. Gandhiji wanted this grief and sorrow to remain private. The desolation of Harilalbhai was part of the private worlds of Harilal, Gandhiji, Kasturba and the extended Gandhi family. The silence was not an attempt to hide, obscure or conceal. The differences were public but the pain and agony were private. We get a glimpse of the acute pain that Harilal, Kasturba and Gandhiji would have felt from the incident at the Katni Station.[3] It is the attempt of fiercely honest, transparent and truthful people to protect and preserve their grief, desolation and the anguish as something personal and private.

Yet, as a satyagrahi and a votary of truth, Gandhiji was committed to Truth. He therefore made no allowance for himself. He does not wish the same protection for himself. His letters to Harilal were preserved – many of them in the diaries of Mahadevbhai – and form part of the *Collected Works of Mahatma Gandhi.*

Chandulal Dalal's biography becomes significant for this reason. He reconstructed a life from letters, family records and archives of the Sabarmati

3. See Appendix 5.

Ashram, and old files of newspapers. He wrote letters and conversed with the family of Harilal Gandhi.

Harilal's life has been the subject of speculation, of fictionalised accounts, theatrical performances and even a film.

In 1988, the Gujarati novelist, Dinkar Joshi, wrote a novel on the life of Harilal, *Prakash no Padchhyo* (Shadow of Light). It presents Harilal as a victim, as a victim of his father's ever-changing fads, his father's desire to appear fair, and his father's unwillingness to comprehend the simple desires of a young man to acquire modern education or to be with his adolescent wife. It is a story that explains Harilal's life as the life of a victim and his conduct as a sign of rebellion. It privileges victimhood and presents it as a moral act.

Based on the novel, Feroz Khan – theatre person, actor, director, producer – directed the play, *Mahatma versus Gandhi*. It made the story of Harilal a subject of intense media speculation.

It created a middle-class critique of Gandhiji as a failed father, an oppressive husband and a tyrannical and whimsical head of the ashram community. Those who blamed Jawaharlal Nehru for creating and perpetuating a political dynasty in the Congress, abused Gandhiji precisely for failing to do the same—that he failed to protect and provide for the self-interests of his family, especially Harilal Gandhi. But the media scrutiny did not give rise to any serious scholarship about the father–son relationship in Indian society or bring any fresh perspective on the relationship between Gandhiji and Harilal.

Keith Heller's novel, *The Woman Who Knew Gandhi,* published in 2003, portrays Harilal as pathetic, poor, woefully and fatally distressed person, who not so subtly tries to extort money from an English woman who once 'knew' Gandhiji.

Neelam Parikh responded to such portrayals of her grandfather and great-grandfather in a manner that is so rare in our public and intellectual life. As the granddaughter of Harilal Gandhi and the great-granddaughter of Gandhiji, she felt it was her unique duty and privilege to speak the truth as she saw it. Her's was a most Gandhi-like method. She put in the public domain *all* material related to the life of Harilal Gandhi. She wrote a short biography *Gandhiji nu Khovayelu Dhan: Harilal Gandhi* (Gandhiji's Lost Jewel: Harilal Gandhi) in 1998 and brought out hitherto unpublished letters of Gandhiji to Harilal. These letters, which are also included here,[4] do not form part of even the *Collected Works of Mahatma Gandhi.* She also published Harilal's letters to Chanchalbehn and his long, pathetic correspondence with his sister-in-law Balibehn.

Neelam Parikh's act is simple, generous and courageous. She and the family of Harilal and Gandhiji have nothing to hide and nothing to be ashamed of. Her desire is to bring Harilalbhai out from a life of shadows. Her plea is direct—the relationship should be understood with empathy and compassion. Her plea is that the pathos of Harilal Gandhi should not be used to attack Gandhiji.

This work originates from a similar impulse. It is an act of translation, and it seeks to go beyond translation. This book has two parts. The first is the life of Harilal Gandhi as chronicled by Chandulal Dalal. In the other part I have chosen to include 12 appendices as Translator's Appendices. Chandulal Dalal's biography, combined with the Translator's Appendices, contains the complete published, un-published and archival material available on Harilal Gandhi. In a way, it seeks to complete the chronicle that Chandulal Dalal had set out to write. It is my tribute to his great scholarship.

In the process I have come to recognise that even for Gandhiji and Kasturba, Harilalbhai was not a part of the underground world of shadows and strange, inchoate voices. The pathos of his life, his suffering, his rebellion, his failures and his short-lived attempts to confirm to Bapu's ideals were integral to their lives as parents and grandparents, and to their service to the country. With this recognition, Harilalbhai was no longer part of my clandestine world. His life and his story have gradually become part of the light that leads me.

Tridip Suhrud
March 2006
Ahmedabad

4. See Translator's Appendix 4.

FOREWORD

Gandhiji's eldest son, the late Harilal Gandhi, from a very early age was displeased with his father's philosophy of life and his values. Harilal believed that his father, for the sake of his values, deprived him and his brothers of routine, commonplace college education of the modern type. This, for him, was his father's fault. Harilal also believed that in so doing, his father had spoilt his career and those of his brothers. He defied Gandhiji and at an early opportunity charted a separate course for his life, on his own volition. This history is well known.

Harilal's opposition to his father increased day by day; it degenerated and became deformed; it recognised no limits and it resulted in the exercise of absolute free will, alcoholism, debauchery and conversion. This too is well known.

Harilal had actively participated in the numerous political agitations that Gandhiji led in South Africa and in India, and had gone to jail. Despite this, he remained steadfast in his rejection of his father's values and in the belief that his father was responsible for all his shortcomings. Gandhiji believed that he had done no injustice to his sons in the manner in which he had raised and educated them. But, he also felt that his own early life was one of the reasons for Harilal's degeneration. He often said so.

But those who understand, in its proper perspective, Gandhiji's faith in truth and his insistence upon it, would not see this as his fault. Those whose sadhana is truth and are willing to sacrifice their all for truth would "sacrifice son, wealth, wife and self"; this is not unusual, they cannot act otherwise. Gandhiji has followed this ancient tradition.

As soon as his sons attained the age of sixteen, following the age-old saying that a son who attains the age of sixteen is a friend, he gave full freedom to them to choose and pursue their careers and vocations in keeping with their desires and abilities. He had explained to each of them – especially to Ramdas and Devdas – the social utility and dignity of the professions of the farmer, the weaver, the tailor, the cobbler, the miller and the scavenger—professions which were very dear and dignified for him. He had urged them to follow one such profession with the deepest force of heartfelt convictions. Despite this, both these brothers expressed their unwillingness and inability to follow any of these professions. Instead, they expressed their desire, like any other person of the modern middle class, to follow a routine profession of being either a lawyer, or a doctor, or a journalist, or an engineer. They willed such a life for their children as well. Gandhiji was shocked by such an attitude. But he absorbed the shock and assured them, with an open heart, that they were free to disregard his counsel and follow their own aptitudes. He also assured them that in such exercise of their free will, the relations between him and his sons would not in the least suffer, and that he would always consider and treat his sons as friends. By such an assurance he made them free from fear.

Throughout Gandhiji's life, his attitude and treatment of his sons was characterised by affection and a friendly disposition. All of us have been witness to this.

It is evident that such magnanimity and generosity is seen in great otherworldly souls.

Members of his family, his well-wishers, his closest associates, co-workers from India and abroad, and writers and biographers, have criticised Gandhiji's attitude towards the upbringing and education of his sons. They claim that Gandhiji was at fault. They have also blamed him for failing in his duty to provide his sons with proper education, by subjecting them to his frequently changing ideas and experiments.

But in this regard, I would only submit this question: What capability do we have to measure otherworldly epochal beings that are more tender than a flower but harder than the vajra? I have said earlier that our limited yardstick is incapable of measuring and comprehending those sadhaks and bhaktas who sacrifice son, wealth, wife and self. We are capable of only stating this.

It was Harilal's fate that he was the first to pass through the constitutive experience of Gandhiji's upbringing. He opposed this and, as stated earlier, he separated from his father. He distanced himself further and further, and became more and more unhappy. It was as if he was banished from society.

Shri Chandulal Dalal has written this book about such a person by gathering every possible information. He has stated in his preface that his attempt is "not to defend Harilal nor is it to criticise anyone. The attempt has been to understand the deformities and degeneration of Harilal...These deformities were not natural to him." For Gandhiji, "institutions and not individuals were greater". He believed that in the interest of the institution, "whatever sacrifice is asked for should be given. If it required the sacrifice of wife, sons or anyone else, he should not hesitate in making such a sacrifice."

When the book was near completion Shri Chandulal came to Mumbai braving many difficulties (the rail route between Valsad and Mumbai was disrupted) despite his weak health, and read out the book to me and sought my suggestions. I was already impressed by his faith in Gandhi, his industry and his capacity for precision.

I was aware of these qualities. I urge the reader to see his *Gandhiji ni Dakshin Africa ni Ladat* for its scholarship; his *Gandhiji ni Dinvari* (1915–1948) for the effort of a chronicler; and the volumes of *Mahadevbhai ni Diary* as a mark of his editorial qualities. Each of these is informed by his industry and concern for precise details.

As for this book, I must state that all information contained therein is substantiated. A reader would appreciate the efforts of a historian, and especially one researching the life of a person who was lost, forgotten and banished. He has shown the same care, concern and commitment, and has put in the same degree of effort that is evident in the *Dinvari* and the *Diary*, in presenting a biography of a person who was un-Gandhian and whose life story does not evoke the most pleasant sentiments and memories. He has judged and evaluated the evidence, and arrived at conclusions with equanimity. Through this effort, he has rendered service to the history of the Gandhian era. I believe that this work gives a new, albeit different dimension to his great contribution of having edited the *Dinvari* and the *Diary*.

Swami Anand
20 April 1975

Kosbad Hill

Preface

The late Harilal Gandhi was the eldest son of Gandhiji. He lived for about sixty years. He went to South Africa twice. He spent eight years there. He earned the reputation of a jail-going satyagrahi in South Africa. When he went to jail in India during the non-cooperation movement he received no publicity or repute. He was unhappy during the last twenty years of his life and he spent those trying to satisfy his bad habits. When he died other newspapers wrote a little about him but the *Harijan* newspaper gave the news in just two to four lines.

I have been quite curious about the members of the Gandhi family, especially his wife and sons.

Much has been written about Kasturba. Manilal was the editor of the *Indian Opinion,* and he has written much. After Kasturba's death a memorial issue of the *Indian Opinion* was published, in which many different persons have written their reminiscences of her. Ramdas has written a book of his reminiscences. Devdas was the managing editor of the *Hindustan Times,* therefore he has also written much.

After Harilal's death, Devdas wrote an essay on him.[1] Ramdas has written about him scantily in his recollections. Vanmalabehn in her book, *Amara Ba,* has a chapter on Harilal. Vanmalabehn's father Narharibhai was a good friend of Harilal's and the chapter was written based on his recollections.[2] Robert Payne's biography of Gandhiji contains two chapters on Harilal. Some scattered writings of other English authors are also available.

The fourth volume of the published diaries of Jamnalal Bajaj covers the period 1934 to 1936. The diaries contain no significant mention of Harilal, though 1935 and 1936 were important years in Harilal's career. Shri Prabhudas

1. Appendix 2 contains the full text of the essay.
2. Vanmalabehn's letter to the author, December 17, 1973.

Gandhi in his book *Jivan nu Parodh* has described in detail his life in South Africa till 1914. But even in this book Harilal's presence is insignificant.

It does not appear that Harilal wrote anything except the 'semi-public' letter to his father.[3] Most of his letters to Gandhiji have not been preserved. Gandhiji himself did not want them to be preserved. After his separation from Gandhiji there has been virtually a 'blackout'[4] on him. In this book, I have presented the facts that I was able to gather.

While reading and thinking about Gandhiji one can feel nothing but reverence and respect for him. The virtues that he tried to cultivate in himself, an endeavour in which he succeeded to a large extent, did not come to him without effort. He strived to nurture these qualities, he reflected on them and internalised them. His mother and his nurse Rambhabai nurtured his deep sense of religion. He did not credit his father for his religiosity. He wrote, "My father was a lover of his clan, truthful, brave and generous..."[5] But, "If you see any saintliness in me it has not come to me from my father but from my mother."[6] Moreover, Gandhiji never claimed to have inherited his sense of religiosity. His qualities were as a result of his context, his own strivings and the efforts of his relatives.

Gandhiji's expectations with regard to his family were high. He wrote, "What I expect from the Gandhi family is that all members should devote themselves exclusively to service work, observe the utmost self-control and have no desire for wealth. They should not marry and those who are married should observe brahmacharya. They should live on whatever they get from service work."[7]

Gandhiji wished such a virtuous life for his son Harilal as well. He made efforts to cultivate such qualities in Harilal, whose disposition was not to his

---

3. Appendix 1 contains the full text of the letter.
4. Translator's note: English term in the original.
5. Reference (Ref.) no. 35, p. 3.
6. Ref. no. 24, vol. 1, p. 67. (Translator's note: Unless stated otherwise, all translations from original Gujarati sources have been done by the translator for the purpose of this translation.)
7. Ibid., p. 354. (Translator's note: Also see, "A Letter, August 7, 1932", *CWMG*, vol. 56, p. 311.)

expectations. Gandhiji wrote in a letter, "If God suffers his drunkenness, what can we do?"[8] It remains a mystery as to why the son of a great man, who cultivated and formed men out of mud, turned to dust from being a man.

Gandhiji felt that his life during Harilal's infancy, full of passionate desires and none too strict in observance of morality, was responsible for this. He has expressed similar views on many occasions.

Is the carnal lust of parents responsible entirely for the immorality of their children?

Was not Gandhiji's own father given to carnal pleasures? Gandhiji has said of his father, "To a certain extent he might also have been given to carnal pleasures."[9] And, "He spoke such abuses in presence of the daughters-in-law that it was unbearable for me."[10] His mother observed strict vows. "My father may not have liked her strict vows and observances."[11] She was his fourth wife. At the time of their marriage Gandhiji's father was forty. "It was difficult even for a karbhari to find a fourth wife. She was found from some village near Junagadh."[12]

Thus, his father was devoted to carnal pleasures. Why was Gandhiji not like him? Are not reasons and factors other than the carnal desires of parents responsible for the good or bad character of a son? Isn't it possible to say that in each instance of conception the parents have succumbed to carnal desires and passionate lust?

There must be other reasons for the moral decline of Harilal. Gandhiji said, "I am a believer in previous births and rebirths. All our relationships are the result of the samskars we carry from our previous births."[13] In a letter he

---

8. Ref. no. 24, vol. 3, p. 185. (Translator's note: Also see, "Fragment of letter to Kasturba Gandhi, March 11, 1933", *CWMG*, vol. 60, p. 27.)
9. Ref. no. 35, p. 3.
10. Ref. no. 24, vol. 15, p. 421.
11. Ref. no. 24, vol. 3, p. 285.
12. Ref. no. 24, vol. 7, p. 10.
13. Ref. no. 7, 10 August 1940. (Translator's note: Also see, "The Case of my First Son", *CWMG*, vol. 79, p. 85.)

wrote about Harilal, Gandhiji indicated that Harilal's karma guided his conduct, "The way he thinks is governed by his past actions."[14]

Moreover, the affection of his father, mother, family and nurse Rambhabai had played an important role in Gandhiji's upbringing. Was Harilal's upbringing devoid of such affection? His wife was better educated than Kasturba. And according to Gandhiji, Chanchi was far superior even to him.[15] Despite this, why was Harilal's moral life so depraved? He was not characterless to begin with.

Gandhiji was displeased with Harilal's marriage. But, when the couple joined him in South Africa he warmly welcomed them into the family. Gandhiji had great liking for his daughter-in-law Gulab. He was also very pleased with Harilal's ability to make sacrifices at the young age of thirteen. Harilal's involvement in the satyagraha in South Africa had gladdened his heart.

But later, the relations between father and son worsened. When the question of sending one person to England for higher education came up, Gandhiji chose a distant nephew over the son. The choice hurt Harilal, who saw it as an instance of personal disregard and neglect. (The opinion that Harilal had expressed when his son Kantilal disregarded Gandhiji's advice and went on to study medicine, and his utterances in an inebriated state at daughter-in-law Saraswati's house bear testimony to these long-harboured feelings.) He left the house, but did not succeed in his attempts to study; he started many business ventures all of which failed. He was fed up. Over time the rift between the father and the son widened; it became deeper. Moreover, the wife whom he loved deeply died at a young age. His father was opposed to his marrying again. He was out of control and there was no one who could exert a tempering influence. He had to send away his motherless children to remain in the care of others. There was no one he could love or receive love from.

---

14. Ref. no. 24, vol. 4, p. 170. (Translator's note: Also see, "Letter to Manilal Gandhi, July 31, 1918", *CWMG,* vol. 17, p. 167. The term 'past actions' translates the word *karma* from the original Gujarati.)
15. Translator's note: Harilal's wife Gulabbehn was affectionately called Chanchi or Chanchal by her family.

The question we need to consider is: Was Gandhiji responsible for Harilal's debasement? Gandhiji believed that the errors of those who were his own should be magnified a hundred fold while the errors of others should be considered insignificant. Gandhiji and Harilal differed on their understanding of who constitutes 'one's own people'.

Harilal wrote to his father, "No attention was paid to us." He further said, "You have never encouraged us in any way." And, "You have spoken to us not in love but always in anger."[16] Ramdas in his reminiscences has written about the six-pence incident where he says, "But for the fear there was no other reason to speak a lie."[17] Harilal has also written that the rule at Phoenix was, "Let the groom die, let the bride die, but do as Bapu says." Those who did not conduct themselves as per this maxim were "despised. This was especially so of us; and among us it was I who was so despised."[18] By 'us' Harilal included his three younger brothers and himself.

Gandhiji said, "I do not discriminate between mine and not mine. All those who follow my path are mine. I do not despise those who choose a different path, but I do not extend help to them." For him the institution was larger than the individual. He believed that all sacrifices should be made in the interests of the institution and in observance of accepted principles. One should not hesitate, he believed, in offering the wife, the sons and the self as sacrifice. No renunciation was larger than the ideals. For the eradication of untouchability he did not hesitate in taking his wife, who believed in untouchability, by her hand and pulling her out of the house.[19] He was against child marriage and suggested without hesitation that Harilal's

16. Appendix 1.
17. Translator's note: Ramdas Gandhi, *Samsmrano* (Ahmedabad: Navjivan, 1967), p. 23. Ramdas Gandhi picked up a six-pence coin from the petty-cash box of Gandhiji's office in Johannesburg. He wanted to ascertain whether the coin was valid. He went to a shop and bought chocolates with it. When asked, he told Gandhiji that someone had bought him the chocolates.
18. Appendix 1.
19. Translator's note: This refers to the incident in South Africa where Gandhiji pulled Kasturba by hand and showed her the door when she refused to clean chamber-pots, believing it to be work fit only for untouchables.

engagement with Gulab should be broken. He had no reservations in selecting a distant nephew Chhaganlal over his sons while choosing a candidate to be sent to England to become a barrister, because he was convinced that the former was more suitable to serve the Phoenix Settlement. When he was convinced that separate electorates for Harijans were not required, he risked his life for the sake of that conviction.

It was not as if Gandhiji had no respect for Harilal. After he left the family house Gandhiji said, "He has an independent mind." In a letter, Gandhiji wrote, "He is a brave boy in one sense, he makes no secret of his vice and his rebellion is an open rebellion."[20] He was aware of Harilal's capabilities. In another letter he said, "If he can get rid of the two vices he can be the best of all brothers."[21]

Harilal also respected his father. When he left the house he carried with him a photograph of his father. According to Devdas, "Outside the family and circle of friends he always respected Bapu and also defended him aggressively."[22] He was proud of a father who did not wish his son to follow him out of fear when the son held a different opinion. Harilal believed that to seek Gandhiji's intervention in his commercial affairs would waste his precious time. He never spoke ill of his father in the presence of his affectionate daughter-in-law. Once he began to dictate his complaints against his father, but he controlled his feelings and tore off the pages. Saraswatibehn records this in her reminiscences of Harilal.

Harilal's vices hurt Gandhiji. Harilal's failure to pay back his creditors was for Gandhiji unpardonable. In a letter, he wrote, "If he had not done his creditors down I will not have minded his other lapses, as I mind this betrayal of creditors."[23]

---

20. Translator's note: "Letter to L. W. Ritch, February 27, 1928," *CWMG*, vol. 36, p. 61.
21. Translator's note: "Letter to Saraswati Gandhi, April 19, 1945," *CWMG*, vol. 79, p. 399.
22. Translator's note: Appendix 2.
23. Translator's note: "Letter to L. W. Ritch, February 27, 1928," *CWMG*, vol. 36, p. 61.

Compared to his feelings for his father and brothers, Harilal loved his mother Kasturba the most. It is apparent from his semi-public letter to his father that it hurt him the most when Gandhiji and others neglected Kasturba. When he adopted Islam, Kasturba wrote him a public letter. Harilal was convinced that this letter was written at Gandhiji's instigation. Therefore, in his response to Gandhiji, he compared Kasturba's situation to that of a camel which is placed between a spiked gate and an elephant that is trying to break it down. The incident at the Katni station when he raised a slogan in his feeble voice, "Mata Kasturba ki jai", is also a poignant example of his affection for the mother.[24]

Harilal's handwriting was certainly much better than Gandhiji's. He had not studied in schools and colleges, but his brothers felt that he was an intelligent person and a good writer. This is also borne out in his letters. In his reminiscences, Devdas has written about Harilal's devotion to the *Gita*, and his courage, endurance, steadfastness and ascetic qualities. Ramdas has said, "The power of his speech was enticing. He argued so well that sometimes even Bapu had to pause and think before responding."[25]

Once while Gandhiji was in jail in India, the jail superintendent remarked that Manilal and Ramdas looked similar and wondered if Harilal and Devdas resembled each other. Sardar Vallabhbhai was also imprisoned with Gandhiji. He remarked, "Those two are Ba's sons; while these two are Bapu's sons." Gandhiji accepted this and said, "It is true. Harilal was born when I was totally Europeanised. How is he to know that despite my lifestyle my heart was not in it? He saw the outward appearances and desired similar pleasures for himself. Therefore he told me, 'Make me a barrister and then see what all I do. See if I can make sacrifices or not?'"[26] In a letter, Gandhiji wrote, "He has crossed all limits, and that, too, openly. I craved inwardly for pleasures of the senses but gradually acquired outward self-control...But how can

24. The incident is recorded in Appendix 5.

25. Ref. no. 26, p. 222.

26. Ref. no. 24, vol. 2, p. 131.

we expect that the changes which took place in me would have any effect on Harilal?"[27]

After Manilal's marriage was fixed, Gandhiji added a postscript in a letter to him, "Write nothing to Harilal."[28] Why did he write this? Was it because he disliked and despised Harilal's conduct? Was it a pragmatic decision to keep him away from the marriage so that no one could get an opportunity to point fingers at him?

It appears that this conflict between the father and the son is also a conflict between two different ideologies. It is a conflict between two powerful personalities. It is a conflict between two very determined individuals. So what if one was a satyagrahi and the other a hathagrahi? Both considered their own position to be true, and despite their mutual respect and affection they were not willing to give up their respective ideas. Gandhiji considered Harilal spiritually diseased. It is possible that Harilal's spiritual and moral debasement shocked Gandhiji. Harilal in his duel with his strong and powerful father broke down and took to vices.

Many in similar situations take recourse to drinking, many become debauched, some commit suicide. Harilal did not commit suicide, but did everything else.

Thus a powerful individual met his end. In Devdas's words, "Death has provided release to an unhappy soul."[29]

It has not been my attempt to provide a defence of Harilal or to criticise anyone in this book. My attempt has been to understand the reasons for his debasement. It is apparent that if he had been guided properly, if he had been allowed to study at the time he wanted to, and if he had found continued warmth from his wife and children, possibly he would have been a different human being. The person who was known in South Africa as the 'young Gandhi' would have brought credit to that name even in India.

---

27. Ref. no. 11. (Translator's note: Also see, "Letter to Jamnalal Bajaj, July 2, 1933", *CWMG*, vol. 61, p. 204.)
28. Translator's note: "Letter to Manilal Gandhi, February 14, 1927", *CWMG*, vol. 33, p. 84.
29. Translator's note: Appendix 2.

No attempt is made in this book to conceal Harilal's vices and degradation. His vices were well known. But one feels that the vices were not natural to him. In this book and in the reminisences of Saraswatibehn there are many instances when he showed genuine repentance and made attempts to go on a righteous path. He possessed many virtues. The effort here has been to bring those to light. By piercing the blackout surrounding his life, an attempt has been made to understand the forces which caused his moral debasement. I have refrained from expressing my opinions and have presented only facts. Proof exists for all the facts and incidents cited here. I leave it to the reader to search the roots of the transformations in the last twenty years of Harilal's life.

The materials on which this book is based have been listed as references. I take this opportunity to thank the institutions, individuals and authors listed therein. I am grateful to the trustees of Navjivan for the permission to cite extensively from their publications. I would like to thank Sri Aurobindo Ashram, Pondicherry, for the letters that they provided.

Shri Kunvarji Parekh, Shri Prabhudas Gandhi, Shri Kantilal Gandhi, Shrimati Manubehn Mashruwala, my friend Shri Rasiklal Chottalal Parikh and the late Shri Swami Anand read and commented upon the manuscript. I am grateful to them. My special gratitude to Swami Anand for having written the foreword.

Chandulal Bhagubhai Dalal
30 January 1976
13, Bharti Nivas Society
Ahmedabad 380 006

1 Childhood and Marriage

Harilal Mohandas Gandhi was the eldest son of Gandhiji.[1] He had three younger brothers—Manilal, Ramdas and Devdas. He did not have a sister. A child was born to his parents before him. The child died within two or three days of its birth. We do not know whether that child was male or female.

His mother's name was Kasturba. The age difference between his parents was not significant. Some texts claim that his mother Kasturbai was older than his father Gandhiji by about six months. His parents were about nineteen when Harilal was born to them.

It has not been possible to ascertain the precise date of his birth. Gandhiji left Rajkot on 10 August 1888 to go to England for his studies. At that time, he left behind an infant of few months with Kasturba. Therefore, Harilal was born before this date. On 18 June 1925, Gandhiji wrote in *Young India* that Harilal had completed thirty-six years. If he was a few months old on 10 August 1888, we can assume that he was born around the month of June in that year.[2]

He was born in Rajkot and probably in the house of the Gandhi family. The first child, which died soon after its birth, was also born in that house. It is normal practice that a woman goes to her parents' house to deliver a child. Therefore, if Harilal was born in Rajkot, in the Gandhi household, that was an exception.

Gandhiji left Rajkot for England in August 1888. He reached Mumbai on 5 July 1891, after completing his studies. Before leaving, he met Kasturba alone in a room, kissed her and took her leave. But we do not know whether he similarly bade farewell to the infant Harilal.[3] We have some letters that he

---

1. In Ref. no. 36, his name has been incorrectly given as 'Hiralal'.
2. In Ref. no. 14 A, it has been mistakenly stated that he was born in 1890.
3. Translator's note: This sentence is not present in the existing edition of the Gujarati book. But the author, C.B. Dalal, revised the text for a possible

wrote from England. It does not appear that he ever mentioned Harilal in any of those letters.

Before Gandhiji reached Mumbai his mother Putlibai had died. This news was conveyed to him after he reached the port of Mumbai. We do not know if anyone gave him any information about his son Harilal. Nor does it appear that he asked after his son. It was 1891, and those were different times. Moreover, the Gandhi family was orthodox. The elders would not speak about such matters and the younger members would not ask; this is quite obvious.

Gandhiji returned to India and started his legal practice. However, his legal career in India was never successful. During those days he got all the children of the household to exercise in order to make them hardy. He liked being with children and found great pleasure in their company. Along with other children, Harilal also benefited from this.

Gandhiji's legal practice did not take off in Kathiawad. Therefore, around 1 April 1892, he went to Mumbai and stayed there for five or six months. His family was in Rajkot. On 28 October 1892, Manilal was born.

Gandhiji did not find success in Mumbai either. He left for South Africa as a lawyer for a Meman firm of Porbandar engaged in trade. He went alone, the family stayed behind in India. Harilal's life was devoid of his father's presence during this period.

Gandhiji had originally planned to stay in South Africa only for a year. But he stayed on to resolve the difficulties faced by the Indian community and also because he felt that his legal practice would do moderately well. He spent almost three years in South Africa. During this period his family was in Rajkot. He does not mention anything about his wife and two sons in his letters home. The sons were growing up in the joint family along with other children.

---

publication of another edition. Some sentences have been taken from his notes. The translation will incorporate the changes suggested by the author. Henceforth such matter will not be annotated. I am grateful to Shri Kashyap Dalal for making available his father's notes for the translation.

When Gandhiji realised that he would have to lengthen his stay in South Africa, he decided to call his family there. His legal practice was doing well; he did not have to worry about the household expenses. Three years had passed since he had left his family behind in India. In July 1896, he came to India to take them to South Africa with him.

After about five months, he left for South Africa along with his family. His wife, his two sons—Harilal and Manilal, and nephew Gokuldas accompanied him. He got fashionable new clothes stitched for all, in keeping with the trend of those days. Harilal was attired in coat, trousers, shoes and socks.

While in India, Gandhiji gave lectures about the hardships faced by Indians in South Africa due to the colour prejudice of the whites. He also published a booklet about it.[4] The whites in South Africa were incensed by this. When the steamer the Gandhis were travelling in reached Durban, they would not allow the passengers to disembark. Finally, when Gandhiji and others disembarked, he was assaulted. The attack was focussed on him; his wife and children were not harmed, and they safely reached the house of Parsi Rustomji.[5]

After some time, the anger of the people subsided and Gandhiji resumed his legal practice without any worries. Life continued in that mode for about five years. During this period two sons were born to Gandhiji and Kasturba—Ramdas and Devdas.

During the later part of 1901 Gandhiji decided to return to India. He wound up his household in South Africa and left Durban with all the members of his family on 19 October 1901.

He had acquired a good reputation during his stay in South Africa. The Indian community had great respect for him. People gave him a grand

4. Translator's note: This pamphlet became known as the *Green Pamphlet* due to the colour of its cover. It was published in Rajkot on 14 August 1896. It was called *The Grievances of the British Indians in South Africa: An Appeal to the Indian Public.* For the complete text of the *Green Pamphlet,* see *CWMG*, vol. 2, p. 2–36.

5. Parsi Rustomji was a merchant of Natal, and an associate and friend of Gandhiji.

farewell and many gifts. The gifts included expensive jewellery. Gandhiji did not think it proper to accept such gifts. He decided to create a trust with these gifts for the benefit of the Indian community.

Kasturba disapproved strongly. Her own jewellery had been sold by Gandhiji; she felt that these ornaments should be kept for the future daughters-in-law. Harilal and Manilal agreed with their father (Ramdas and Devdas were still very young). Harilal was about thirteen years old, he was no longer a child. Since the sons agreed with their father, Kasturba could do nothing; the ornaments were given to the trust.

After his return to India, Gandhiji started his legal practice and set up his household in Mumbai.

The sons were growing up. Gandhiji was concerned about their education. This question had arisen when they were in South Africa. All the schools there had been for white children, non-whites did not get admission into those schools. Even if admission had been granted because of Gandhiji's status, the children would have been without company. The medium of instruction was not Gujarati; Gandhiji did not approve of this in the least. So he had not got his sons admitted in one such school. He had decided to teach them himself. But he found that he did not have enough time for this. He had then thought of hiring a teacher for them, but could not find a suitable person. Most Indians in South Africa were merchants, they were only functionally literate and could not teach. Moreover, they were economically well off and did not need employment. The Indians who worked as clerks were not fit to be teachers; they had neither the capability nor the time for it. In those days, women were not allowed to study, so Kasturba was illiterate. (Later in life she learnt to read and write a little, this was due to Gandhiji's and her own efforts.) Kasturba therefore could not be the teacher. So long as they lived in South Africa, the question of the children's education could not be resolved.

The problem remained even after they came to India. Gandhiji did not discriminate between his son Harilal and his nephew Gokuldas. They were equal in his eyes. Where should they be sent for their education? He had Gondal and Banaras as two options. He could not decide who should be sent where. He called a child from the neighbourhood and gave him an one-rupee coin and an one-paisa coin. He then asked the child to hide these coins in separate places in the house. The child did as he was told. Gandhiji asked Harilal and Gokuldas to find these coins. Gokuldas found the one-rupee coin, while Harilal found the one-paisa coin. Gandhiji sent Gokuldas to Banaras and Harilal to Gondal.

Gandhiji was not satisfied with the boarding school in Gondal, so he called Harilal back home after sometime.[6]

At that time, Chhaganlal,[7] a nephew three generations removed, was staying with Gandhiji. He taught Harilal and Manilal. Ramdas and Devdas were very young and the question of their studies did not arise.

The Gandhis were pulling along some how. But soon they had to wind up their Mumbai household. Before leaving South Africa Gandhiji had promised the Indian community that in case of need he would return.

They truly needed him. They sent him a wire and some money. Towards the end of November 1902, he left Mumbai. He left his family behind thinking that he would not be needed in South Africa for more than a year. This time too his estimation was wrong. After reaching there, he realised that the stay would be longer.

Before leaving, he had informed his friend, Barrister Shukla,[8] who was practising in Rajkot, that as soon as Rajkot was free of plague, his family would come to Rajkot. Gandhiji requested his friend to look after the boys, arrange for their studies and allow them to use his tennis court. But the family stayed on in Mumbai and Gandhiji's stay in South Africa was extended. Finally, it was decided that the family would move to South Africa. In 1904, a wire came, calling them to South Africa. The Mumbai household was wound up and Kasturba, accompanied by Manilal, Ramdas and Devdas left

---

6. "Gandhi received reports so distressing that he almost disowned him and brought him back." Ref. no. 37, p. 89.
7. Chhaganlal was the grandson of Gandhiji's uncle Jivanchand, and the son of Khushalchand.
8. Dalpatram Bhagwandas Shukla.

Mumbai for South Africa. Harilal was left behind in Mumbai for the sake of his studies.[9]

Gandhiji set up a house in Johannesburg, in the Transvaal province. He did not interfere in the running of the household; he did not have the time to do so. But he took care to ensure that the boys cultivated certain habits. He taught his three sons to grind grain, clean toilets and care for the sick. Harilal was not with the family and was thus deprived of such an education.

Two families were prominent in the Modh Bania community of Rajkot: the Gandhi family and the Vora family.

Haridas Vakhatchand Vora was a leading reformer and citizen of Rajkot. He was of Gandhiji's caste and also a friend. The Modh Bania community had excommunicated Gandhiji when he had gone to England. Haridasbhai was instrumental in re-admitting him into the caste on his return, after Gandhiji performed the purification rituals. Gandhiji had returned to India in 1896 for a short period. On 9 July he came to Rajkot, among the people who received him at the Rajkot station were Haridasbhai and his son Chhaganlal. Haridasbhai was an advocate of girl's education. In those days, in a backward province like Kathiawad, he had educated his daughters.

He had three daughters. The eldest was Balibehn.[10] Gulabbehn was younger to her, and the youngest was Kumibehn or Kumudbehn. Balibehn was betrothed. They were looking for a groom for Gulabbehn.

Gulabbehn was like a daughter to Gandhiji. She had played on his lap. While Gandhiji was in India, he and Haridasbhai had discussed the question of Gulabbehn's engagement. We do not know whether Harilal was explicitly mentioned. But later, Harilal's name was discussed in Haridasbhai's family;

---

9. On page 8 of Ref. no. 26, it is stated that all the four brothers went to South Africa. On page 10, it is stated that after reaching Johannesburg, Gandhiji made arrangements for the education of Harilal and others. On page 16, it is written, "we four brothers were living there." All these statements are factually incorrect; Harilal did not join his family at this point in time.
10. Her name was Jivibehn. She was called Balibehn by her family.

all looked upon him with approval. At this time, Gandhiji was in South Africa. Therefore, Harilal was betrothed to Gulabbehn with the consent of Gandhiji's elder brother Lakshmidas.

This engagement took place with the consent of the elders of both families, and all the ceremonies were performed. We know that Gandhiji and Haridas had discussed the matter, and Gandhiji felt that "even if one were to search, where would one get a girl wiser then Gulab?"[11] Since he believed that it was not harmful to betroth boys and girls at a young age, he welcomed this engagement.

In April–May 1903, Harilal fell ill. At that time he was at Gandhiji's sister Raliyatbehn's house. There were no men in the household. When Haridasbhai came to know of this, he took Harilal to his home. Harilal was well cared for there. When Gandhiji learnt about this he wrote a letter on 30 June 1903,[12] and thanked Haridasbhai and Revashankarbhai.[13]

Harilal has written about the time that he spent recuperating from illness at his future father-in-law's house. "I was not entirely unaware at that time. Haridasbhai's family was considered reformist. I knew that I was at my in-laws. Naturally, I desired to see what kind of girl was destined for me. I saw a photograph. A thought entered my mind that I have not been engaged to an unsuitable girl, and the in-laws' family is also good. After some days I desired to see the girl face-to-face. I saw her. Time did the rest. As we got more opportunities we talked and joked. The bond of love bound us."[14]

---

11. Ref. no. 1.
12. Translator's note: Gandhiji wrote, "During my self-imposed exile, I have been overwhelmed with kindness of friends in India. I know that you and Revashankarbhai have supplied my place to Harilal. I do not wish to enlarge upon that subject. I can only wish that he was here to be attended to by me, and regret that he should have been a source of anxiety and worry to either of you." *CWMG*, vol. 3, p. 128–29.
13. Revashankar Jagjivan Jhaveri was the elder brother of Gandhiji's friend Dr. Pranjivandas, and uncle of Shrimad Rajchandra. He was the owner of 'Mani Bhuvan' where Gandhiji stayed whenever he was in Mumbai, after his return to India.
14. Appendix 1.

After recovering completely, Harilal returned home. How were Gulab and Harilal to meet now? They began exchanging letters.

On the other hand, Gandhiji wrote from South Africa that Harilal should join him. In the letter of 30 June cited above, Gandhiji suggested that Kasturba and their sons should leave India for South Africa in November 1903.

On 18 November 1903, Gandhiji wrote to Chhaganlal and told him to buy a sari for Chanchi if he had not already done so.[15]

Kasturba, Manilal, Ramdas and Devdas sailed for South Africa, and Harilal stayed back in India to continue with his studies.

When he was studying in the fifth standard at the Esplanade High School in Mumbai, Kishorlal Ghanshyamlal Mashruwala was his classmate. Harilal's stay in India was uncertain and he told his classmates that he would soon join his father in South Africa.[16]

His mind was in South Africa. The time for his departure neared; he was corresponding with Gulabbehn. Their mutual attraction was growing. Both were in a quandary. What could be done? Harilal felt that if he were to leave for South Africa he would take at least five years to return. Gulabbehn and her family must have felt that there would be criticism if she were to remain unmarried for so long. The decision was made to get them married.

Harilal wrote a letter to Gandhiji wherein he stated, "I have the letter written in 1915,[17] which proves under what considerations the decision was made...I am ready to show it whenever asked for."[18]

Gandhiji believed that they were too young to be married. Whatever might have happened in his case, he felt that it would be wrong for his sons

---

15. Ref. no. 1.
16. Ref. no. 31, p. 80.
17. Gulabbehn must have written this letter to Harilal. The year mentioned is 1915, nine years after the marriage of Harilal and Gulabbehn. It is possible that the year mentioned is incorrect, or by mistake the year 1905 was noted as 1915. It is also possible that the letter was written in 1915.
18. Appendix 1.

to marry at a tender age; he felt that Harilal's welfare lay in delaying the marriage. He wanted Harilal to join him in South Africa as soon as possible. His letters instructed that Harilal should be sent with any of their acquaintances travelling from India to Africa.

Harilal remained in India.

Meanwhile, the Zulu rebellion broke out in Natal. Gandhiji wrote to the Natal government on 24 April 1906, offering his help in establishing an Indian Ambulance Corps. He set about making preparations for it and spent the period between 15 June 1906 and 20 July 1906 at the war front.

In India, preparations were on for Harilal and Gulabbehn's wedding. Gandhiji felt that marriage had become almost inevitable for them.

After the date of marriage was fixed, Gulabbehn wrote a letter in verse to Harilal.

> Dear Husband—the basis of my life, Salutations.
>
> My heart adorned with virtue, resplendent like the moon
> shines in the beautiful land of Porbandar.
>
> An ocean of truth, born in a high family,
> I am blessed in having him as my husband.
> (It takes many lives of good deeds to get such a one.)
>
> I, Gulab, offer from Rajkot my pranams.
> I have not had a glimpse of you for so long,
> not even in my dreams.
> Yet, the gods know that our hearts are one.
>
> The thought of our union is nectar to my mind,
> accept the love I offer you.
> (How I wait for) the eighth day of the Sud Paksha of Vaishakha—
> the moment of our union.
>
> Come soon my spring, my soul Harilal,
> like a night without a moon, I long for you.
> Dear, the moon has risen in the sky, the moonlight is resplendent,
> my mind is enthralled with your thought, my heart filled.

Beauty, youth, virtue, character and knowledge unite in you,
I am blessed by the gods, my being is fulfilled.

Your virtues flow as a river and surround me,
they envelop me like the fragrance of sandalwood and kasturi.

Consider me your slave, overlook my shortcomings,
free me from pangs of separation.

I hope you are in good health. God willing we shall meet soon.
I plead your forgiveness for this late letter. You may give me
the punishment that I deserve.

Written in love by one craving for the moonlight, longing for
her moonlike lover,

Gulab[19]

It appears that the consent of neither Gandhiji nor Kasturba was obtained before the marriage. It is easy to understand that Kasturba was not consulted. She was the daughter-in-law of an orthodox Hindu family, where is the need for her consent? She need not be asked. That, one can comprehend. But Gandhiji was not even asked before the date of the marriage was fixed.

Gandhiji wrote to his elder brother Lakshmidas on 27 May 1906, "It is well if Harilal is married; it is also well if he is not.[20] For the present at any rate I have ceased to think of him as a son."[21]

Why did he write so? Did he write this in anger or in order to taunt his family because he and Kasturba were neglected on this occasion? Or was it because Harilal was sixteen years old and he believed that a sixteen-year-old son should be like a friend, and he considered Harilal his friend and felt that

19. Song to be sung in the raga of "Guru Govind na Mahina" (in the original). Translator's note: I am grateful to G.N. Devy for his comments on the translation of this letter in verse.
20. In an open letter to Gandhiji (see Appendix 1) Harilal wrote, "You were prepared to have my engagement broken." Probably, he is referring to this letter by Gandhiji.
21. Ref. no. 23. (Translator's note: *CWMG*, vol.5, p. 353.)

he ought not impose his views on him? It is difficult to determine what Gandhiji's feelings were while writing this letter.

Harilal and Gulab were married on 2 May 1906.[22]

---

22. a. In Ref. no. 30, p. 77, it is mentioned that, "Harilalbhai resumed his studies on returning to the country...Meanwhile he married on the advice and help of uncle and other relatives. He gave up studies after failing in the matriculation examination once or twice and took up some business."

    This is factually correct, but inaccurate with regard to dates. Harilal returned to India after separating from Gandhiji in 1911. He was married before this. His first child – daughter Ramibehn – was born in South Africa. He returned to India after that and made attempts to study.

    b. Ref. no. 38, p. 185, incorrectly mentions that Harilal's marriage took place in 1907.

2 'Young Gandhi' of South Africa

After about three months of his marriage Harilal went to South Africa. Gulabbehn stayed behind in India. He borrowed about ten pounds from a cousin of Gandhiji, Khushalchand. He booked his own passage as a deck passenger. He made all the arrangements for the journey. Gandhiji was pleased with him. In September or October of 1906, he reached South Africa.[1]

Gandhiji had not liked his views being disregarded in the matter of Harilal and Gulab's marriage. Moreover, he also got to know that his elder brother Lakshmidas had spent a lot of money on the marriage. He had asked Gandhiji for money and Gandhiji had expressed his inability to send money. Later, after Harilal had reached South Africa, in a letter dated 20 April 1907, he wrote to Lakshmidas, "Since Harilal is already betrothed,[2] I have nothing to say against it. At the same time I cannot say that I am pleased about it."[3]

Thus Gandhiji was disappointed with the marriage of Harilal and Gulab. But once the marriage had taken place he tried not to let it bother him.

Harilal joined Gandhiji's office in Johannesburg. We have a letter that was signed by him on behalf of Gandhiji. Simultaneously he tried to further his studies. It was not possible to join a school, therefore Gandhiji taught him.

---

1. Ref. no. 38, p. 149, states that Harilal was sixteen when he reached South Africa. If this were correct, the year of his arrival should be 1904. But, in 1904 he was still in India. Therefore, the statement is incorrect.
2. The translation 'already betrothed' in *CWMG*, vol. 6, p. 431, is incorrect. In Gujarati, the term is 'vivah', which means 'marriage' and not 'betrothal' or 'engagement'.
3. Translator's note: "Letter to Lakshmidas Gandhi, April 20, 1907", *CWMG*, vol. 6, p. 431.

After that he went to the Phoenix Settlement, and there he worked in the printing press and the office of the *Indian Opinion.* He moved between Johannesburg and the Phoenix Settlement, but kept indifferent health. He was newly married, but had left his wife behind in India. He was eighteen years old. His wife was also an adolescent. It is natural that he desired to have his wife with him. It is possible that Kasturba also wished that.

Gulabbehn also wrote that she was very anxious. It is possible that since Gandhiji had expressed displeasure at the marriage, his relatives were not very welcoming. Gandhiji wrote that she should be sent to South Africa with someone known and suitable. They waited for the telegram informing them of her journey. It is likely that no suitable travel companion was found. Finally, Harilal was sent to India. This was in either May or June 1907. He must have returned soon to South Africa, accompanied by Gulab.

Gulabbehn was pregnant. Her father reached the Phoenix Settlement on 4 September 1907. He was unwell and had come to Phoenix on Gandhiji's invitation. He might have come to take Gulabbehn back with him. But she remained in Phoenix.

At this time, in the political sphere of South Africa, and especially of Transvaal, a movement against the Indian community was on the rise. The South African parliament had passed an act against the Indian community. Gandhiji led a delegation to England to ensure that the act did not receive royal assent. He succeeded in his efforts, but the success was shortlived. The parliament passed the Asiatic Registration Act. The Indian community under the leadership of Gandhiji began a satyagraha by refusing to submit to the registration. On 27 December 1907, Gandhiji was arrested and sentenced to simple imprisonment for two months.

When this news reached the Phoenix Settlement, they were celebrating the seemant of Gulabbehn.

With a view to reach a compromise, the South African government released Gandhiji on 30 January 1908. As he was going to voluntarily register himself as per the terms of the agreement, an Indian called Mir Alam attacked him out of ignorance. Gandhiji was injured. At this time Harilal was not with him.

On 10 April 1908, Gulabbehn gave birth to a girl. She was born on Ramnavami and hence was named Rami.[4]

The government of Transvaal did not honour the terms of the settlement. The Indian community recommenced the satyagraha, and made a bonfire of the certificates they had obtained through voluntary registration as the first step of the struggle.

Possession of a license to trade was required in Transvaal. As part of the satyagraha, Indians started hawking without license. Those who hawked were no ordinary Indians, but prominent merchants of the community. Hawking without licenses was the second front of the struggle.

The struggle continued on both these fronts. Gandhiji appeared in court for the defense. His presence as a counsel for defense was inspiring, and it enthused people.

A third front was opened. Under the Immigrants Restriction Act, an educated Indian could not enter the country and those who violated the act could be arrested. This law too was breached. The struggle was taking place on three fronts.

Harilal was watching the developments, he understood the significance of the struggle and was impatient to join it. He left Phoenix to join the struggle. According to Devdas, "His sendoff was heart-wrenching. He looked handsome, his hair were parted in the middle and locks of hair flew around on his forehead."[5]

On 24 July 1908, Harilal entered Transvaal from Natal and started hawking without a permit. He was arrested on 27 July and on the next day he was tried along with other satyagrahis. Gandhiji appeared in the court as counsel for defense. He said to the court that the accused had "asked him to ask for a severe sentence. If a light sentence was imposed, as soon as they came

---

4. Devdas in his article (Appendix 2) says that he and his elder brother's daughter were of the same age and therefore they shared toys. Devdas was born in May 1900. Rami was born in April 1908. About eight years separated them. Devdas' statement, therefore, is incorrect.
5. Appendix 2.

out, they intended to repeat the action. It would be a saving of time to give them a long sentence."[6]

The magistrate did not accept his arguments and imposed a fine of £1 on Harilal, and if he did not pay the fine he was to face imprisonment for a week with hard labour. Harilal chose imprisonment.

Harilal was twenty years old at that time. Many people asked Gandhiji why he allowed his son to go to jail. Gandhiji explained,

> I have received inquiries from many quarters as to why I sent Harilal, my son, to gaol. I give some reasons below:
>
> 1. I have advised every Indian to take up hawking. I am afraid I cannot join myself since I am enrolled as an attorney. I therefore thought it right to advise my son to make his rounds as a hawker. I hesitate to ask others to do things which I cannot do myself. I think whatever my son does at my instance can be taken to have been done by me.
> 2. It will be a part of Harilal's education to go to gaol for the sake of the country.[7]

Gandhiji wrote in a letter that Harilal "did a very good thing by coming here and going to jail. Since I could not go, I could be happy only if Harilal went. I think it has been a very good experience for Harilal himself."[8]

Harilal was freed on 3 August 1908. He was re-arrested on 10 August and was produced before the court. He was charged with the offence of not possessing the certificate of registration. Gandhiji was present in the court as counsel for defense. He said that Harilal had no desire to leave Transvaal. But he requested that the accused be given twenty-four hours to leave the

---

6. Ref. no. 4, August 1, 1908. (Translator's note: See also "Trial of Harilal Gandhi and Others", *CWMG,* vol. 8, p. 405–06.)
7. Ref. no. 4, August 8, 1908. (Translator's note: See also "Letter to *Indian Opinion*", *CWMG,* vol. 8, p. 432–33. This was published under the title "Why he Sent his Son to Gaol: Mr. Gandhi's Explanation.")
8. Ref. no. 1. (Translator's note: See also "Letter to Maganlal Gandhi", *CWMG,* vol. 91, supplementary vol. 1, p. 76.)

colony.[9] Gandhiji made this request because the registration of two other Indians was due to expire in a few days. If all the cases were tried together, Gandhiji felt it would be more convenient for the court. The court accepted the request and ordered Harilal to leave Transvaal within seven days.

Harilal did not leave Transvaal. On 18 August, he was sentenced to one month's imprisonment with hard labour. This was his second jail term.

Harilal was to be released from jail on 17 September 1908. Gandhiji was eager to meet him. Gandhiji enquired about the time of release; he did not receive a reply from the jail authorities. Gandhiji assumed that Harilal would be released as per the jail regulations and went to the jail in the morning to receive him. On reaching there, he was informed that Harilal had been taken away to some place at about 7 a.m. in the morning. Gandhiji came to know that Harilal had been taken towards Natal by rail and at every station en route the windows of his compartment had been closed.

Gandhiji wired Harilal and instructed him to re-enter Transvaal. Harilal was now known as 'young Gandhi'. He was equally eager to meet his father. Before he was deported to Natal he had requested the jail authorities to allow him to meet his father, but the request had been declined.

The very next day he reached Charlestown.[10] In about ten minutes he caught a train to Transvaal. He was detained at the Volksrust station.[11] The hearing of his case was postponed till 22 September. The magistrate was willing to release Harilal if he furnished a bond for £50. Harilal declined to

---

9. Ref. no. 4, August 15, 1908. (Translator's note: *Transvaal Leader,* August 11, 1908, reported, "Mr. Gandhi, on behalf of the accused, said that the latter had no desire to leave the Colony, but nevertheless he was desirous that the Court should make an order for the accused to leave the Colony within 24 hours. He made the request because two other Indians whose time under the Act would expire on Wednesday would be ready to go to gaol. He [Mr. Gandhi] hoped His Worship would adopt this course, as the accused's affairs were in his hands. Mr. Jordan ordered the accused to leave the Colony within seven days." See "Trial of Harilal Gandhi-II", *CWMG,* vol. 8, p. 436.)
10. It is the last railway station in Natal on the route to Transvaal.
11. It is the first railway station in Transvaal on the route from Natal.

furnish the bond and chose a jail term. Meanwhile, on 21 September, the prosecution withdrew its case and Harilal was released.

The struggle was gaining strength. Finally, the Transvaal government arrested Gandhiji on 6 October 1908, and on 14 October he was given a choice of a fine of £25 or two months of jail sentence with hard labour. To protest against this a public meeting was held in Johannesburg on 18 October. Harilal was also present. In his speech he said,

> I am proud of my respected father. As British subjects we are sons of Britain; but because of this black act of the Transvaal government I am ashamed to call my self her son today. It was a happy day for me when my father was sentenced. It is ridiculous to ask for the fingerprints[12] of a man who has practised law in South Africa for thirteen years. As well wishers of Britain we shall abide by truth and fight till the end. Some whites allege that Indians are a threat to the Empire. Others[13] have shown this to be false. But to my mind, it is true that Indians are a threat to the Empire. Because Satyagraha always poses a threat to the false; who does not know this? Their politics is not beneficial to the Empire. It might even lead to its collapse. We sought redress from the higher government about the Transvaal act, what did we get from them? The promises of His Majesty's government have been washed away. Then why should we seek help from anyone but god? The government says that we are demanding doors to be opened for all Indians. The government wants to prolong the struggle by such false claims. But after today's meeting the truth of our struggle will shine forth. Till truth is established we shall fight with all our might. The entire civilized world accepts the justness of our struggle.[14]

Gandhiji was kept in the Volksrust jail. He was transferred to the Johannesburg jail on 25 October in connection with another case and was produced before the court on 28 October. Harilal went to the court and met him.

---

12. Providing fingerprints was a requirement for the registration certificate.
13. There were also whites who supported the Indian struggle.
14. Ref. no. 4, October 31, 1908.

Kasturba was living in the Phoenix Settlement. She fell ill. Gandhiji sent a telegram to Harilal when he learnt about her illness. Harilal left Johannesburg and reached Phoenix to nurse his mother. Gandhiji was released from jail on 12 December 1908, and in a few days began to nurse Kasturba.

We have seen that Gandhiji was displeased with the marriage of Harilal and Gulab because his views had been disregarded. But with time, it no longer rankled Gandhiji. Harilal had joined the struggle and supported his father. This had given Gandhiji much satisfaction, and his affection for his son and daughter-in-law increased everyday. Gulabbehn was like a daughter to him. She was now a daughter-in-law and also a mother of a child; often he wrote letters of advice to her.

After Kasturba had recovered a little, Gandhiji went to Johannesburg for public work. He was detained at the Volksrust station on 16 October 1909. But on account of Kasturba's illness he furnished a personal bond and was released. He wrote a letter to Gulabbehn and advised her that she should for the time being give up the idea of staying with Harilal because it would be good for both of them. He also addressed her in her capacity as the mistress of the house, "Do not forget that we are very poor."[15]

Gandhiji had returned to the Phoenix Settlement after he was released because Kasturba's health had worsened. On 25 March 1909, he appeared before the court and was sentenced.

Harilal joined the struggle, leaving behind his mother who was on her deathbed. Along with the others he entered Transvaal on 1 December 1908. They were arrested and produced before the court. He told the court that he had nothing to say in his defense. The court ordered that he be deported. He was kept in the prison for two days and on the third day he was deported from Natal. He caught a train from Charlestown and entered Transvaal within ten minutes of deportation. He was produced before the court on 9 December and the court again ordered his deportation. He returned on 10 December and was produced before the court on the same day.

15. Ref. no. 1. (Translator's note: See also "Letter to Chanchalbehn Gandhi", *CWMG*, vol. 9, p. 150.)

Due to a legal complication his case was adjourned. On 31 December 1908, he was deported, and the very next day he re-entered and was arrested. Harilal, along with the others, was sentenced to six months imprisonment on 10 February 1909.

Father and son were in the same jail. Gandhiji thought of his daughter-in-law and granddaughter while in the jail. On 28 February, he wrote to Chanchal and advised her to feed Rami at the breast for a few more days.[16] He wrote to Manilal, from the jail on 25 March 1909, that he thinks of Chanchi everyday. He requested Manilal to look after her and make sure that she does not miss Harilal too much.[17] In a letter to Henry Polak on the 26 April 1909, he asked, "Is Chanchi cheerful? Or does she brood over her separation from Harilal?"[18]

In those days, people were sentenced arbitrarily. Harilal was sentenced to prison for six months, while Gandhiji who was the leader of the movement was given three months in prison. Gandhiji was released on 24 May 1909, but Harilal and others who were sentenced before him were still in jail. On his release he said, "I am not happy at being released; rather, I am unhappy...For... others, including, if I may be personal, my eldest son Harilal,[19] are still in

---

16. Translator's note: This letter was written on 26 and not 28 February 1909. See *CWMG,* vol. 9, p. 200.
17. Translator's note: "Letter to Manilal Gandhi", *CWMG,* vol. 9, p. 205.
18. Translator's note: "Letter to Henry Polak", *CWMG,* vol. 9, p. 214. Henry Salomon Leon Polak was one of the closest European associates of Gandhiji in South Africa. He was born in a Jewish family at Dover, England. Henry Polak and Gandhiji met in 1904 in a vegetarian restaurant in Johannesburg and soon became close friends. It was Polak who gave Gandhiji John Ruskin's *Unto This Last,* a book that changed the course of Gandhiji's life and led to the establishment of the Phoenix Settlement in 1905. He articled as a solicitor to Gandhiji in Johannesburg (1905–08) and his marriage to Millie Graham Polak was solemnised with Gandhiji as a witness. Henry Polak worked as the editor of the *Indian Opinion* from 1906 to 1916. Despite divergent political views the two retained a deep friendship that lasted till Gandhiji's assassination.
19. In jail, Harilal was given the task of cooking.

gaol...I request you again to fill the gaols and not rest till our demands are conceded."[20]

Gandhiji led a delegation to England. When he left from Johannesburg on 21 June 1909, Harilal was still in the jail. The delegation returned empty-handed on 2 December 1909.

Harilal was released on 9 August 1909. At that time his younger brother Manilal was unwell, so he went to the Phoenix Settlement to nurse him.

---

20. Ref. no. 4, May 29, 1909. (Translator's note: See also "Speech at Pretoria Meeting", *CWMG,* vol. 9, p. 216.)

3 Harilal Leaves Home

While Gandhiji was in England, his friend Dr. Pranjivandas Mehta was also there. Dr. Mehta offered to bear the expenses for study in England for one person from the Phoenix Settlement and one of Gandhiji's sons. Gandhiji was not in favour of the second offer. But without naming any person, he insisted that the opportunity to study in England should be given to any Phoenix settler. He also said that if he felt that his son Manilal deserved the opportunity he would not object to it being given to him.

Dr. Mehta acceded to Gandhiji's conditions. Gandhiji selected his nephew Chhaganlal and informed Dr. Mehta.[1] At that time Henry Polak was in India advocating the South African cause. On Gandhiji's instructions Chhaganlal first went to India and travelled around the country with Polak for some time. He left India for England on 1 June 1910.[2]

---

1. a. Ref. no. 15, Part 1, sr. no. 3, fn., mentions that the discussion about sending Chhaganlal to England had been going on since 1905. But Gandhiji's letters of that period do not provide any substantiation.

   b. Gandhiji had the following expectations from Chhaganlal.

   > He should, before embarking, take a definite and formal vow of poverty. He should also take the vow that he will not use the learning acquired here as a means of livelihood, the latter being always found from Phoenix and that he should dedicate his life to a realization of the Phoenix ideals...He should live, if necessary, in a house in one of the suburbs and there do his own cooking and everything.

   Ref. no.1. (Translator's note: See also "Letter to HSL Polak, September 29, 1909", *CWMG,* vol.10, p. 438–40.)

2. Chhaganlal left South Africa on 17 September 1909. After going to India he must have changed his mind and might have expressed his desire to leave the Phoenix Settlement. In response, Gandhiji wrote to the effect, "You have struck me harder then Mir Alam. How can you leave Phoenix?" Ref. no. 1.

We do not know if Harilal was aware of these developments. But, we can say that the seeds of the discontent between him and Gandhiji were sown in 1909, when Gandhiji was in England and Harilal was in and out of jail in South Africa.

When Chhaganlal left South Africa for India, Harilal was out of jail. He must have been aware of Chhaganlal's departure. He may not have known all the details about the arrangements. He was deeply involved in the struggle. With Manilal's recovery, Harilal entered Transvaal once again and was sentenced to six months imprisonment on 1 November 1909. Gandhiji was in England at that time. He was happy hearing the news and even expressed it to Tolstoy in a letter of 10 November 1909.[3]

Discussions had taken place about forming a trust for the Phoenix Settlement even before Harilal's jail term. Harilal had agreed to be a settler and live according to the ideals and norms of the Settlement.

Harilal was kept in the Volksrust jail. Later he was transferred to the Johannesburg jail. He was taken from the Volksrust jail to the railway station and from the Park Station of Johannesburg to the Fort Jail in handcuffs. He was asked to carry his own luggage, including books, and also the luggage and blanket of the warden.

He was released on 30 April 1910. On 6 May 1910, he went to the Phoenix Settlement to meet his mother, wife and daughter.[4] Meanwhile, the Tolstoy Farm was being established and Gandhiji was living there.[5]

---

3. Translator's note: Gandhiji sent a copy of Joseph Doke's biography of him and sought the support of the Count for the struggle and its method. He referred to Harilal's recent imprisonment and wrote, "I may add that my son has happily joined me in the struggle and is now undergoing imprisonment with hard labour for six months. This is his fourth imprisonment in the course of the struggle." *CWMG*, vol. 9, p. 529.
4. Ref. no. 38, p. 242–43, states that during the imprisonment Harilal was filled with concern for his two children. This is incorrect; at that time, he had only one child.
5. Translator's note: The Tolstoy Farm was the second ashram-like community established by Gandhiji in 1910. It was situated some twenty-two miles from

Harilal spent the month of May and twenty days of June at the Phoenix Settlement. During this period Gandhiji was either at the Tolstoy Farm or in Johannesburg.

Gulabbehn was pregnant again. She was to be sent to India along with her daughter Rami. Gandhiji gave instructions to this effect on 15 June 1910. Harilal wanted them to go by second class, Gandhiji agreed to this.[6]

Harilal rejoined the struggle. On 20 June 1910 he entered Transvaal. He was arrested and on 23 June he was sentenced to three months imprisonment. He was released on 22 September 1910. Gulabbehn and Rami had by then reached India.

Harilal entered Transvaal one more time and was arrested. On 10 October 1910, he was sentenced to three months imprisonment. He was kept in the Volksrust jail. Here he had to face harassment; through his own efforts he secured a transfer and was sent to the Johannesburg jail.[7] He was released on 9 November 1910.

During this period, that is from 1 November 1910 to 9 January 1911, Gandhiji was not in jail.

Johannesburg and was built on 1100 acres of land belonging to Gandhiji's friend Herman Kallenbach. Families of satyagrahis lived there. Gandhiji experimented with community living on the Tolstoy Farm. The Farm was abandoned in early 1913. Some of its inmates joined the Phoenix Settlement.

6. Translator's note: Gandhiji wrote to Maganlal Gandhi, "I have decided to send Chanchal to India. Please find out some company for her and send her immediately. I am not likely to go there. Harilal wants a second-class ticket to be bought for her and we shall do so...Chanchal may go even in the company of some good man. If she has the courage, she need not wait for me." *CWMG*, vol. 10, p. 273.
7. In Ref. no. 24, vol. 1, p. 19, Gandhiji is quoted as saying, "He had fasted for seven days to secure a transfer from the jail and had succeeded." In Ref. no. 4, November 26, 1910, English section, p. 395, there is a mention of a seven-day fast by Surendra Bapubhai Medh. There is no mention of Harilal's fast. It is hard to believe that Surendra's fast was noted but not Harilal's. Gandhiji was referring to the incident – quoted in Ref. no. 24 as having taken place around 15 March 1932 – after twenty-one to twenty-two years. It is probable that due to the time gap Gandhiji might have not remembered the name correctly.

It had taken some time to ensure that Gulabbehn and Rami could travel to India in good company. While in jail, Harilal had suggested that he would accompany his wife and daughter to India, but Gandhiji refused to grant him permission. He felt that they were not rich enough to spend so much money. Moreover, one who is committed to the struggle may not leave it, for however short a period. They were sent to India while Harilal was still in jail.

After his release Harilal spent time at both the Tolstoy Farm and the Phoenix Settlement. Gandhiji was preoccupied with the new law that the government was about to enact. He spent time in Cape Town in connection with this work. Harilal, to the extent it was possible for him, looked after Gandhiji's responsibilities.

On 6 April 1911, a phone call was received from a hospital that an Indian patient had died there. The hospital had no information about his kin, as there had been no one taking care of him. Harilal arranged for a proper cremation of the dead body.

Reverend Phillips and Albert Cartwright, the editor of the *Transvaal Leader*, both well-wishers of the Indian community, were leaving for England on 10 April 1911. Harilal was present at the Johannesburg railway station to bid them goodbye as Gandhiji's representative. On 17 April 1911, Harilal was present at the gates of the prison to welcome the freed satyagrahis.

Joseph Royeppen was to leave Transvaal on the resolution of the struggle. The Vande Mataram League gave him a farewell and a scroll of honour on 1 May 1911. Gandhiji presided over the function, and Harilal was also present.

But his mind was restless. He had been deeply dissatisfied with Gandhiji for some time. When he was married at the age of eighteen in 1906, his father had shown no joy or enthusiasm. Instead he had written, "It is well if Harilal is married; it is also well if he is not. For the present at any rate I have ceased to think of him as a son."[8] It is probable that Gandhiji might have written this

8. Translator's note: "Letter to Lakshmidas Gandhi, May 27, 1906", *CWMG*, vol. 5, p. 353.

thinking of Harilal as a friend rather than as a son, but it would not be surprising if Harilal had felt slighted.

After sometime Harilal and Gulab had come to South Africa and lived with Gandhiji. Even after that, Gandhiji had written, "Since Harilal is already betrothed, I have nothing to say against it. At the same time I cannot say that I am pleased about it."[9]

Even after he reached South Africa, differences with regard to his education persisted between Gandhiji and Harilal. It is true that Gandhiji believed it was better to be uneducated than receive the kind of education that was available to Indian students. He also felt that school atmosphere was not conducive to education. For these reasons Gandhiji might have remained indifferent to the education of his sons. To Harilal, it must have appeared as lack of concern on Gandhiji's part. He thought, "Bapu is highly educated. Why does he not then give us good education? Bapu speaks of service, simplicity and character building. But if [he] had not received the kind of education that he has would he have been able to serve the country as he does today? Even we will serve the country after receiving education and lead a simple life after achieving qualification. We are not opposed to a life dedicated to service and simplicity. But how are we to serve the country by remaining unlettered?"[10]

Gandhiji's apparent lack of concern bothered not only Harilal but also others. Polak and Kallenbach were also worried and expressed their doubts to Gandhiji.[11] Some other friends had also asked Gandhiji what was the harm in

---

9. Translator's note: "Letter to Lakshmidas Gandhi, April 20, 1907", *CWMG*, vol. 6, p. 431.
10. Ref. no. 30, p. 75.
11. Translator's note: Herman Kallenbach (1871–1945) was born in a Jewish family in East Prussia and went to South Africa as an architect in 1896. Gandhiji and Kallenbach met sometime in 1903 and became soulmates. Gandhiji described him as "a man of strong feelings, wide sympathies and child-like simplicity". Kallenbach also shared Gandhiji's first penitential fast at Phoenix in 1913 over the 'moral lapse' of two inmates of the Settlement. He accompanied Gandhiji and Kasturba on their return to India in 1914, but

his sons becoming barristers? He was also asked what rights he had to clip their wings.[12]

This discontent was also present among Harilal's three brothers and Kasturba. Ba was ambitious that her sons receive good education and be regarded as important men. Gandhiji's neglect bothered her a great deal. She asked him, "What is it that you intend to do? Do you want to keep the sons illiterate? Do you want them to wear a loincloth? Do you want them to remain poor beggars?"[13]

Gandhiji was not unaware of such feelings and opinions. Gandhiji was aware that all his sons had this complaint against him to a lesser or greater extent. But, he believed that as per his ideas he was correct. He was firm in his belief that they should be educated as per his ideals. Seventeen-year-old Manilal was perplexed. What should he say if asked, "What class are you in?" Gandhiji retorted, "Can you not give an answer to the question, 'What class are you in?' Henceforward you may say that you are in Bapu's class."[14]

Manilal was probably silenced by such a response; he might have even suppressed his desires. But Harilal, twenty-one years old, was not to be silenced; he could not suppress his desire to be educated.

If this were not enough, when Dr. Pranjivandas Mehta expressed his eagerness to bear the expenses of education in England for one of Gandhiji's sons, Gandhiji had said that if Manilal was a deserving candidate, then Gandhiji would not have any objection to his taking up the opportunity. Even at that time, Gandhiji had thought of Manilal and not Harilal. Harilal

---

was detained in London as an enemy alien. He visited Gandhiji in India in 1937 and again in 1939.

12. Ref. no. 35, p. 273.
13. a. Ref. no. 32, p. 106–07.
    b. Ref. no. 26, states that Gokhale had recommended to Gandhiji that Harilal be sent to England to train as a barrister. Gokhale had gone to South Africa after Harilal had returned to India. So, if such a recommendation had been made, it was after Harilal had reached India.
14. Ref. no. 23. (Translator's note: See also "Letter to Manilal Gandhi, October 22, 1909", *CWMG,* vol. 9, p. 495.)

must have come to know of this; it is possible that Manilal's selection may not have hurt him, but Gandhiji selected his nephew Chhaganlal.[15]

---

15. a. Devdas does not mention Dr. Pranjivandas Mehta's offer in his essay. On Harilal's desire to become a barrister, he has written, "Having renounced this worldly happiness Bapu did not have enough money to spend." See Appendix 2. This reason is irrelevant. Gandhiji did not have to spend any money. The expenses were to be borne by Dr. Mehta.

    b. After Harilal left his father's house, which we shall discuss shortly, Gandhiji in his letter of 8 May 1911 to Dr. Pranjivandas Mehta said, "He [Harilal] did not like going to England with your money and under any binding." (Translator's note: *CWMG,* vol. 11, p. 65.) We can surmise that Gandhiji would have discussed the issue with Harilal. But when? It is not possible to ascertain when the discussion took place. Dr. Mehta's offer is discussed for the first time in a letter to Polak written on 2 September 1909. (Translator's note: Gandhiji wrote,

    > Dr. Mehta, however, has promised much more. He intends to give a scholarship that would cover the expenses of educating and boarding an Indian lad at Phoenix...The idea arose from his desire to take over the training of one of my own boys. I told him that I could not accept any such thing, but I would be pleased to accept the expenses, to be used for the best person in Phoenix, and that, if I considered that Manilal was the most suitable for the purpose, I should not hesitate to send him also.

    CWMG, vol. 9. p. 382.)

    In another letter to Polak, dated 29 September 1909, Gandhiji mentioned his expectations from Chhaganlal if he were to go to England. During this period, Gandhiji was in England. It is therefore not possible that he discussed this matter with Harilal before the selection was made. Chhaganlal went to England, but his health suffered there. He returned to India by 20 January 1911. It is possible that after his return, the father and son discussed the matter and Harilal declined to be bound by any conditions.

    Later it was decided that Sorabji Shapurji Adajania would be sent to England on the money provided by Dr. Mehta. He left South Africa for England on 21 July 1912. This decision hurt Harilal. On 16 October 1912, Gandhiji wrote to him,

    > You have not understood the step I have taken regarding Sorabji. The chief thing is that he is a Parsi, and it befits a Hindu to encourage

Gandhiji did not permit Harilal to accompany Gulabbehn to India. His reason for refusal was financial and perhaps justified. On the other hand, Harilal might not have wanted to express his discontent openly—therefore, his suggestion that he accompany Gulabbehn on her journey to India. He might have thought that he would otherwise not be allowed to leave South Africa. If he were to leave on his own, his departure would not be appreciated by anyone. Accompanying Gulab was a good excuse and he thought of taking advantage of that. But he did not succeed.

He was fed up.[16] He decided to leave his father's house and run away. On 10 February 1911, Gulabbehn gave birth to a boy, Kantilal, in India. It is possible that on receiving this news Harilal became eager and restless to go to India.

But his main desire was to study. He did not expect his father to earn, accumulate wealth and bequeath it to his sons. At the age of thirteen he had felt that the ornaments received by his father could not be considered the family's personal property. He felt that they should be used for the service of others and be given back to the people in the form of a trust. "He did not want to live his life on the earnings of his father. He wanted to study, educate himself and work for a living."[17]

Harilal must have thought of leaving for India without informing anyone, and as soon as his jail term was over he must have started planning. His wife was not with him. There was no one in whom he could have confided his innermost thoughts. He must have been in a turmoil.

> him. If Sorabji succeeds in becoming a barrister, his responsibilities will increase. Sorabji's services cannot be used beyond a certain point, but this is not true of Medh. That is why I would not encourage Medh to be a barrister. How then could I ever encourage you [to become one]? If I did, all my ideas would go by the board; though, at present, you will not appreciate them.

Ref. no. 1. (Translator's note: See also *CWMG*, vol. 11, p. 333.)

16. Ref. no. 26. Devdas writes, "This selection had 'shocked' the three brothers, but Harilalbhai was most affected by it."
17. Ref. no. 30, p. 76.

He spoke to Joseph Royeppen. Royeppen was born in Natal colony. He had studied for nine years in England and was a barrister. He had gone to jail often as a satyagrahi during the Transvaal struggle. It possible that he and Harilal had met often in Johannesburg and had spent time together in some jail. Harilal had met him during a farewell given in his honour on 1 May 1911.

Royeppen left for Durban on 20 May 1911. Before he left, Harilal spoke to him in Johannesburg and informed him about his decision to leave South Africa. He also requested Royeppen to inform Gandhiji. But soon after that – before 8 May 1911 – he collected some of his belongings, which included a photograph of Gandhiji, and left Johannesburg without informing anyone.

Before leaving, he wrote a note addressed to Gandhiji. Gandhiji was pained on reading it. He said, "This was the result of reading *Sarasvatichandra*.[18] He had also left leaving a letter of farewell for his father."[19]

Surendra Medh and Pragji[20] searched all over Johannesburg, but in vain. They could not find him. Finally they got the information that Harilal had borrowed £20 from a Parsi friend.

The news spread like wildfire. People around them had expected some such incident. Many Muslim merchants came to remonstrate with Gandhiji, "You should have sent him to England for further studies. We would have paid all the expenses."[21]

In a letter written on 8 May, Gandhiji said that Harilal had taken an extreme step. He felt that the fault lay with him; Harilal was not to be blamed.[22]

That evening Gandhiji returned to the Tolstoy Farm from his office in Johannesburg. On the train journey, Gandhiji said to his associates, "Don't say

---

18. A Gujarati novel by Govardhanram Madhavram Tripathi.
19. Ref. no. 25, p. 83–84.
20. Both were associates of Gandhiji in South Africa.
21. Ref. no. 25. p. 83.
22. Translator's note: Gandhiji wrote to Maganlal Gandhi, "Harilal has taken a most extraordinary step. The fault lies with me. Perhaps one may blame the circumstances. In any case, Harilal is not to blame." See *CWMG*, vol. 11, p. 68.

anything about Harilal's disappearance to Ba. I myself will reveal the fact to her in my own way."[23]

Harilal took a train from Johannesburg and reached Lourenco Marques (Delagoa Bay).[24]

He had changed his name, lest someone recognise him as Gandhiji's son. He did not have enough money to travel to India. He went to the British Counsel and sought aid, as a poor Indian, for a passage to India. He was recognised there.

In a few days, a message was received that he was at Delagoa Bay. Kallenbach offered to bring him back. Gandhiji declined the offer. Gandhiji sent Harilal two telegrams requesting him to come back.

On 15 May, Harilal returned to Johannesburg.[25] The father and son spoke to each other with open hearts. Harilal remonstrated Gandhiji. Giving an account of this conversation Gandhiji wrote, "He feels that I have kept all the four boys very much suppressed, that I did not respect their wishes at any time, that I have treated them as of no account, and that I have often been hard-hearted...Unlike other fathers, I have not admired my sons or done anything specially for them, but always put them and Ba last; such was the charge."[26]

Gandhiji tried hard to allay his anxieties. They spent the night of the 15th in a long exchange of views. Harilal was not convinced. On the 16th, after breakfast, Gandhiji announced that Harilal would leave for India the next day. Harilal left Johannesburg on the 17th. Gandhiji was at the railway station, along with others, to bid him farewell. As the train was about to leave Gandhiji told him in tearful voice, "Forgive your father, if you think he has done you wrong."[27] Those gathered there were in tears. The train moved, father and son separated with heavy hearts.

23. Ref. no. 25, p. 83.
24. A Portuguese port on the east coast of Africa.
25. In Appendix 2, Devdas incorrectly mentions that Harilal reached Durban.
26. Ref. no. 23, (Translator's note: See also, "Letter to Maganlal Gandhi, May 18, 1911", *CWMG*, vol. 11, p. 407–08.)
27. Ref. no. 25, p. 84.

Gandhiji arranged to pay for Harilal's expenses. This arrangement continued till Gandhiji left South Africa for India for the final time.

Harilal felt that he had been neglected when Gandhiji decided not to send either him or Manilal to England at Dr. Pranjivandas Mehta's expense. Due to the mental turmoil his behaviour had changed; the settlers and co-workers at Phoenix had observed these changes and complained about him to Gandhiji. Gandhiji wrote to Maganlal Gandhi, on 19 March 1911, to have more love for Harilal as more of his faults were discovered.[28]

Moreover, Chhaganlal had been selected to go to England. This must have displeased Gandhiji's family as well as other associates and settlers in the Phoenix Settlement and the Tolstoy Farm. They must have all whispered about it to each other. These murmurs must have reached Gandhiji's ears. He was afraid that Harilal's decision to leave home would unleash an upheaval amongst family and associates; members of the family would charge and accuse each other and as a result those who were so charged would leave.

He felt it necessary to clear the air by placing the facts before all. He did not want discontent to simmer. He was afraid that Maganlal might also leave the Phoenix Settlement. That would have been a great catastrophe. Gandhiji wrote to Maganlal on 15 May, the day Harilal returned. This letter was written even before Gandhiji had a talk with Harilal. "I can well understand the varied feelings surging within you. Please consider this: If Harilal's or Manilal's or Ba's being unhappy with you, or their bitter words, make you think of leaving, you will be behaving as one separate from us and I shall find it difficult to do my duty to them and to you...If you decide on leaving, Harilal's and Manilal's best interests cannot but suffer...The responsibility is

---

28. Translator's note: Gandhiji wrote, "The more defects you discover in Harilal, the more love you should have for him. One requires a great deal of water to put out a big fire. To overcome the baser element in Harilal's nature, you have to develop in yourself and pit against it a more powerful force of goodness. Give him the coat too when he asks for a shirt." *CWMG,* vol. 10, p. 476.

entirely mine. I alone will be to blame for any false step of mine...But the fruits of my error will be for me alone to taste."[29]

En route, Harilal was recognised at the Zanzibar port. The Zanzibar Indian community took him to Valimuhmmad Nazarali's house and looked after him well. He was given a scroll of honour; in response, Harilal said that the struggle in Transvaal had demonstrated the efficacy of satyagraha. If the government were to betray the people again, satyagrahis would gather from all corners of the world to join the struggle.

---

29. a. Ref. no. 23. (Translator's note: See also *CWMG,* vol. 11, p. 74–75.)
    b. After about eight years, Gandhiji wrote to Maganlal, "With Ba things are as you say and I am unhappy about it. So long as she does not consider you all with the same regard as Harilal, her staying in the Ashram is in vain. But we cannot escape the situation and, therefore, must submit to it and feel compassion for Ba." Ref. no. 23. (Translator's note: See also "Letter to Maganlal Gandhi, December 7, 1919", *CWMG,* vol. 16, p. 334.)

4 Studies in Ahmedabad

Joseph Royeppen met Gandhiji after Harilal left Johannesburg without informing anyone. Harilal had arranged for this meeting. Royeppen informed Gandhiji that Harilal intended to study somewhere in Punjab after reaching India. Gandhiji was doubtful whether Harilal knew anything at all about Punjab. He therefore suggested that if Harilal wanted to return to India in order to study, he should study in Ahmedabad. When Harilal reached Mumbai, Revashankarbhai suggested that he should study in some commercial class in Mumbai. The prospectus of the Dawar College of Commerce was obtained. Gandhiji did not think it was appropriate. Dr. Pranjivandas Mehta suggested that Harilal go to Rangoon and study. This too did not meet with Gandhiji's approval. He wrote suggesting that it would be good for Harilal if he were to stay independently and study. He should gain experience of India and if he were to tire of it, he could go either to Rangoon or to South Africa. But he did not like the idea of his son staying in Mumbai.

Even after reaching India, Harilal's anger and frustration did not subside. He perhaps did not write to Gandhiji informing him that he had reached India; and if he had, the news did not reach Gandhiji. After he arrived in India, Harilal met Chhaganlal Gandhi. Chhaganlal reached South Africa in the later half of July 1911; he gave Gandhiji news about Harilal.

At last Harilal reached Ahmedabad and joined the New English School.[1] His intention was to appear for the matriculation examination. In Mumbai he had studied up to English fifth standard. He must have progressed in his studies and therefore could join the matriculation class.

He selected French as the second language for his examination. When Gandhiji learnt of this, he wrote, "I cannot help feeling that the time and money spent on French are being wasted. I can give you no idea of how

1. The J.L. New English School of today.

much better it would have been if you had spent this valuable time on Sanskrit...I should be happier if you would reconsider the matter even now and start on Sanskrit, sacrificing a year and spending Rs. 8 instead of Rs. 7 on private coaching."[2]

In the beginning, Harilal lived in the Agakhan house on the western banks of the Sabarmati.[3] At that time his wife and children were not with him.[4] After that, for sometime, he lived in Sheth Miyakhan's house situated in Munjal Mohalla of Kalupur area. This family owned a firm in Durban called Gulam Hussein Miyakhan & Co; Harilal might have been acquainted with them.[5] The family refused to take rent from Harilal. When Gandhiji learnt about this he wrote to Harilal that he should forcefully request the family to accept rent.

Later, when his wife and children came to live with him, he rented a house in Dhanasutar ni Pole. It was the first house on the southern side of Chokhwatiya ni Pole. He rented the third floor of the house. He lived in this house and rented a room to study in a house situated in Toda ni Pole within Raja Mehta ni Pole. That house belonged to a temple. There was a cowshed on the ground floor, and Harilal Gandhi and his friends used the upper floor. Two other students, Rambhai and Gangaram, came there to study with Harilal.

Harilal began preparations for the matriculation examination. But he must have felt embarrassed. He was twenty-three or twenty-four years old. He had to study with students who were sixteen or seventeen years of age. Moreover, he was married and was the father of two children. The other students were mostly free from such responsibilities. It is doubtful if his mind was really in studies. The room in Raja Mehta ni Pole was hardly used for studies; friends

---

2. Ref. no. 1. (Translator's note: See also "Letter to Harilal Gandhi, September 5, 1912", *CWMG,* vol. 11, p. 316.)
3. This information was given to the author by the late Shri Mulchand Bhagat.
4. Ref. no. 38, p. 246, incorrectly mentions that while Harilal was in Ahmedabad his wife was in South Africa.
5. Gandhiji had good relations with this family. When Polak was in Ahmedabad in 1909, he had visited the family. After coming back to India in 1915, Gandhiji visited them on 2 February 1915.

gathered there, drank tea, chatted with each other and passed time.[6] Harilal was fond of playing chess. A neighbour of his in Dhanasutar ni Pole once remarked, "Look, his father is such an expert barrister and his son is so useless!"[7]

Harilal must have whiled away his time. He appeared for the matriculation examination but failed to pass it. He did not inform Gandhiji of his failure. Gandhiji came to know about it through someone else. Gandhiji wrote to him, "I have not felt disappointed over your failure. Since you have resolved to pass that examination, go on working for it again."[8]

Around 4 January 1913, Gulabbehn gave birth to their third child, a son, Rasikbhai.

Meanwhile, the events in South Africa were fast reaching a climax. Gopal Krishna Gokhale reached South Africa on 22 October 1912. He met many political leaders there and left for India on 17 November 1912 with hopes of early resolution of the conflict. He reached Mumbai on 13 December 1912. The next day he gave a lecture in Mumbai on the South African situation; Harilal was present at the lecture.

After Gokhale left South Africa, the political situation turned against the Indian community. There were signs that the satyagraha would have to be recommenced.

In January 1913 Gandhiji closed down the Tolstoy Farm and returned to the Phoenix Settlement.

The South African government refused to recognise the validity of Indian marriages. To protest against this, a group of women under the leadership of Kasturba offered satyagraha; they were sentenced to three months of imprisonment on 23 September 1913. It was unprecedented that women

---

6. The author was given this information by a person who lived in Harilal's neighbourhood.
7. This remark was made to a friend of the author, who in turn told the same to the author.
8. Ref. no. 1. (Translator's note: See also "Letter to Harilal Gandhi, January 26, 1913", *CWMG,* vol. 11, p. 449.)

offer satyagraha and be jailed for it. This shocked people; all experienced a new energy. The atmosphere turned sombre.

During this period Harilal's health turned indifferent. Gandhiji wrote, "Still I must advise you to shake off this craze for examinations. If you pass, it won't impress me much. If you fail, you will feel very unhappy...It is not surprising that you have lost your mental powers. The education there is useless because it is ill-conceived...Where the aim is merely to pass an examination, the result is bound to be unhappy."[9] Harilal might have written to him about his desire to join the struggle. In response, Gandhiji wrote, "If you give up the thought of examinations and if, when you get this letter, the struggle here is continuing, come here along with Chanchi, both of you prepared for imprisonment. Chanchi has otherwise no right to come now."[10]

On 6 November 1913, Indians marched in Transvaal, under Gandhiji's leadership. He was arrested and, on the 11th, he was sentenced to nine months of imprisonment. On the 14th, three additional months of imprisonment were added to his sentence. Kallenbach, Polak and the others were also imprisoned. The struggle became more pronounced; the government lashed out violently at the marchers.

The South African government was criticised all over the world. Pressed from all sides, the government appointed a commission of enquiry. On the commission's recommendation, Gandhiji was released from jail on 18 December 1913. Indians did not find the commission acceptable; the situation was volatile. After his release, Gandhiji spoke in a public meeting.

> I hope you will hold yourselves in readiness to respond to the call the Government may make by declining our just and reasonable requests, and then, to again force the pace by again undergoing still greater purifying suffering...Then, if the Government does not grant our request, this is the proposition I wish to place before you this morning: That all of us, on the

---

9. Ref. no. 1. (Translator's note: See also "Letter to Harilal Gandhi, September 18, 1913", *CWMG*, vol. 12, p. 190.)
10. Ibid.

> first day of the New Year, should be ready again to suffer battle, again to suffer imprisonment and march out.[11]

Harilal's heart was in a turmoil. In Zanzibar, on his way back to India, he had said that if satyagraha were to be offered again, satyagrahis from all over would come and join the struggle. On 22 November 1913, a meeting was held in Ahmedabad under the chairmanship of Divan Bahadur Ambalal Sakarlal, where Harilal was one of the speakers. He said, "I have been a witness to the Satyagraha. I have been to jail in that struggle. My family is in jails there. When I left I had promised that I would return, and now I am eager to go back."[12]

He met Gokhale on 25 December 1913. Gokhale threw cold water on his enthusiasm and prevented him from going back to South Africa. The next day, Gokhale sent a telegram to Gandhiji informing him that he had advised Harilal to continue with his studies and not leave for South Africa. He also said that he was solely responsible for such advice and sought Gandhiji's forgiveness for having interfered.

Gokhale was perhaps aware of the political and diplomatic efforts to resolve the conflict, and that the struggle might be called off. He was also certain that a new struggle would not be required. And it so happened that the South African government stopped the arrests. The satyagraha that was to recommence on 1 January was postponed. The march was also likely to be postponed by two or three weeks.

The struggle continued. So, on 3 January 1914, Gandhiji sent a telegram to Gokhale requesting him to give permission to Harilal to join the struggle because the latter had taken a vow as a satyagrahi, and a vow must be honoured. If Harilal went to jail in the process, wrote Gandhiji, he would gain in both experience and education, which according to him was true education.[13]

---

11. Ref. no. 4, special issue of December 24, 1913. (Translator's note: See also "Speech at Mass Meeting, December 21, 1913", *CWMG*, vol. 12, p. 275–76.)
12. Ref. no. 8, November 30, 1913, p. 13.
13. Translator's note: Gandhiji sent a cable, "Subject your sanction feel Harilal should come. He vowed see struggle through as resister. Should be permitted

Meanwhile, the situation in South Africa was improving. The Commission of Enquiry released its report. Its recommendations were a victory for the satyagraha struggle of the Indian community. The satyagraha was therefore called off.

One of the commission's recommendations was that even in religions that permitted polygamy only one wife would be considered the legal spouse at any given time. Gandhiji had accepted this in the settlement. This had angered some Muslims. While Gandhiji was in Cape Town he heard rumours that a conspiracy to kill him was being hatched in Johannesburg. In a letter dated 11 March 1914, he wrote at length regarding the objectives of his life, his aspirations, and the arrangements to be made for the maintenance and future of his family. He said that in event of his death, "Harilal will have to fend for himself...If Harilal takes upon himself the burden of maintaining Ba, let him by all means..."[14] But such an eventuality did not arise.

The South African parliament passed a bill incorporating the recommendations of the Commission of Enquiry on 1 July 1914 and Gandhiji made preparations to return to India.

It is likely that Harilal was in a quandary about going to South Africa. He wanted to join the struggle but Gokhale advised him to stay in India. Harilal wrote to Gandhiji that he was anxious to meet him and Kasturba. Gandhiji felt that this was sheer hypocrisy. On 2 March 1914, he wrote in response, "I don't believe that you are impatient to see us both; equally, this idea that you were to come here sounds insincere to me. Does one who really means to come trumpet it aloud? Now, of course, your coming is pointless, as you say."[15]

Perhaps Harilal was facing financial difficulties. In the same letter, Gandhiji suggested that he meet Revashankarbhai.

---

fulfil obligation. My opinion gaol other experiences substantial education." See "Cable to GK Gokhale, January 3, 1914", *CWMG*, vol. 12, p. 316.)

14. Ref. no. 32, p. 303. (Translator's note: See also "Letter to Chhaganlal Gandhi, March 11, 1914", *CWMG*, vol. 12, p. 382–83.)
15. Ref. no. 1. (Translator's note: See also "Letter to Harilal Gandhi, March 2, 1914", *CWMG*, vol. 12, p. 368.)

Harilal once again failed the matriculation examination,[16] so he once again thought of joining the Dawar commerce classes. Gandhiji wrote, "Do you think it will be much of an achievement to pass the matriculation examination?...If, indeed, you wish to go ahead with your plan for studies, you should have Chanchi stay with me...Think of Chanchi when you turn your mind to earning."[17]

With the completion of the struggle in South Africa, Gandhiji left that country with Kasturba on 18 July 1914 for India. They were travelling via England. Some of the Phoenix settlers left South Africa on 7 August 1914 and came to Mumbai without breaking journey. Among those who returned were the three brothers of Harilal—Manilal, Ramdas and Devdas. Harilal met them and spent a week with them in Mumbai before returning to Ahmedabad. It is said that Ramdas went to Harilal's house in Dhanasuthar ni Pole to meet the other members of his family.

Harilal went to Mumbai again to meet his parents, when they landed there. Gandhiji was to stay in Mumbai at the house of Sheth Narottamdas Morarji. They did not know of Gandhiji's food habits. Harilal went to their house on 8 January 1915 and acquainted them with Gandhiji's food habits. The next day Gandhiji and Kasturba landed at the Mumbai port. Harilal was among those who received them. He was with his parents till they left Mumbai on 15 January. On the 12th Gandhiji had called upon Dadabhai Naoroji. Harilal had accompanied his father to this meeting.

Gandhiji too was pleased to meet Harilal.

Harilal accompanied Gandhiji when he left Mumbai. He went with his father to Wadhwan, Wankaner, Rajkot, Gondal, Jetpur, Dhoraji and Porbandar, and returned to Ahmedabad on 1 February 1915. On 4 February, Gandhiji left Ahmedabad. Harilal did not accompany him, but stayed on in Ahmedabad.

Gandhiji reached Mumbai on the evening of 4 February; and on the 6th, he settled all his accounts with his brothers. This included the money given to

---

16. He failed the matriculation examination in 1912, 1913 and 1914.
17. Ref. no. 1. (Translator's note: See also "Letter to Harilal Gandhi, March 2, 1914", *CWMG*, vol. 12, p. 369.)

Harilal since he returned to India. It appears that after 6 February there were no financial dealings between father and son.

After this, Gandhiji went to Poona, Shantiniketan and Calcutta. Harilal accompanied his father. During this period their relationship was not further embittered, but they could not resolve their differences either. Finally, on 13 March 1915, in Calcutta, Harilal decided to separate from his father.

Meanwhile, Gulabbehn gave birth to their fourth child, a son, in her natal home in Rajkot, before 31 March 1915. He was named Shantibhai.

We have earlier looked at some of the causes for the differences between Gandhiji and Harilal. After his father returned to India, and especially after the property- and money-related arrangements within the family were settled, Harilal published a letter titled "My Open Letter to My Father M. K. Gandhi (Bar-at-Law)"[18] in the form of a booklet. This 32-page booklet was printed on Antique paper. He wanted to publish this letter in newspapers, but Narandas[19] who was in Mumbai prevailed upon him, and Harilal himself "could not become sufficiently harsh".[20] He did not publish the letter in newspapers, but sent copies to all those concerned with Gandhiji. Gandhiji received a copy of the letter when he reached Shantiniketan from Rangoon on 31 March 1915.

This letter has been reproduced as Appendix 1 of this book. Vanmala Parikh in her book, *Amara Ba,* has included Narhari Parikh's comments on the letter:

> Given the style of that letter and the arguments given therein I formed a high opinion of Harilal's abilities. Harilalbhai has poured out his anger by describing the injustice done to Ba, his younger brothers and himself by Bapu. He pleaded with Bapu "You did not educate me, but educate my younger brothers." Given Bapu's fondness for vows, those who took vows in the ashrams, ate salt-less diet, ate one meal a day or became a fruitarian would become Bapu's favourites and Bapu would in

18. 'Bar-at-Law' was placed within brackets in the original.
19. Chhaganlal Gandhi's brother.
20. See Appendix 2.

his enthusiasm give honorifics like 'Rishi,' 'Muni,' 'Tapasvi' to them and these 'Tapasvis' got licence to criticise others. Harilal has described all these in a humorous way.

He has also described his anger at those who took difficult vows in their enthusiasm but soon gave up those vows, norms and even the ashram, and later criticised Ba saying, "Ba uses lot of sugar" or "Ba drinks coffee."

Moreover, Manilalbhai and Ramdasbhai would be given other responsibilities in [the time] allocated for [their] studies and if this did not satisfy Bapu he would say, "You are nursing...and therein lies your best education. The man who performs his duties is constantly educating himself. You claim that you have to give up your studies; but that is not true. While serving you are studying. Literacy training can be acquired later but the opportunity to serve does not come always." Harilal [has] said that by saying such things their father was misleading his younger brothers and did not allow them to further their education.

There is a saying 'Let the groom die, let the bride die, but feed the Brahmin.' The ashramites behave similarly, 'come what may, but please Bapu'. By writing…such matters he brought out in public what for him was the hypocrisy of the ashram.

He has also described in this letter how he got married while he was a student and could not study further.[21]

---

21. a. *Amara Ba* was published in 1945. Narharibhai died on 15 July 1957. He must have seen and verified the quote attributed to him. In his foreword to the book Gandhiji wrote, "I see she has painstakingly collected her facts and ordered them neatly." Therefore, he too must have read the book.
    b. Harilal published his letter in 1915. Ten years later, Mirabehn (Miss Slade) came to the Sabarmati Ashram and lived there. In the second year of her residence she told Gandhiji that the lives of the ashramites were not in keeping with the objectives and ideals of the ashram. Two or three years later the ashram advanced the common-kitchen ideal. She criticised the conduct of the ashramites. She wrote, "The Udyog Mandir people...are apparently trying to do all sorts of things because they feel you want them to, not because it is natural to them, or that they have conviction in that matter." (Translator's note: Letter of October 27, 1928, Sevashram,

On reading the letter Maganlal formed the impression that the letter spewed venom on him, Chhaganlal and Jamnadas.[22] Gandhiji was attacked, but nothing was said about his vows. In the letter, Harilal admitted that Gandhiji's life was pure; but he severely criticised Gandhiji's associates who observed vows following his example.

After 13 March 1915, Gandhiji proceeded to Rangoon, while Harilal returned to Mumbai. Following Gandhiji's instructions, he wrote a letter to Maganlal from Mumbai that he should reach Calcutta before Bapu returned from Rangoon. At that time Maganlal was at Rajkot. He went to Mumbai on his way to Calcutta and met Harilal on 30 March 1915. Harilal poured out his grievances to Maganlal.

When Gandhiji received the aforementioned 'open letter' he was deeply pained, but he felt that Harilal had displayed his weakness by writing it. Devdas has written, "[Harilal's] decision to not go further with the letter was influenced by the awareness that his case was weak."[23]

It is normal for both parties to feel embittered after such a letter. But no such feelings remained in this case. Gandhiji felt that writing the letter had helped Harilal calm himself and find peace. In a letter to Narandas, Gandhiji mentioned that Harilal repented having written the letter.[24]

Benares, accession no. SN 26816, Archives of the Sabarmati Ashram.) Some time later she wrote about the experiment of the common kitchen at the Ashram: "I threw myself heart and soul into the Common Kitchen, and made one supreme effort to mix with the women and children in the daily life. Then the real Purgatory began...I saw what glorious possibilities lay before us if only the people would rise to the occasion...But my nerves began to give way." (Translator's note: Letter of November 15, 1928, Bettiah, accession no. SN 26828, Archives of the Sabarmati Ashram.)

22. Jamnadas was Chhaganlal's youngest brother.
23. See Appendix 2.
24. Translator's note: See "Letter to Narandas Gandhi, April 25, 1915", *CWMG,* vol. 13, p. 62–63.

5 Residence in Calcutta and Demise of Gulab

Harilal realised that it was impossible for him to study further. There was no hope of receiving monetary support from Gandhiji. When he parted from Gandhiji on 13 March 1915, Gandhiji had given him forty-five rupees. He decided to enter into some profession.

It appears that he met Sheth Narottam Morarji with this hope and joined his Solapur mill for a short time—either to learn the profession or as a regular employee.

Harilal thought of setting up a household in Solapur, but his work required him to travel from one town to another. He was in a predicament as to what should be done. It was difficult to move from place to place with young children. Therefore, he decided that Gulabbehn and the children should continue to stay in Ahmedabad. There were difficulties in this as well; moreover, Gulabbehn did not like this arrangement.

Harilal wrote to her on 6 September 1915 that he was going to be in Ahmedabad and she should come there to meet him. Together they would discuss the matter. Harilal assured her,

> I will come often to Ahmedabad to meet you, have no doubt regarding that. Ba would like that. You would be able to stay for a longer time with Ba. She would be happy at heart and others would stop criticising. You will face no misery staying with Ba, I am certain of that…If you are unhappy in Ahmedabad, if you are not treated well, and if I am convinced of it, I will take you away from there immediately. This my word to you. You know that nobody could come in my way if I do not want you to stay there. I am miserable in your pain and joyous in your happiness. How will I remain a spectator if you are unhappy in Ahmedabad—I am your beloved. 'Come and fetch me'—I would rush to you on hearing these words.[1]

1. Ref. no. 3.

Harilal reached Ahmedabad on 15 September, and on the next day Gulabbehn arrived with the children.

In those days, the ashram was at Kochrab. It had been established for about four months. After discussions, Harilal and Gulabbehn decided that they should, at least for the time being, stay in Ahmedabad.

Meanwhile, Harilal was given a job in Sheth Narottamdas's Calcutta office. It was decided that he would set up a household in Calcutta.

Gandhiji did not like this city mainly because of the animal sacrifice practised at the Kali temple. Gandhiji's advice was that Harilal should not set up household in Calcutta; his advice was disregarded.

Gandhiji went to Mumbai from Ahmedabad on 19 September1915 to receive C.F. Andrews. Harilal accompanied him to Mumbai and from there he went to Calcutta. He called his family there after locating a house.

Gulabbehn's mother wished for her to spend some time in Rajkot before she left for Calcutta. Therefore, towards the end of October, Manilal escorted Gulabbehn and the children to Rajkot.

Harilal wrote to Gulabbehn with instructions about the household items she would need to bring with her and the arrangements for the journey. He wrote to her about things that she should carry, gave her advice about how to pack and how to pass through the checkpoint at Viramgam with all their belongings.[2]

On Gandhiji's instruction, Manilal went to Rajkot and accompanied Gulabbehn and the children to Calcutta. It is not possible to ascertain the exact date on which they reached Calcutta, but it is certain that they had reached Calcutta by the end of April 1916.

After returning from Calcutta, Manilal sent some money to Harilal from Mumbai. This amount was not lent to him, but was given to him so that he could buy household goods.

---

2. In those days all passengers travelling from Kathiawad to Gujarat by train were searched at the Viragam station.

There are two possibilities with regard to the source of this money. According to Reference no. 36, this money belonged to the ashram.[3] Given Gandhiji's emphasis on probity and financial discipline this appears unlikely.

Gulabbehn in one of her letters mentions that Manilal had sent his personal money, which he had kept in the custody of Narandas.[4]

Harilal sent a receipt for the money. This receipt fell into Gandhiji's hands. He was stunned. He had not been informed that money had been sent to Harilal. He cross-examined Manilal. When he realised that Manilal had in fact sent the money, he fasted for three days. In June, Manilal was sent to Madras to learn weaving.[5]

Harilal and Gulabbehn set up household in Calcutta. Initially three of their children were with them. Rasikbhai was left with Gandhiji in the ashram. Gandhiji and Rasikbhai were fond of each other. Later Rasikbhai too was sent to live with his parents in Calcutta.

They passed their days happily. When Gulabbehn suffered an eye ailment, Harilal cared for her and despite his uncertain pecuniary circumstances did not spare any expenditure for her treatment. He himself taught his children. So far as possible he did all the work himself. In a letter, he wrote about Kantibhai, "He likes to play the games that girls play, no one is to be blamed for it."[6] Kantibhai's pet name was 'Bhabho', which was later changed to 'Khutiyo'. Gulabbehn was from Rajkot, so Harilal would tease her by saying that women from Porbandar were better. Gulabbehn looked after their servant well. He teased her for this, "You are very affectionate towards him." After Gulabbehn's demise,[7] he wrote in a letter, "I not only loved

3. Translator's note: Louis Fischer, *The Life of Mahatma Gandhi*, (New York: Harper and Row, 1983), p. 207.
4. Ref. no. 3.
5. Subsequently Manilal and Ramdas returned to South Africa to look after the publication of the *Indian Opinion*.
6. Ref. no. 3.
7. This will be dealt with later in the chapter.

her, I worshipped her. I was afraid of her, she guided me, and I was guided by her."[8]

Thus, Harilal's desire to lead a happy conjugal life was fulfilled.

But he did not meet with the same success in monetary matters. It appears that he faced hardships from the very beginning. Initially, they did not face much difficulty. The Sheth paid Harilal Rs. 120 per month. He had to pay Rs. 27 as rent for the house; the monthly expenditure was Rs. 80, including the rent. They could meet all the expenditure quite easily, though Gulabbehn felt that things were very expensive.

Gulabbehn's mother had lent three thousand rupees to someone at a monthly interest of eight annas. She wanted to take the money back because she was not receiving the interest. She asked Gulabbehn as to what should be done. In consultation with Harilal, Gulabbehn wrote to her suggesting that the money be reclaimed and sent to Harilal instead. Harilal would pay her the interest of Rs. 15 every month. She also mentioned that he received a monthly salary of Rs. 120, which was sufficient for their needs. Therefore, she should not harbour any fears that her money would be lost forever. Harilal wrote to his mother-in-law that if she had any fears that he would squander away the money, he would invest the money in some reputed firm in her name and would draw some amount out of it for his business with her consent.

Harilal had a job but he wanted to start a cloth business to earn some additional income. He wrote to Gulabbehn's mother that by borrowing a few hundred rupees he would be able to earn a profit of fifty rupees. Later he wrote that he would need five hundred rupees.

Gulabbehn's mother sent the amount to him. Harilal used the money, but could not earn any profit from it. He could not even send the monthly interest payment of fifteen rupees. There was some correspondence regarding this as well.

There were uncertainties regarding his job at Sheth Narottam's office. There was talk of him being transferred to another place, but Harilal did not

---

8. Ref. no. 3.

want to move from one place to another. If necessary, he was willing to give up the job and start a business of his own.

During this period, or perhaps a little earlier, Harilal had borrowed Rs. 2000 from Soni Rugnath Kalidas of Ranavav.[9] He repaid Rs. 1500, but while returning the money he said, "I will need this amount." This made the creditor suspicious but at that time he took the money that was returned. Later he got a sum of Rs. 82. Harilal still owed him Rs. 418. Harilal could not return this amount and asked for a further loan of one thousand rupees, which was refused. The creditor travelled to Calcutta to claim the remaining amount of Rs. 418. Harilal told him, "Today is Saturday and the bank is closed. I will send the money to you on Monday by wire." Harilal did not send the money. As a last resort that man wrote a letter to Gandhiji on 16 June 1917. Rugnath wrote that before Gandhiji got involved with the struggle in Kheda he had travelled to pay obeisance to Gandhiji, where he had met Harilal. He described the events narrated above. He requested Gandhiji to pay him the remaining amount of Rs. 418. He said in his letter, "I ate the fruits by looking at the tree."[10]

We do not know if Gandhiji replied to this letter or if he did respond what his reply was. This must certainly have perturbed him. Harilal must have fallen in his eyes even further. That year, on Diwali day, he wrote to Harilal from Motihari to convey his blessings for the new year. "I wish that all your aspirations are fulfilled and that all of you increase in your wealth of character, and pray that you realize more and more that this is the only real Lakshmi and our highest good lies in the worship of this alone."[11]

He did not write anything else. It was a letter of three lines. The next day he wrote a letter conveying his blessings to Maganlal Gandhi. This was a long letter comprising thirty lines, albeit it contained large quotes from the Bible.

---

9. Ranavav is situated about ten miles east of Porbandar.
10. This incident is based on Soni Rugnath's letter to Gandhiji. I have not been able to ascertain facts from other sources.
11. Ref. no. 24, vol. 4, p. 7. (Translator's note: See also "Letter to Harilal Gandhi, November 14, 1917", *CWMG,* vol. 14, p. 89–90.)

Harilal was involved in some financial irregularities in the office of Sheth Narottam. Shri Manu Subedar was an employee of the Sheth. He met Gandhiji in Nadiad on 19 April 1918, and again on the 23rd and the 24th of the same month, in Mumbai, to discuss the misconduct. During the same period, Harilal sought Manu Subedar's recommendation for some work in Calcutta.[12] Mahadev Desai was present, and did not object to Harilal's suggestion. Mahadevbhai informed Gandhiji of this on 25 April. Gandhiji remonstrated with him, "You are very kind. For me this is a failing and not a quality. You ought to have told Harilal immediately that such a thing cannot be. You ought to have admonished him. This is a failing of yours." The next day he told Mahadevbhai, "You acted out of love, hence what more can I scold you? But I must say that spiritually it was a wrong act."[13]

Either Gandhiji sought Harilal's explanation on the misconduct or Harilal wrote to him explaining his conduct. Gandhiji received this letter in Delhi. On 1 May 1918, he wrote to Harilal.

> Since you are emphatic that you did not commit the theft, I may believe you but the world will not. Bear the world's censure and be more careful in future. You should give up your notion of what the world means. Your world is your employer. Have no fear if you are tried in a court of law. If you take my advice, do not engage a lawyer. Explain everything to the advocate on the other side.
>
> You had in your hand a diamond which you have thrown away, thanks to your rash and impatient nature...If you are speaking the truth, don't lose your faith in it. There is no God but Truth. One's virtues are no dead matter but are all life...I would have died broken-hearted if I had no other sons.[14]

---

12. Harilal would have sought Manu Subedar's note of recommendation or sought a note from someone on Manu Subedar. The source is not clear on this. This was either on 19, 23 or 24 April.
13. Ref. no. 24, vol. 4, p. 85.
14. Ibid., p. 99. (Translator's note: See also "Letter to Harilal Gandhi, May 1, 1918", *CWMG,* vol. 14, p. 385.)

On 23 June, Manu Subedar met Gandhiji once again in Nadiad. Having read all the relevant papers and discussed the matter, Gandhiji told Subedar, "As an impartial man I feel that Harilal has committed the crime. You proceed against him in court without any hesitation."[15]

Gandhiji wrote to Sheth Narottam to the same effect on 29 June, "I also do not think that the boy is innocent. If you would please me, see that he has justice[16] in a court."[17]

When Harilal came to know of this he wrote to Gandhiji calling him 'cruel'. In response Gandhiji wrote, "If it was cruel to say what I felt was true, then certainly my letter was cruel. I repeat that the world will most emphatically not consider you innocent. Whatever you may have said in your sincerity,[18] Narottam Sheth could have had no idea about your speculation. You have followed one wrong thing with another. It was not enough for you that you had lost ten thousand rupees. But there is no use arguing with you. May God give you wisdom. If I have made a mistake, I will set it right. If you think you can point out any, do so even now."[19]

It was later revealed that Harilal had lost about thirty thousand rupees of Sheth Narottam's out of mere idiocy.[20]

Sheth Narottam thought it proper to act against Gandhiji's counsel. After all Harilal was Gandhiji's son! Harilal knew that his case was weak. He wrote

15. Ref. no. 24, vol. 4, p. 119.
16. The term 'justice' is used here in the sense of the 'judgement of the court'—if the court is convinced, Harilal ought to be penalised.
17. Ref. no. 24, vol. 4, p. 130. (Translator's note: See also "Fragment of a letter, June 29, 1918", *CWMG,* vol. 14, p. 459.)
18. Translator's note: The original Gujarati reads: "Whatever you said in Sakchi." The author has annotated it as an old village near Jamshedpur. While the *CWMG* has annotated it by stating, "The original is not clear at this point." See *CWMG,* vol. 14, p. 480, fn. 1.
19. Ref. no. 24, vol. 4, p. 151. (Translator's note: See also "Letter to Harilal Gandhi, July 9, 1918", *CWMG,* vol. 14, p. 480.)
20. Ref. no. 38, p. 469, mistakenly states that, "Harilal stole Rs. 30,000 from a Madrasi merchant." Ref. no. 24, vol. 4, p. 170, mentions Sheth Narottam by name; there is no mention of either a theft or a Madrasi merchant.

a letter to Sheth Narottam accepting his guilt. Sheth did not take him to the court but relieved Harilal from his employment.

On 22 April 1917, Gulabbehn gave birth to a daughter—Manubehn. She was born in Calcutta in Harilal's house. Kasturba was present at the time of birth. After that Gulabbehn went to her natal home and stayed there for a very long time. It is possible that her family had insisted that she stay longer. They might have done so either because of Harilal's uncertain monetary circumstances or because of Gulabbehn's indifferent health. Gandhiji did not like this. He felt that by leaving his wife in her natal home for such a long time Harilal had surrendered his autonomy. He also believed that it would be proper for Harilal to pay off his debts and start a new business by selling off his wife's ornaments. In times of difficulty, he felt, such an act is not proscribed; and also because these ornaments were given to Gulabbehn by her father-in-law. He himself had sold Kasturba's ornaments to pay for his education in England. Why should Harilal not act in a similar fashion? Harilal did not do so and let his wife remain at her natal home for a long period of time. Gandhiji felt that it was akin to being a ghar jamai.[21] Gandhiji also believed that such a person was as good as lost.

Gulabbehn came to live at the ashram either on or before 24 June 1918. That evening, Gandhiji, Mahadevbhai and Kasturba left for Nadiad. Mahadevbhai informed them that Gulabbehn had been crying. Gandhiji said, "Each one is crying for himself. But we have to lament for everyone. But if we bemoan for each one all twenty four hours of the day would go in crying."[22]

Mahadevbhai said, "How dependent women are! She has to accept whatever her husband does; she is bound to suffer its consequences."[23]

To which Gandhiji replied, "This is the lot of women all over the world. But I do not see that as the cause of suffering. That is her duty."[24]

---

21. Translator's note: A derogatory term used for a son-in-law who either stays with his in-laws or lives off the in-laws' money.
22. Ref. no. 24, vol. 4, p. 127.
23. Ibid.
24. Ibid.

Gulabbehn returned to her natal home when Kasturba went to Nadiad. There was an outbreak of influenza in Rajkot and she too caught it.

Harilal went to see her. Gandhiji met him either at Ahmedabad or at the Nadiad railway station. He wrote to Devdas on 1 July 1918 that Harilal "has lost all his tenderness. Do not be pained by it; but watch out how much a man falls once he starts falling."[25]

Harilal was to travel back from Rajkot to Mumbai the next day. Gandhiji was in Nadiad that day. He went to the station in the evening to meet Harilal, but he was not in that train. He went again in time for the night train. Harilal was asleep in the second-class compartment. He must not have expected anyone to come and meet him. He was awakened. Father and son talked for a while. Gandhiji was deeply pained. He said, "This boy's face has altered completely."[26]

If for nothing else, Gandhiji was proud that Harilal had an independent mind. He could not take pride even in that quality any longer.[27]

During this period Gandhiji was recruiting soldiers for the First World War. In August Gandhiji fell ill with severe dysentery. Harilal wrote and asked after his health. Gandhiji wrote in response on 29 August 1918 that his health was improving and there was no cause for anxiety. His health improved, but suddenly took a turn for the worse. His condition steadily declined. On October 1, both Harilal and Devdas were summoned with telegrams;[28]

---

25. Ibid., p. 134–35. (Translator's note: This sentence is not included in either the Gujarati version of the collected works *Gandhiji no Akshardeh* or the English *CMWG.* This letter is dated 2 July 1918 and not 1 July 1918 as mentioned by the author. This is corroborated in *Mahadevbhai ni Dairy,* vol. 4, p. 133–34; *Gandhiji no Akshardeh*, vol. 14, p. 413–14; and *CWMG*, vol. 14, p. 466–67. But it is recorded by Mahadevbhai in his entry of 2 July 1918, that Gandhiji wrote these sentences to Devdas.)
26. Ref. no. 24, vol. 4, p. 134–35.
27. Ibid.
28. Manilal and Ramdas were in South Africa.

the next day Gandhiji felt better and wrote letters to both of them. To Harilal he wrote,

> I have a feeling that I am now going. I have very little time left. The body is becoming weaker and weaker. I am not able to eat anything. But my heart is at peace and so I do not find the going at all difficult. I think whatever inheritance I am leaving to you brothers is appropriate. What would you have gained if I had left money? But the inheritance of character which I am leaving to you is invaluable in my view. I wish you to cherish it. Follow the path of religion. I have written a letter to Devdas. Ask for a copy of it. If you think you can apply that letter to yourself, do so.[29]

During Gulabbehn's illness Harilal cooked his own food in Calcutta. Gandhiji was pleased with this. In his letter of 29 August he wrote, "I was very pleased to learn that you cook your own food and that you enjoy doing so. Maybe you will find this an instructive experience; understand through it the secret of life and, repairing past mistakes bring light into your life."[30] In yet another letter he wrote to Harilal, "It is true that cooking takes some time but I believe that this time is not wasted...Do not imagine that I write this to suggest that you should always cook yourself...I can have no objection to your calling Chanchi, having good things to eat and enjoying life, within limits. Only see that you do not repeat your mistakes. I want you not to be too eager to get rich quickly."[31]

Gulabbehn's health worsened day by day. Her son Shanti too was unwell. They were taken to Padadhari[32] for a change of climate. Shantibhai died there in the second half of October 1918. After a week or so, Gulabbehn also died.[33]

---

29. Ref. no. 1. (Translator's note: See also "Letter to Harilal Gandhi, October 2, 1918", *CWMG*, vol. 91, supplementary vol. 1, p. 171.)
30. Ref. no. 24, vol. 4, p. 195. (Translator's note: See also "Letter to Harilal Gandhi, August 29, 1918", *CWMG*, vol. 15, p. 36.)
31. Ibid., p. 203–04, (Translator's note: See also "Letter to Harilal Gandhi, September 9, 1918", *CWMG*, vol. 15, p. 46–47.)
32. A village about fifteen miles from Rajkot.
33. The year of Gulabbehn's demise has been incorrectly given as 1920 by Devdas in his essay and in Ref. no. 30.

6 Gandhiji and the Daughter-in-law

Harilal was not present at the time of Gulabbehn's death. He went to Rajkot on receiving the news. He was in Rajkot on 31 October 1918. Gandhiji was unwell at this time. He was so weak that he could not write letters; despite his weakness he wrote almost daily to Harilal after Gulabbehn's death.

Gandhiji's health was showing signs of improvement. He was required to travel – for a change in climate – to help restore his health fully. He desired to meet Harilal before setting out on his journey. He wrote to Harilal, "Your responsibilities have increased, your trials have increased and your temptations will increase likewise. To a man with a family, the fact of being such, that is, having a wife, is a great check. This check over you has disappeared...I shall give you the full benefit of my experience; you may accept what you can. All this after you come."[1]

After Gulabbehn's death, the question of raising their children became pressing. Harilal and Gandhiji differed on many issues, so Harilal thought very carefully before deciding to leave the children with Gandhiji. He was embarrassed as well. He realised that at that juncture it was best to leave the children with Gandhiji and Kasturba. He gave his consent to such an arrangement.

This did not please Balibehn and she wrote a long letter to Harilal protesting against such an arrangement. Responding to her from Calcutta, on 31 December 1918, he said that the present arrangement was the best in his opinion and further clarified that the children had not been handed over to the Ashram but were living with his own parents. He also suggested that she should go to the Ashram often to meet them. Balibehn was not too pleased with such a response. Harilal again wrote to her that it was in the best interests of everyone that the children live in the Ashram.

---

1. Ref. no. 24, p. 215–16. (Translator's note: See also "Letter to Harilal Gandhi, November 26, 1918", *CWMG*, vol. 15, p. 55–56.)

Kasturba raised and cared for all of Harilal's four children: Ramibehn, Kantibhai, Rasikbhai and Manubehn. Gandhiji went to Matheran for the improvement of his health and later went to Mumbai for an operation for his piles. The four children accompanied him. Later they stayed at the Ashram and were raised there. Balibehn did not approve, but she was helpless as Harilal himself had arranged for them to stay at the Ashram. Gandhiji also wrote to her and suggested that she should come to the Ashram often and meet them. Her visits, he said, would benefit all.

Gandhiji was engaged with recruiting soldiers for the First World War. He wrote to Harilal suggesting that he too should enlist, but Harilal declined. In a letter written to him on or before 8 July 1918, Gandhiji said, "I understand what you say about your enlisting. I made the suggestion at a time when I did not doubt your truthfulness.[2] I do not think I have any interest in it now. I can give you no idea of what my condition has been since I began to doubt your truthfulness."[3]

Gandhiji had immense respect and affection for his daughter-in-law Gulab. We have already noted that Gandhiji was displeased at the early marriage of Harilal and Gulab. But he harboured no prejudice against Gulab. His displeasure and anger were directed against the elders of the family who had arranged for the marriage without seeking Gandhiji's consent. He wrote to her from the jail and discussed with her minute details about bringing up her daughter Rami and advised her about the need for leading a simple life.

---

2. He is referring to the problem with Sheth Narottam.
3. a. Ref. no. 24, vol. 4, p. 151. (Translator's note: See also "Letter to Harilal Gandhi, July 9, 1918", *CWMG*, vol. 14, p. 480. The *Gandhiji no Akshardeh*, vol. 14, p. 427 and the *CWMG* give the date as 9 July. Mahadev Desai has reproduced the letter under the entry of 8 July in his diary. Mahadevbhai's diary is the source for both the *Gandhiji no Akshardeh* and the *CWMG*.)

   b. Ref. no. 8, July 21, 1918, mentions that while enlisting recruits Gandhiji gave a speech at Kathalal on 11 July 1918, where he said, "I have sent my elder son, who is married and is a father of five children for protecting the country." This speech was given on 11 July, while the letter to Harilal was written either on or before 8 July. It is difficult to understand the purport of the speech in the context of the letter.

He also wrote to others that they must ensure that in the absence of Harilal – he was in jail at that time – Gulab should not feel neglected. He once wrote to Gulab,

> It is not right that you should think you are away from your father's house.
>
> I consider you to be my daughter, not a daughter-in-law. Had I considered you as my daughter-in-law, I would have looked upon you as a child. I take you to be my daughter, and hence I do not want to accept that you are a child. You have not been able to understand that. Just as I do not consider Manilal a child, so also I would not consider you one. Had I kept up our relations as between father-in-law and daughter-in-law, that is, had I kept up such a distance between us, I would have, in accordance with my usual nature, first tried to win you over and would have taken work from you freely only when a sense of oneness with the family had developed in you. But I had taken it for granted that you would forget our relationship of father-in-law and daughter-in-law as I have fondled you in my lap as a daughter long before you marriage to Harilal. You have not forgotten that. Try to forget it now.[4]

Gulabbehn returned to India from South Africa and some time later Harilal had also left South Africa for India. They had set up household in India. During this period Gandhiji showed his affection for Gulab and often asked about her well being.

While she was in India and staying at her father's home Gulabbehn wrote a long and affectionate letter to Gandhiji. In his reply of 8 January 1911, Gandhiji wrote that everyone had read the letter with interest and further added, "Do you ever go out for a walk? It is good that you have kept up the habit of reading. I wish you not to wear jewellery for fear of being criticized if you don't. There is no beauty in jewellery...Our custom of wearing ornaments

---

4. Ref. no. 1. (Translator's note: See also "Letter to Chanchalbehn Gandhi, January 28, 1909", *CWMG*, vol. 9, p. 174.)

on the nose and the ears seems to me barbarous."[5] In this letter he gave her Harilal's news and asked about her relatives.

After Gulabbehn returned to India with Rami, both Gandhiji and Kasturba felt a certain emptiness. Kasturba longed for them. When Kantibhai was six months old, Gandhiji wrote to Harilal on 25 July 1911 that he should send Gulab and the children to South Africa whenever they felt inclined to make the journey and he should take the money for their passage from Revashankarbhai.

When Gulabbehn set up her household in Dhanasuthar ni Pole, she maintained cordial relations with her neighbours.

When Kantibhai was about a year old she fed him Mellin's Food. Gandhiji wrote to her, "Personally, I do not like your giving Kanti Mellin's Food."[6]

During Harilal's involvement with the struggle and his imprisonments, in order to reduce her pangs of separation, Gandhiji often wrote to Gulab, offering solace. Once he wrote, "Harilal will grow by staying apart and will perform his other duties. Love for you does not consist only in staying with you."[7]

In another letter he sang praises of women who were separated from their husbands,

> There have been innumerable women in India who saw their ultimate good in separation from their husbands. Damayanti became immortal on account of her separation from Nala. Taramati separated from Harishchandra and that separation led to the good of both. Draupadi's separation from the Pandavas proved a blessing to them and the entire Hindu

5. Ref. no. 1. (Translator's note: See also "Letter to Chanchalbehn Gandhi, January 8, 1911", *CWMG*, vol. 10, p. 397.)
6. a. Ref. no. 1. (Translator's note: See also "Letter to Chanchalbehn Gandhi, February 18, 1912", *CWMG*, vol. 11, p. 237.)
   b. Though during Gandhiji's illness he consumed Mellin's Food—on 5 October 1918.
7. Ref. no. 1. (Translator's note: See also "Letter to Chanchalbehn Gandhi, January 16, 1909", *CWMG*, vol. 9, p. 150.)

> nation sings the praises of her resoluteness...By these examples I only want to show you that your separation is not going to do you any harm. That it would cause you mental agony is quite natural. That is a sign of love...[8]

Gandhiji was deeply pained by her death. Despite his ill health he sent Kasturba to spend time with Harilal. Prabhudas Gandhi has recalled in an essay written in 1953 that Gandhiji shed tears at the news of her death. He wrote in a letter, "Yes, Harilal has been sorely stricken. Chanchi was far superior to me."[9]

---

8. Ref. no. 1. (Translator's note: See also "Letter to Chanchalbehn Gandhi, January 28, 1909", *CWMG,* vol. 9, p. 174.)
9. Ref. no. 24, vol. 5, p. 27. (Translator's note: See also "Letter to Sonja Schlesin, February 23, 1919", *CWMG,* vol. 15, p. 97.)

7 Merchant in Calcutta

The demise of his wife was a major milestone in Harilal's life. His life altered with her death. He had respected and loved his wife. He was aware that his wife had forgiven many of his sins, including adultery. So long as she was alive, he had a wife and a family. He had her support and warmth during good and bad times; there was someone in whom he could confide. With her death all these vanished. He was separated from his children. He had deep love and regard for his mother Kasturba, so he would not have been perturbed to leave the children in her care; but the support and warmth of family life were no longer available for him.

With that, the limits that conjugal life imposed also vanished. After the death of his wife Harilal remained in Calcutta and practised his trade.

He started a firm called Satyagrahi Brothers. Surendra Medh and Pragji Desai joined as partners. They drew up a partnership deed but it was not signed. Each one felt that the firm was an experiment and formalities could be completed if the experiment succeeded. Meanwhile, Harilal assumed total responsibility for the business.

All three men were 'satyagrahis' and therefore called their firm Satyagrahi Brothers. Its head office was 22, Amratala Street, Calcutta. Harilal looked after the head office. The firm had branches in Mumbai (32, Apollo Street) and Madras (4, Narayan Mudli Street). Surendra Medh and Pragji Desai took turns in looking after the branches.

The telegram address of the Calcutta office was 'AGRAHI'. The firm had its own symbol as well—a large elephant sitting in the middle of the street being pushed from behind by a steamroller. The elephant is so large and powerful that the steamroller is unable to move forward. On the top of this drawing there was a picture of Hanuman taking a great leap and sunbeams streaking down. Below the symbol, the typography read 'Satyagrahi Brothers'.

It appears that this symbol drew upon a cartoon published in a South African newspaper[1] during the satyagraha in South Africa. In this cartoon Gandhiji is shown riding an elephant; the words 'Indian Community' are inscribed over the elephant. A steamroller is shown trying to push the elephant. The steamroller is driven by General Jan Smuts. The steamroller is shown belching steam and letting out whistles, but unable to move forward. The elephant has a smile on its face and it is saying, "Stop ye, tickling Jan."[2]

In a letter dated 23 February 1919, Gandhiji addressed Harilal as "The Most Worthy Firm of Satyagrahis."[3]

It was a firm of importers, exporters, general merchants and commission agents.

The firm was established before 23 February 1919. Later, Harilal's mama – that is, Kasturba's brother – Madhavdas Gokuldas Kapadia either joined the firm or had business relations with the firm.

At this time Madhavdas was living in Mumbai. He was a wealthy man. He had three bungalows in Walkeshwar in Mumbai and had spent Rs. 1200 in getting a swing made.

Around the same time, Gandhiji announced a satyagraha against the Rowlatt Act. Gandhiji was the first signatory to the Satyagraha Pledge. He began travelling around the country to cultivate public opinion. He intended to travel to the Punjab province. He was detained at Palvel station on 9 April 1919, and was brought to Mumbai and released on 11 April 1919.

---

1. Translator's note: *Sunday Times.*
2. a. Jan refers to General Jan Christian Smuts.
   b. For the cartoon see, "Golden Number", *Indian Opinion*, 1914.
3. Ref. no. 24, vol. 5, p. 23. (Translator's note: See also "Letter to Harilal Gandhi, February 23, 1919", *CWMG*, vol. 15, p. 100–01.) The editor of the fifth volume of *Mahadevbhai ni Diary*, Narhari Parikh, has written in the footnote, "Harilalbhai and some of his friends who went to jail during the Satyagraha in South Africa have been called a Firm of Satyagrahis in jest by Gandhiji." (Translator's note: The same footnote has been reproduced in *CWMG*, vol. 15, p. 100.) It is more appropriate to assume that Gandhiji was translating the term 'Messrs Satyagrahi Brothers'.

When Gandhiji visited Mumbai again around 5 May 1919, Madhavdas went to see him, and along with other matters he talked about Harilal. Gandhiji learnt from him that Harilal was facing financial difficulties. It is possible that Madhavdas might have expressed his willingness to lend some money to Harilal. Gandhiji wrote to Harilal that he should manage without others extending monetary help. "You think nothing of risks and want to get rich quickly...Hence it would always be my wish that you did not depend on other people's money for your ventures."[4] Harilal had expressed his desire to go to South Africa. Gandhiji wrote in response, "I do not like your idea of going to South Africa. My own wish is that all of you, having called yourselves satyagrahis, should content yourselves with lower profits and do business only in swadeshi goods."[5]

Meanwhile the Khilafat Movement was launched. The two struggles became one. It was decided that a countrywide strike would be observed on 17 October 1919. Gandhiji send this pamphlet to Harilal.

Harilal and Madhavdas engaged in business relations against Gandhiji's advice. Madhavdas also extended financial assistance to Harilal. He told Harilal, "I have no children, and I consider you my son. Whatever is mine is yours."[6] He also told Harilal that he would arrange for him to get married again.

Madhavdas lent six thousand rupees to Harilal in July 1919. Harilal invested the amount in tobacco. Madhavdas had told him that tobacco would take a long time to sell, that he should recover the invested money as and when the tobacco is sold, and that he should not be impatient in this trade.

Madhavdas traded in foreign cloth. He cabled Harilal that he should take delivery of twenty-seven boxes from a certain merchant. The telegram contained no other information or instruction. He was not asked to check the quality of cloth, or whether it was damaged or stained. Harilal, as instructed,

---

4. Ref. no. 24, vol. 24, p. 74–75. (Translator's note: See also "Letter to Harilal Gandhi, May 5, 1919", *CWMG,* vol. 15, p. 278.)
5. Ibid.
6. Ref. no. 1.

took delivery of the goods. The cloth was found to be stained. Harilal wrote this in the receipt.

Subsequently Madhavdas asked for an explanation as to why Harilal had taken possession of inferior goods.

Madhavdas went on a pilgrimage. He also visited Calcutta. He visited the Calcutta markets. He felt that the prices would go up. He instructed Harilal to dispose the goods when the prices went up. He left Calcutta with these instructions. The markets went into a recession and the prices fell. The prices improved after a while. Madhavdas asked Harilal to sell off the goods at the prevailing market prices. Harilal did as he was told and sold the cloth.

He had acted as per the instructions of Madhavdas. But Madhavdas did not get the price that he had expected. He felt that Harilal was at fault. As luck would have it, two bales were stolen.

In these transactions, either Harilal had been careless or Madhavdas had become suspicious of his conduct. Harilal offered to pay for the stolen goods but sought some time to make the payment. Madhavdas was not pleased. Both exchanged angry words. Madhavdas felt that either Harilal was incapable or he was dishonest.

Madhavdas asked for Rs. 3000 by banker's cheque. He had not got the price he had expected for the goods and hence wrote a letter to Harilal admonishing him.

Harilal was indignant. On 29 November 1919, he wrote to Madhavdas, "As I gain in experience I realise that softness and generosity in business is taken advantage of. Generosity is considered foolishness. Hard-headed selfishness is considered a quality." He further wrote, "It cannot be carved in stone that business transactions would always lead to profits."[7]

Madhavdas had taken Pragji also to task. He went to the Mumbai office of the firm. He told Pragji that Harilal had not paid his debts and so long as the debts were unpaid Pragji could not break the partnership as he held both men responsible for his money.

---

7. Ref. no. 1.

Pragji wrote to Harilal about this incident. Harilal mentioned this as well in his letter of the 29th. "Pragji listened to you and would listen to you in future because he is my friend. It is futile to tell him 'return my money at once.' You go and make such attacks and allegations at the office...this does no credit to either of you."[8]

Harilal was given to angry outbursts. He did not stop at this. He further wrote, "First you raise me, then discredit me and push me down. Meat eaters fatten cows, goats and chicken before killing them for food; this is considered a delicacy. If that dumb animal knew that after being fattened it is to be killed it would not touch even the most delicious feed. The one who kills cannot be praised for fattening the animals."[9]

Madhavdas was seething in anger. He spent his rage on Pragji.

Having written angry words to Madhavdas, Harilal thought that the matter should be placed before Gandhiji, especially because he had entered into business with Madhavdas against Gandhiji's advice.

At that time Gandhiji was travelling through Punjab for the Khilafat Movement. Harilal informed him by telegram that he was coming to meet him. The father and son met on 10 December 1919 in Lahore and discussed Harilal's business dealings at length. The next day, both left Lahore. Gandhiji stopped at Delhi. Harilal proceeded to Calcutta from there.

In Calcutta he received a letter from Madhavdas dated 13 December 1919. Madhavdas had threatened Harilal that he would place the matter before his father. But Harilal was not the one to give in. On the 16th he wrote, "It is natural that I should be afraid of Bapu. But, even Bapu would not like [it] if I were not to act according to my views in matters where I differ conscientiously from Bapu because I am afraid of him. Therefore you are free to place all my letters before Bapu. If it pleases you, you may even place this letter before him. If Bapu asks for my explanation, I would give him a satisfactory answer within my limits. If I were to ask him to mediate in every dispute that I have in my business, it would amount to wasting his time."[10]

8. Ibid.
9. Ibid.
10. Ibid.

The day Gandhiji reached Delhi, a deputation from British Guyana called upon him. They had come with a proposal to settle some Indians in the colony. Some Indian settlers from British Guyana were on their way to Calcutta by the steamer *SS Sutlaj*. To ascertain their views and experiences Gandhiji suggested to the deputation that some of those coming by the steamer should meet Harilal in Calcutta, who would send him a report. Gandhiji informed Harilal of this either when they parted in Delhi or subsequently through a letter. So two of the settlers who had travelled by the steamer met Harilal in Calcutta. Later Harilal wrote about his impressions to Gandhiji. He said that these people praised British Guyana so much that he doubted if they were speaking the truth.

When Madhavdas received Harilal's letter of 16 December 1919, he felt that he would have to be more strict. On 7 January 1920 he threatened Harilal with legal action. Harilal was not a person to be scared easily. On 10 January he responded, "I cannot think of what to write. You are free to take legal recourse...legally very small sum of yours is outstanding on me. In terms of purely financial benefits I desire to pay you as little as possible. Bhai Pragji and Medh...are not responsible for any dealings of the Satyagrahi Brothers...Even if they are; I have owned up the responsibility and freed them. Considering this, take whatever legal actions you wish to against me... I alone am fully responsible."[11]

Meanwhile, Madhavdas wrote to Gandhiji at length. Pragji also wrote and placed the case before him. Gandhiji sent all the papers to Harilal. Harilal received the papers on 10 January 1920. The very same day he wrote to Gandhiji and narrated the events in detail. In explanation he wrote, "If I had money and even if I were to become a pauper after that; given the cruelty of my mama towards me through his letters and conduct I would give him all the money that he might ask for and I would have no dealing with him ever again."[12]

It is not possible to ascertain whether Gandhiji responded to this letter and how the entire episode was resolved.

---

11. Ibid.
12. Ibid.

We know that Madhavdas went to the Agakhan Palace prison at Yeravda to meet Kasturba before her death on 22 February 1944. Once a wealthy man, Madhavdas was then a pauper; he had lost all his wealth in speculation during the Second World War. Kasturba was breathing her last when he reached the prison. Kasturba recognised her brother; tears filled her eyes, but she was unable to speak. Harilal was also present. Why did she have tears in her eyes? Out of affection for her brother? Had she felt pained by his sorry condition? Or was it because she remembered her brother's harsh attitude towards her son?

Gandhiji wrote a letter to Madhavdas on 4 August 1945. "Ba's last words to me about you were: 'You have done what you could for Madhavdas, I did what I could as his sister, and made you do what you could for him. Now you need not do anything for him.' This is what she said about you and Harilal."[13]

The episode of Harilal and Madhavdas ended thus.[14]

In the year 1920, Harilal thought of starting a limited company. For this he turned to Jamnalal Bajaj. Harilal went to Wardha and explained the plan to him. Jamnalalji advised him to stay in Mumbai. Harilal was displeased with his response. After returning to Calcutta, Harilal wrote about the enterprise to Jamnalalji—perhaps regarding purchase of shares. Jamnalalji replied that he had left the decision of considering the matter and providing appropriate assistance to the Calcutta office. We have no information whether any assistance was provided.

Harilal established a limited company called All India Stores Limited. It was well publicised. Taken in by the publicity that its director Harilal Gandhi was Mahatma Gandhiji's son, people from different parts of the country purchased its shares. Its head office was again 22, Amratala Street, Calcutta. It had a branch in Rawalpindi and a factory in Amritsar.

13. Ibid. (Translator's note: See also "Letter to Madhavdas G. Kapadia, August 4, 1945", *CWMG,* vol. 81, p. 71.)
14. Madhavdas went to Delhi after Gandhiji's murder. He died on 2 February 1962.

A special session of the Congress was held in September 1920 in Calcutta. The session was convened to discuss the commencement of the Non-cooperation Movement. The Khilafat Movement and the Muslim League were also in session at the same time. Gandhiji reached Calcutta on 2 September to participate in the session. He stayed with Harilal at 4, Pollock Street.

The Non-cooperation Movement touched Harilal as well. Before that he had given a speech about the Khilafat Movement. The secret police raided the Calcutta office of the Khilafat Committee on 15 March 1920 to get a copy of Harilal's speech. From August 1921 Harilal started wearing a khadi cap. In August 1921 Gandhiji toured Assam. On 17 August, father and son met in Calcutta and talked for a long time. Harilal was arrested on 11 December for his role in the Non-cooperation Movement. Gandhiji sent a congratulatory telegram from Ahmedabad on hearing the news. Harilal was given six months imprisonment. This pleased Gandhiji. In a letter, he wrote, "Harilal has done good work."[15] Harilal sent a message to Kasturba through a visitor that he was perfectly all right in jail and that she should not worry about him.

Harilal was released on 10 June 1922.

Before that Gandhiji was arrested and on 18 March 1922 he was sentenced to six years imprisonment. When Harilal was released Gandhiji was in prison. Harilal went to visit Gandhiji in prison on 1 July 1922, and he went again a week later.

Ramibehn was growing up. Harilal had started thinking about her engagement even before Gulabbehn died. In a letter to Balibehn, Gulabbehn had written, "Even we will have to save little by little for Rami."[16] She trained Ramibehn in household work as well.

Harilal was worried about this after Gulabbehn's death. Ramibehn was not very old, but soon after she turned ten Harilal had started making

---

15. Ref. no. 1. (Translator's note: See also "Letter to Devdas Gandhi, December 15, 1921", *CWMG,* vol. 22, p. 32.)
16. Ref. no. 3.

some arrangements. On 31 December 1918, he wrote to Balibehn that she should be on the lookout for a suitable groom. He suggested that a boy from coastal Kathiawad would be more desirable as he did not have good opinion of the others.[17]

He wrote again after two months. Balibehn might have suggested that Kasturba and Gandhiji should be consulted. In response, he suggested to Balibehn that she should discuss the matter directly with Kasturba. "At present, a direct approach from me is unlikely to succeed. If you write to Ba, Bapu's attention will be drawn."[18] Harilal feared that Gandhiji would not approve of an engagement at such a tender age.

But the matter did not progress much. On 13 August 1920, Harilal wrote to Balibehn, "My Ba and Bapu lead a life of asceticism. It is not for us. Therefore, such burdens should be borne more by us. I bear my share of the burden. I need a woman's help."[19] After the death of Gulabbehn, the children had been living with Gandhiji and Kasturba. Gandhiji's imprisonment for six years might have added to Harilal's anxieties. He went to Ahmedabad and took all his children, except Manubehn, with him to Mumbai. He stayed with his mama Madhavdas and after a few days he took the children with him to Calcutta. Time passed. In October 1922, Kasturba, Ramdas and Manubehn travelled to Calcutta and spent some time with Harilal. He and Kasturba might have discussed Ramibehn's engagement, but nothing came of it.

Harilal's anxiety was growing. He wrote to Balibehn, "I keep feeling that I should come there and settle matters for Rami."[20] Later, on 28 June 1923, he wrote to Balibehn, "I can leave from here around Magasar or Posh. We will settle Rami's marriage then."[21]

Meanwhile, Kunvarji Khetji Parekh of Morbi was suggested as a possible groom for Rami.

---

17. Ibid.
18. Ibid.
19. Ibid.
20. Ibid.
21. Ibid.

Harilal went to Rajkot in January 1924.[22] He met Kunvarji; all other matters appeared satisfactory to him and he decided on the betrothal of Ramibehn with Kunvarji. Kunvarji was acquainted with Balibehn. It is possible that it was she who suggested the match and therefore Harilal had gone to Rajkot.

At this time Gandhiji was in the Sassoon Hospital, Poona. Harilal visited him there and received his consent for the betrothal. He then went to Calcutta. The betrothal ceremony took place on 10 February 1924. Kantibhai went to Morbi from Rajkot with the ceremonial coconut.

Gandhiji was released from the sentence on 5 February 1924 after his appendicitis operation and before the engagement.

Ramibehn and Kunvarji were married on 24 May 1925 at the Sabarmati Ashram. Ramibehn was not yet seventeen years old. But her in-laws had insisted on an early marriage, therefore Gandhiji did not create any obstacles, though he did not like her getting married at such a young age.[23] Harilal was not present at the marriage. He sent his blessings through cable from Calcutta.

While Gandhiji was in jail, the Congress was divided between the Swarajists and the No-changers. Gandhiji went to Calcutta on 4 November 1912 to resolve this division. He stayed with Deshbandhu Das. Mahadevbhai, who had accompanied him on the trip, looked for Harilal. He was not at the station. Mahadevbhai was to go to Harilal's house in search of him. We do not know whether he was able to do so.

During this period we have little information about the limited company that Harilal had established. When Ramdas visited Calcutta in 1922 he had

---

22. There is information that on 23 December 1923 Gandhiji wrote to Harilal, with the permission of the jail superintendent, that Harilal should meet him. Perhaps it was in connection with the engagement.
23. After Rami's marriage, Gandhiji wrote, "Didn't I myself wish to give Lakshmi a string of beads, when I was reluctant to give anything to Rami?" Ref. no. 15, vol. 2, sr. no. 301. (Translator's note: See also "Letter to Narandas Gandhi, March 16, 1933", *CWMG*, vol. 54, p. 95.)

observed the functioning of the company and according to him it was being managed well. On the other hand, we also know that in 1923 Harilal started a new business—H. M. Gandhi & Co., Coal Merchant and Commission Agent. The address of the company was again 22, Amratala Street, and the telegraphic address was also 'AGRAHI'. The reader would recall that the Satyagrahi Brothers and the limited company also operated from the same address.

Harilal's financial difficulties continued. Either his money was locked in bad investments or he was very extravagant in his expenditure. In a letter dated 9 June 1923, he wrote, "Surely I don't have money bearing trees."[24]

The limited company also met a similar fate.

A Muslim had brought shares of the company through its agent in Rawalpindi. After which he received no information regarding the company. He therefore wrote a letter to the company's office at 22, Amratala Street, but did not receive any response. Finally, he placed his case in the hands of a lawyer from Lyallpur. The lawyer also wrote to the company's address. The post office returned the letter. It came back from Calcutta as a 'dead letter'. This lawyer wrote about the matter to Gandhiji. The lawyer raised doubts whether such a company had ever existed; he also expressed his apprehension that his client had been cheated of his money by fraud.

Gandhiji received this letter either before or during May 1925. Gandhiji was in Calcutta between 4 and 7 May. He met Harilal during his stay and they discussed various matters for over three hours. Harilal suggested to him that Kasturba, if she was planning to come to Calcutta, should not do so as he had moved out of his house and was staying with a friend of his. During their discussions Gandhiji must have brought up the issue of the letter from the lawyer from Lyallpur. Otherwise, Gandhiji might not have felt the need to spend three hours discussing matters with him. Harilal might have moved out of the house so that neither his shareholders nor the postal department would have his residential address.

---

24. Ref. no. 3.

Gandhiji felt that others like the Muslim shareholder might have also bought shares and undergone similar experiences. He wrote an essay on this issue in *Navjivan*.[25] He wrote that it was true that he was Harilal's father, but that his ideals were different from Harilal's and for a long time they had been living separately. Gandhiji disclaimed all responsibility for Harilal's commercial transactions. He admitted that Harilal might have taken advantage of his 'sonship' and that fruits might have been sold in the name of the tree. He expressed his sympathies with all those who had invested money in Harilal's enterprise. He felt that if Harilal were truly honest he would not rest until he had paid back all the creditors in full. If Harilal held different views regarding honesty he might seek protection under the law of insolvency. He assured the public that "nothing crooked will have countenance from me." He also said that he would like to see Harilal reformed. He wrote, "The protection of a human father has its decided limitations. That of the divine father is ever open to him."[26] Harilal, Gandhiji wrote, should seek divine protection and that he would find it.

Finally, he wrote that he pitied all those who had bought shares without studying the solvency of the enterprise just because Harilal was his son. He warned the others not to be taken in by big names.

After the publication of this essay Harilal met Jamnalalji in Calcutta on 21 July 1925. We have no record of their conversation. The episode of the limited company thus came to an end.

Harilal might have floated this company to pay back the Pathans and other creditors from whom he might have borrowed money. Chirranjan Das[27] was a friend of Harilal. We know that during this period he paid up all of Harilal's debts.

---

25. Ref. no. 6, June 21, 1925. (Translator's note: See also "A Domestic Chapter", *CWMG*, vol. 27, p. 259–62. This was originally written in English and published in *Young India*, June 18, 1925; and was subsequently translated and published in Gujarati in *Navajivan*, June 21, 1925.)
26. Ref. no. 6, June 21, 1925. (Translator's note: See also *CWMG*, vol. 27, p. 261.)
27. Son of Chittaranjan Das.

Towards the end of 1925, a Congress session was held at Kanpur. Sarojini Naidu was the president of the Congress. Gandhiji had gone to Kanpur to attend the Congress.

On 25 June Harilal was in Calcutta. It appears that he no longer had an office. Gandhiji wrote to him on that day and addressed the letter to the office of M.M. Bhagat at 72, Canning Street. On 11 December 1925, Harilal wrote a letter to his brother Devdas from this address. Devdas had written to him, "We would be obliged if some day you were to write to us." Harilal in response wrote, "So be it. I am writing to you today. How is your health?... What is Ramdas up to? How you serve the parents! I do not serve them, hence I am unhappy and make all of you suffer."[28]

Devdas might have suggested to him that he should visit the Sabarmati Ashram. In his letter Harilal wrote, "Is this impure body befitting [to enter] the ashram? I am going tomorrow to meet Bapu at Wardha. I will come to the ashram if he permits. It is my wish that Ba and all of you should come to Kanpur. We shall meet there."[29]

We do not know whether they met as suggested.

---

28. Ref. no. 1.
29. Ibid.

8 Concerns for the Children

During a large part of 1926 Gandhiji had withdrawn from active political life. He spent this year mostly at the Sabarmati Ashram, rebuilding it. After Gulabbehn's death, Gandhiji and Kasturba raised Harilal and Gulabbehn's children. Their masi – mother's sister – Balibehn visited them often at the Ashram. Sometimes the children went to their maternal home with their masi. At times Harilal visited them.

Harilal had reasonably good relations with everyone in the family, except of course his father. He had deep affection for his mother. He felt similarly towards Manilal, Ramdas and Devdas. We have noted that once Manilal had sent him money without Gandhiji's consent.

After Harilal's departure from South Africa and before Gandhiji's return to India, Manilal was involved in some misconduct for which he had to bear the wrath of Gandhiji.[1] Gandhiji had also undertaken fasts on account of this misconduct. He had also, as punishment, decreed that Manilal should not marry for a specified number of years. Manilal had accepted this punishment. Gandhiji softened when Manilal was thirty-four or thirty-five years old and gave him permission to marry. Manilal's marriage took place in India on 6 March 1927.

He then lived in South Africa and looked after the affairs of the *Indian Opinion*. Before his marriage in 1926, he had been in love with a Muslim girl in South Africa.[2] Gandhiji did not find this relationship acceptable. Manilal

---

1. Translator's note: The year was 1913. Manilal was involved in a sexual relationship with Jayakunwar Manilal Doctor, known to all as Jeki, married daughter of Gandhiji's friend Dr. Pranjivandas Mehta. Gandhiji was deeply perturbed by this 'moral fall' at the Phoenix Settlement. See Uma Dhupelia Mesthrie, *Gandhi's Prisoner? The Life of Gandhi's Son Manilal* (Delhi: Permanent Black, 2004), p. 105–10.
2. Translator's note: Fatima, or Timmie as she was called, was a member of the Gool family, old friends of the Gandhis in Cape Town. See Mesthrie, *Gandhi's Prisoner?* p. 174–77.

wrote to Ramdas about this. He might have even written to Harilal or else Ramdas might have informed Harilal. Harilal wrote to Gandhiji making a case in favour of this marriage. In his response of 30 May 1926 Gandhiji wrote,

> "I cannot think just now how inter-marriages will ever become possible. How can we have a family in which one member is a vegetarian and another a non-vegetarian? In which tradition will the children of such a couple be brought up? Problem alliances of this kind will raise many other issues besides these. Any attempt at this time to persuade people to act upon your suggestions will furnish one more ground for opposition or make the achievement of political unity impossible. How unwise it is to imagine a connection between political unity and other issues where none exists![3]

This matter ended with this letter.

In 1926 another significant incident took place.

We have noted earlier that financial dealings between Gandhiji and Harilal ended in 1915. During that period the ancestral property, including the house at Rajkot,[4] was divided. Gandhiji surrendered his rights to the ancestral house and had sent all the papers to this effect to Barrister Shukla in Rajkot. According to the partition deed, the rights of the house were vested in Samaldas (son of Gandhiji's elder brother Lakshmidas) and Jethalal alias Kakubhai (son of the other brother Karsandas).

In 1924, when Harilal visited Rajkot for the betrothal of Ramibehn he was in financial difficulties. He borrowed ten thousand rupees from the Thakore Saheb of Rajkot.

When Samaldas and Jethalal wanted to sell the ancestral house, the money lent to Harilal by the Thakore Saheb was accounted as outstanding debt by the State Treasury. So long as this debt remained unpaid, the Counsel of People's Representatives declined to transfer the property in the name of the purchaser.

---

3. Ref. no. 1. (Translator's note: See also "Letter to Harilal Gandhi, May 30, 1926", *CWMG,* vol. 30, p. 512.)
4. This house is today called 'Kaba Gandhi no Dahelo'.

In fact, Harilal had no claims on the property and therefore the sale could not be withheld. Perhaps the partition deeds were not clear, and therefore it became necessary to clarify that all claimants to the property had surrendered their rights. Jethalal complained to Gandhiji in a letter dated 7 June 1926 that Harilal had declined to commit in writing that he had no right to the property. Harilal subsequently went to Rajkot and clarified that he had borrowed ten thousand rupees on his sole and personal responsibility, and since Gandhiji had surrendered his right to the property, he had no claims on it. Thakore Saheb agreed to consider the loan as a personal advance. The sale deed was validated after that.[5]

After this incident related to the sale of the house, in July–August of 1926, Harilal spent a little over a month with Gandhiji at the Sabarmati Ashram. Manilal came to India in December. When the two brothers met, Manilal gave Harilal ten rupees. Gandhiji came to know of this while he was travelling. This time he did not show the same anger that he had shown in 1916. Gandhiji wrote to Manilal on 10 January 1927 to the effect that he would have done a good turn to Harilal if he had not given him those ten rupees. He said that often strictness results in real kindness and kindness results in cruelty. If every one of them were to be lovingly strict towards Harilal, his eyes would open sooner.

---

5. a. The Council of People's Representatives, in its proceedings between 16 and 27 August 1926 had passed the following resolution: "This meeting of the Council of People's Representatives requests His Highness the Thakore Saheb to adopt a practice underwhich whenever within this State, a Sale Deed or a Deed of Mortage comes to be presented before the Court for the registration thereof, the same shall be admitted for scrutiny only after the receipt or calling of the report, stating the accounts showing the transactions with the State from the Manager of the Rajkot State Bank."

   The Thakore Saheb approved of this resolution. It is possible that this resolution became necessary after the dispute regarding the sale of Gandhi property.

   b. For more information on this incident see Appendix 3.

Manilal's marriage was fixed to take place on 7 March 1927 at Akola. Gandhiji was travelling when the decision was made. He wrote to Manilal on 14 February 1927 and instructed him to "write nothing to Harilal".

It appears that around this period the rift between Gandhiji and Harilal widened further. They wrote and met each other even less.

Harilal's sister-in-law Balibehn had been widowed at a young age.[6] After Gulabbehn's death, the children lived with Kasturba at the Ashram. Balibehn visited her nephews and nieces often at the Ashram. At times the children went with her to Rajkot and spent time at either her house or the house of their maternal grandparents. Harilal disapproved of this. Once Gandhiji had to write to Balibehn, "You both feel very unhappy because I cannot make arrangements for the children as desired by you...I should like you...to go to Sabarmati, stay in the Ashram and be happy with the children."[7] Once when Kantibhai had gone to Rajkot, he was persuaded by his relatives to stay on. Gandhiji had to send a telegram to Balibehn that Kantibhai should be sent back to the Ashram. Balibehn's younger sister Kumibehn visited the Ashram and insisted that the children accompany her to Rajkot. Again, Gandhiji had to insist that the children should be sent back to the Ashram after some days.

It appears that Harilal's relationship with his in-laws, especially Balibehn, was not cordial. He often wrote to Gandhiji about this. In his letter of 4 June 1927, written from Bangalore, Gandhiji wrote to Kumibehn,

> I share your unhappiness. But I can offer no consolation except to ask you to bear with it. Chi. Harilal's last letter is worse than even his previous ones. You and I should look upon him as a sick man and take no notice what he writes. I believe he will return to his senses some day. I do hope neither of you two sisters thinks that I have said anything

---

6. Her husband, Manilal Laxmichand Adalja, died around 7 October 1911. Her in-laws lived in Rajkot.
7. Ref. no. 24, vol. 5, p. 8–9. (Translator's note: See also "Letter to Bali, January 21, 1919", *CWMG*, vol. 15, p. 75–76.)

> anywhere about you and him. I do not remember having said anything about the plight you are in to anyone except Harilal himself. And I am amazed at what he writes about Chanchi. I have looked upon you all girls as my daughters...There is no question of my defending myself against Harilal's attack. But if you so much as feel that I have done something that adds to your unhappiness, please do not let such a thought ever cross your mind. Just for this reason I write all this. I do not worry because you sisters are both brave...If Bali reads Harilal's letters, let her read this letter too. But if you have taken the precaution of not letting her read his letters, there is no need to let her read this one either. But if she has read them, ask her not to be unhappy on account of Harilal's letter.[8]

Three days later he wrote to her again.

> He was born during what I regard, relatively, as my period of indulgence...therefore, myself and Ba, to the extent that she was a willing partner in indulgence, are responsible for the condition in which Harilal lives today. Why, then, blame Harilal?...It is certainly bad of him to make this charge against Chi. Bali...Personally, I believe that Harilal will wake up from his deep slumber and reform himself...[9]

Gandhiji knew that Harilal had rights over his children and that they could stay with him only so long as Harilal wanted them to. If Harilal wanted to take the children away no one would be able to deny his right to do so.

Harilal once considered taking care of the children himself. He was then working as a salesman for Godrej in India, Burma and Ceylon. He was successful at that job due to his abilities and hard work. He also earned well.

---

8. Ref. no. 1. (Translator's note: See also "Letter to Kumi, June 5, 1927", *CWMG*, vol. 33, p. 441. Both the *CWMG* and *Gandhiji no Akshardeh*, vol. 33, p. 414, give the date of the letter as 5 June 1927.)
9. Ref. no. 24, vol. 11, p. 9. (Translator's note: See also "Letter to Kumi, June 8, 1927", *CWMG*, vol. 33, p. 455.)

Like Gandhiji, he too desired that his sons should receive the best education. But they differed in their idea of what was the 'best' education. Gandhiji preferred the education that was given in the Ashram, while Harilal's idea of education was contrary to the Ashram education. He felt that if Kantibhai were to receive college education he would be better able to serve the country later.

Harilal was earning rather well at that point of time and was in a position to pay for the expenses of such an education.

He wrote to Kantibhai about this and also said that he would be able to arrange for him to stay in a hostel.

Harilal was aware that his life was on the wrong path. He also desired that, if possible, his sons should be prevented from taking the path that he had taken. Therefore, he suggested that Kantibhai stay in a hostel.

Kantibhai wrote back expressing his willingness. Gandhiji was in Bangalore during that time for reasons of health. Kantibhai wrote to him and asked, "Shall I go?" On 17 June 1927, Gandhiji responded to his query:

> I got your letter. You want my permission to go and see Chi. Harilal. A son need not seek his grandfather's permission to see his father. No one can stand in the way of a son's wishes. You have now come of age, and that is another reason why there should be no question of my giving you permission.
>
> All I can do is to explain to you your responsibility, and this is my advice in regard to your seeing Chi. Harilal. I believe he is at present following a wrong path. He leads an immoral life. He has become an addict. He has forgotten his dharma, and, therefore, he is not fit to exercise his right as a father. I regard him as suffering from a kind of disease. His disease is not physical but spiritual, and spiritual disease is more dreadful than a physical ailment. It is not, therefore, your duty to go to him to comfort him; on the contrary, it is your duty to keep away from him. You, I and his friends and well-wishers should employ spiritual non-co-operation against him. If you have intended to go to him to reform him I regard your idea as

worthy of support, and in that case I would facilitate your going. But just now it seems that you wish to go because of that letter. I feel, therefore, that your going to him will mean your encouraging him in his intention.

Moreover, if you wish to go to him in order to reform him, you are not yet, from a practical point of view, fit and sufficiently mature to undertake such a task. From that point of view, you are yet a child. You are still studying. It is my desire, and also my effort to see that as you study, you should so develop your soul that you may acquire the power to do what I could not in regard to Harilal, and you should so impress him that the moment he sees you he would abjure his evil habits. I have been bringing up both you brothers with that aim in view. If you have the capacity, you will be able to benefit from such education. I would, therefore, advise you to write to Harilal and tell him firmly that until he gives up his addictions and his immoral life and is able to support you all, or until you are able by the power of your tapascharya to awaken him from his slumber, you cannot go and see him. I do not, however, insist that you should forthwith accept my advice.

So far, Harilal used to admit his weaknesses, and has been saying that he would try to shake them off; but now he has started writing letters against me in the papers. I have not seen those letters, but I know their purport. Harilal says that it is I who have forsaken my dharma, not he, and that I have been propagating the Buddhist faith.[10] And he holds that such propaganda is harmful to people's welfare and, therefore, regards it as an evil. His rebellion, he says, is against that evil. And he intends to take you brothers away from under my undesirable influence at the first opportunity.

As such are his views, you are likely to be assailed by doubts. If you have the slightest doubt whether my ideas are

10. Harilal wrote a series of articles in a Gujarati daily, *Hindustan Prajamitra,* entitled, "Amaro Balvo yane Mahatma no Budhhavatar" ("Our Revolt or Mahatma's Incarnation as the Buddha").

right or Harilal's, I think you should not be led away by my ideas. Hence this is my further advice to you that you should humbly consult the teachers under whom you have studied or those among the elders with whom you have come in contact in the Ashram and who command your confidence. Put all your problems before them and act as they advise. If you ask me to solve your problems, I too will help. The *Gita* which all of us study daily, which you have been learning by heart and trying to understand with great devotion, says that we should get our problems solved with the help of those whom we regard as our elders by earnestly questioning them with humility. We should have faith in them, accept what they say as true and act accordingly. I wish, and I advise you, that you should do what I have suggested. Do not reach a hasty decision. Do not act with childish immaturity. Try to understand what your duty at the present moment is, and act with courage and determination in accordance with that duty. Consider, not what you would like to do, but what you should do. You may show this letter to anyone you may wish to consult. I shall wait for your reply. Let me know how both of you are.[11]

The matter ended with this letter.

Ramdas' wedding took place on 27 January 1928 at the Sabarmati Ashram. Harilal was present at the marriage. He and Devdas spent about ten days together, after which Harilal left the Ashram. It appears that even after the marraige Harilal visited the Ashram occasionally.

Harilal's other son, Rasikbhai, was also living in the Ashram. When he grew up he was sent to Delhi to assist Devdas. He reached Delhi on 3 September 1928. Devdas was then at Jamia Millia. Rasikbhai worked there and taught

11. Ref. no. 24, vol. 11, p. 18–21. (Translator's note: See also "Letter to Kanti Gandhi, June 17, 1927", *CWMG*, vol. 34, p. 18–19.)

spinning. Rasikbhai was sixteen or seventeen years old. He contacted typhoid while he was in Delhi. His condition worsened day by day. He expressed his desire to be sent back to the Sabarmati Ashram. He was hopeful of being cured there. But he was kept in Delhi, under the care of Dr. Ansari.

Gandhiji was in the Ashram when he was informed of this illness. On 2 February 1929 he left the Ashram for his tour of Sindh. Subsequently the Ashram received the news that his condition had deteriorated. A telegram was sent from the Ashram to Gandhiji informing him of Rasikbhai's condition. Kantibhai and Kasturba were with him on this journey. When the news reached them, Kasturba and Kantibhai got down from the train at Marwad junction and went to Delhi. Gandhiji continued his journey towards Sindh. Gandhiji did not like Kasturba thus going to Delhi. He believed that because of railways and such other conveniences people travel too much and such unjustifiable expenditure should be incurred as the last resort. But he did not say anything at that time. Rasikbhai's masi, Balibehn, also rushed to Delhi from Rajkot. Harilal also reached there when Rasikbhai was breathing his last. All the treatment and nursing was in vain; Rasikbhai died on 8 February 1929.[12]

Harilal was in the habit of quarrelling with his brothers; but never on such occasions. He only blamed himself. He was extremely courteous to everyone. He was deeply pained, but he had no complaints against anyone. He thanked the doctor and other friends.

The day Rasikbhai died, Gandhiji was in Shikarpur in Sindh. Kasturba, Harilal and Kantibhai stayed in Delhi waiting for his arrival. Gandhiji reached Delhi on 17 February. At that time Harilal was in Delhi. After some days he went to Kanpur, and again returned to Delhi. He was to go to Lahore from Delhi.

Thus Harilal lost two of his sons. Shantibhai had died earlier, and Rasikbhai too died. Kantibhai was his only surviving son.

Before leaving Delhi, Harilal asked Kantibhai, "Do you want something?" Kantibhai expressed his desire to buy a camera. Harilal took out forty rupees from

---

12. Devdas in his essay (Appendix 2) mentions the year as 1928. This is an error.

his pocket. Kantibhai had acquired good deal of knowledge of photography. He knew that a reasonably good camera would cost Rs. 125. He said so to Harilal. Harilal told him, "Keep these forty rupees for now. Keep saving for it. Otherwise even this amount will not remain with me." But Kantibhai declined, "You keep the money. You will face difficulty. I am in no hurry."[13]

Harilal wrote to Gandhiji asking him to send Kantibhai to him. He also expressed his wish to buy him a camera. Kantibhai at that time was working in the dairy of the Sabarmati Ashram. Gandhiji was touring south India. On 2 May 1929, he instructed the Ashram that Kantilal should be allowed to go if it does not inconvenience the work in the dairy. On the issue of the purchase of a camera, he said that he was not inclined to ask Kantilal to refuse it.

Harilal went to the Sabarmati Ashram on 7 June 1929. He went to Rajkot on 18 August 1929 and returned to the Ashram, on his way to Mumbai, where he met everyone.

---

13. Kantibhai's communication with the author.

9 On the Path to Addiction

On 12 March 1930, Gandhiji marched to Dandi. He was arrested and released, and after protracted negotiations he went to London for the Second Round Table Conference. He returned from it empty-handed and was again imprisoned on 4 January 1932.

We have no information about Harilal, his activities and whereabouts during this period. We know that during January 1931, when Sardar Patel was imprisoned in the Arthur Road Prison in Mumbai, Harilal had paid him a visit. Harilal was intoxicated and Sardar felt that this had been planned by the government. He had declined to meet Harilal.

Harilal's younger daughter Manubehn had been with Kasturba since childhood. She did spend some time with Balibehn. This incident took place in 1932 when Manubehn was about fifteen years old. She had been staying with Balibehn either at her house or at the house of her maternal grandparents. One day Harilal went there intoxicated, and misbehaved. Manubehn witnessed this incident. She wrote to Gandhiji about it. Balibehn also wrote to Gandhiji and said that the girl had not stopped crying since the incident. Gandhiji responded to Manubehn's letter on 4 April 1932.

> You need not be scared. It was very good that you saw the woeful condition of Harilal with your own eyes. I knew all about him. However, we should not give up hope of anyone's future. Nothing is beyond God's power. If there is still some merit to Harilal's credit earned through good deeds in the past, it will bear fruit one day. We should not pamper him or have false pity on him, but should make our hearts purer day by day. That will have an effect on Harilal too. You have got to harden your heart and write to him and tell him plainly that, as long as he does not give up drinking, he will have to assume that you do not exist. If all of us adopt such a course, Harilal

> might take heed. Often a drunkard gives up his evil habit when he is greatly shocked.[1]

Manubehn wrote another pathetic letter. She informed Gandhiji that her masi had slapped Harilal three or four times. Gandhiji wrote to her on 10 April. He advised her not to fear Harilal and to forget him altogether. He said that Balibehn was a brave woman, "Her slapping [your father] was not an act of violence, but showed her deep love."[2]

He wrote so to Manubehn. But he was deeply pained and shocked by Harilal's conduct. The next day, on the 11th, he wrote to the Ashram that Harilal should be permitted to stay in the Ashram only on the condition that he gives up drinking. He also wrote to Harilal that henceforth he would not find a shelter in the Ashram.

Balibehn, having slapped Harilal, either felt remorse or she wanted to clarify what had happened. She visited Gandhiji in jail.

On the other hand, Harilal complained that he was assaulted by Balibehn and asserted that Gandhiji was culpable for her behaviour. Moreover, he demanded that Manubehn be released from Balibehn's clutches. Gandhiji wrote in response on 27 April 1932:

> I will still not give up hope of your reformation, for I have not given up hope about myself. I have always believed that I was a bad man when Ba carried you in her body, but after your birth I have been doing greater and greater penance for my former life. How can I, therefore, give up all hope? I will continue to hope as long as you and I are alive. And hence, contrary to my usual practice, I am preserving your letter so that, when you have awakened, you may see the insolence of your letter and weep over it and laugh at your folly. I am not preserving this letter to throw it on your face then, but only that I may laugh at it, if God wills that I should see that day.

1. Ref. no. 24, vol. 1, p. 73–74. (Translator's note: See also "Letter to Manu Gandhi, April 4, 1932", *CWMG*, vol. 49, p. 269.)
2. Ref. no. 24, vol. 1, p. 92. (Translator's note: See also "Letter to Manu Gandhi, April 10, 1932", *CWMG*, vol. 49, p. 292.)

> All of us are full of short-comings. But it is our dharma to overcome them. I pray that you do so.[3]

Manubehn wrote another long letter and poured out her pain to Gandhiji.

Harilal too wrote a letter to Gandhiji. It was as insolent as the previous letter. He defended his misconduct and blamed Balibehn for the incident. Gandhiji knew well that Balibehn was like a mother to Manubehn. If Manubehn were to be taken out of her care, as Harilal desired, it would cause suffering to both.

It appears that Harilal was on good terms with Jamnadas.[4] When Harilal had written that semi-public letter to Gandhiji,[5] it had affected Jamnadas and his accusations had pained him. It appears that Jamnadas was kept aware of the frequently changing addresses and accommodations of Harilal. Gandhiji had sent the letter of 11 April 1932 to Harilal through Jamnadas.[6] Gandhiji knew that Harilal sought shelter wherever he could, satisfied his passions and addictions, and moved on to another place leaving his forwarding address with his previous host.

Jamnadas was aware that Balibehn had slapped Harilal. Either he was present when the incident took place or he was informed of it later. Perhaps it was Harilal who informed him. Jamnadas wrote about this incident to his elder brother Narandas who in turn might have informed Gandhiji; or Jamnadas might have directly written to Gandhiji. He gave his opinion on the matter. It is possible that according to him Harilal was not at fault. Gandhiji received reports from others that Harilal had broken free from all limits and restraints. Gandhiji felt that Harilal was cheating the people around

---

3. a. Ref. no. 24, vol. 1, p. 125–26, (Translator's note: See also "Fragment of a Letter to Harilal Gandhi", *CWMG*, vol. 49, p. 374–75.)
   b. It appears that either the government detained the letter or caused delay in sending it from the jail. Gandhiji had lodged a complaint regarding this.
4. The youngest brother of Chhaganlal Gandhi.
5. See Appendix 1.
6. Translator's note: This letter does not form part of either *Gandhiji no Akshardeh* or the *CWMG*.

him. In order that no injustice is done to Harilal, Gandhiji decided to ask Jamnadas' views on the incident. He wrote to Jamnadas on 16 May 1932 that he had come to know of Harilal's beastly behaviour, but wanted to know the details from Jamnadas.[7]

Three days later, Gandhiji wrote to Narandas that he should write his opinion on the matter so that Gandhiji does no injustice to Harilal.[8]

But Harilal was falling rapidly. Alcohol and adultery had become commonplace for him. A letter that he wrote to Gandhiji during this period was full of errors, the signature was incomplete and writing was shaky as if written in a fit of passion or in an inebriated state.

His demand to take possession of Manubehn was becoming more and more insistent and aggressive. Harilal spewed his anger on Balibehn. He might have either written to Manubehn that she should go and stay with him or might have sent such a message to her. Manubehn asked Gandhiji to advise her. He told her that she must write to Harilal that she did not want to stay with him.

Gandhiji also felt that despite his harassment, Harilal did not really want the children to go and stay with him—his monetary condition did not allow for their stay. He wanted to extract money by any means. His threat to file a complaint against his in-laws and Balibehn was without substance—it was a ploy. It appears that either Harilal had incurred some debts or made some purchases and had promised that the money would be paid by Balibehn. It is also possible that it might have been his wish. The creditors asked Balibehn to repay them. Balibehn wrote to Gandhiji. He responded on 24 August 1932 and told her that she must refuse to pay any bills in Harilal's name that she might receive.

Manubehn still longed for her father. Gandhiji wrote to her on the same day he wrote to Balibehn that she should stop crying for Harilal.

Gandhiji was in prison. He wrote to the Secretary of the Home Department, Government of India, on 1 May 1933, that he would undertake a fast

7. We do not know if there was a reply to this letter.
8. It appears that even this letter remained unanswered.

for twenty-one days from the 8th. He also declared that the fast was not against the government or any individual, but for self-purification. The government released him on the morning of the 8th and escorted him to Lady Thackersey's bungalow.

Harilal wrote the following letter to Gandhiji when he came to know of the proposed fast. This letter was written from a hotel located on Frere Road, Mumbai:

> In the service of Pujya Pitashri,
>
> Your fasts has posed a question to all, 'What is my dharma?' This question is natural to those who believe in you. What is my dharma as a son? I am ready to fast on your behalf. You can ask of this body anything that it is capable of. My question is unconditional. I would be happy if you could find a way where undertaking this fast is not imperative for you. I am eager to receive your response.
>
> Your obedient son
>
> Harilal's Dandvat.[9]

This letter was written from the Nizamiah Hotel of Vazir Mohammad.[10] Harilal converted to Islam about three years after this event. But he wrote this letter from a Muslim hotel! Gandhiji knew this, he also realised its meaning, but immediately responded by telegram. His response was of the kind that would cause a change of heart.

> YOUR LETTER TOUCHES ME. IF THIS FAST MEANS YOUR RETURN TO PURE LIFE IT WOULD BE DOUBLY BLESSED. SEE ME. I SHALL TRY GUIDE YOU. GOD BLESS YOU.[11]

---

9. Ref. no.1.
10. He had been staying here since or before 16 April 1933.
11. Ref. no. 1. (Translator's note: See also "Telegram to Harilal Gandhi, May 6, 1933", *CWMG,* vol. 55, p. 128.)

Gandhiji told Kakasaheb Kalelkar who was in jail with him, "I am ready to fast for forty-two days if Harilal is to return."[12]

Harilal responded to the telegram with a letter.

> I have received your telegram. My pecuniary condition is extremely precarious, making it difficult for me to leave from here. It is my prayer; send your instructions for me through a letter. I have full faith in the legitimacy and success of your fast.
>
> Your Obedient Son
>
> Harilal's Dandvat.[13]

After Gandhiji's fast, a decision was made—to disband the Sabarmati Ashram on 1 August. It was arranged that all the Ashram children would stay with Ansuyabehn Sarabhai. Of Harilal's children, only Manubehn was at the Ashram. Gandhiji sent instructions that in Manubehn's case Balibehn's opinion should be sought, and that Manubehn should go to Wardha if Ansuyabehn had any reservations. If Manubehn wished to be either at her maternal grandparents' house or with Balibehn, she should be allowed to make her choice. Gandhiji wrote to Ansuyabehn, "Take Manu with you; if she wants to go to Rajkot let her go. But do not give her any money. Perhaps Balibehn will come. If Manu wants to go back with her let her do so. But Manu does not want that Masi will be able to do nothing."[14]

It appears that Manubehn did not go to Ansuyabehn's house.

---

12. Ref. no. 24, vol. 3, p. 292.
13. Ref. no. 1.
14. Translator's note: This letter is included neither in *Gandhiji no Akshardeh,* nor the *CWMG,* nor *Mahadevbhai ni Diary.* The author's research notes indicate that he saw the letter in the office of the Majoor Mahajan Sangh (Textile Labour Union).

10 A Change of Heart?

We have very scant and scattered information about Harilal and his family during this period.[1]

We know that Harilal went to Pondicherry either during January or the early part of February 1934. It is possible that he stayed at the Ashram of Sri Aurobindo. There, he begged for money. He got some money as well. It is possible that some Gujarati inmate might have given him some money. He also drank alcohol there. Perhaps for this reason he was driven out of the Ashram.[2]

---

1. 1932–33.
2. Here is a letter that Harilal wrote to the Mother. It is undated. It appears that he wrote this letter subsequent to his banishment from the Ashram. His address is marked as 'The Monk, Pondicherry'. It has not been possible to ascertain whether it is the name of a person or a hotel.

   My Revered Mother,

   I know that you would like me to beg pardon. You know that I have sought forgiveness and as penance I gave a promise to Sri Aurobindo, a promise that I give unto you as well, that I shall not commit the same mistake ever again. I shall unconditionally live by this promise all my life.

   Yours Filially

   Harilal

   In the postscript, Harilal mentions a dream that he had, in which he was called to the Sabarmati Ashram. We do not know if this letter received a reply. (Translator's note: The original of this letter is untraceable in the archives of the Sri Aurobindo Ashram, Pondicherry. However, another letter from Harilal to the Mother and his letter to Sri Aurobindo are preserved in the archives, and have been reproduced in the original elsewhere in this book. I am grateful to Dr. Peter Heehs, Director of Archives and Research Library of Sri Aurobindo Ashram for making the letters available. The letter given above is my translation of Harilal's letter from the Gujarati.)

After this Harilal lived in south Hydrabad and worked as an insurance agent for a company called Sun Life of Canada. Gandhiji visited south Hydrabad on 9 March 1934. Harilal went to see him. We do not know the details of their conversation. It appears that Gandhiji suggested he should go to Pondicherry.

Harilal wrote a letter on 5 May 1934 to the Mother.[3]

> C/o Rayjyar
> Shop Tuljaprasad
> Nampally
> Hyderabad (Deccan)
>
> My Revered Mother,
>
> Gandhiji has asked me to go to Pondicherry. I cannot come now. But my heart is there. When will I fall at your feet? This is just to pray for your blessings. Please give my love to Kantilal.
> My obeisance to Shri Arbindo.
>
> Kindly give me a word of advise. I am awaiting it at the above address.
>
> Yours Filially
> Harilal Mohandas Gandhi
>
> Excuse p.s.: I call out to thee, Mother, Mother. Would the Mother still not respond? What can be done about it?[4]

Harilal's financial condition was extremely precarious and his health too was indifferent. On the 5th, he also wrote a letter to Balibehn in which he pleaded with her.

> C/o M. Abbas Ali
> Old Lakdi Mandi, House No. 5832
> Nampally, Hyderabad (Deccan)

---

3. Translator's note: Original reproduced. Courtesy, Archives and Research Library, Sri Aurobindo Ashram, Pondicherry.
4. Translator's note: This postscript was written in Gujarati. The Mother did not read Gujarati.

5 May 1934

Affectionate Balibehn,

Possibly Bapu wrote to you that I am in Hydrabad. I met him when he was here. Chi. Bhai Ramdas wrote that Kusum has died. Rami and Manu must be in good health. Chi. Kunvarji, Tulsidas and Kamubehn must be well. After meeting Bapu this time, my rage about you has receded. I do not write this to flatter you, but it is a true statement.

I write this out of my own need. My health no longer holds. I have had fever for the past eight odd days. I work, having settled here, for Sun-Life-Of Canada, an insurance firm. But fate does not favour me. I have no money. I have no clothes or cover. It would be an act of great kindness if you were to send by telegraphic transfer Rs. 50, upon receipt of this letter. I will return it in two months. I understand that you spend money over Rami and other children. To care for each other is a human obligation. Do care for me now. I eat at an eatery on credit promising to pay with the money that you would send.

Please remember me to Nanabhai and send through him Rs. 50 by telegram to the above address. Convey my regards to Anandlalbhai, Harishankarbhai and all others. I hope your health is good.

Regards,

Harilal

Harilal did not receive any money from Balibehn. Instead she wrote a letter chastising him.

Harilal wrote another letter full of pathos:

C/o Seth Tulsiram

Opp. Custom House

Nampally

Hyderabad[5]

---

5. He wrote a letter to the Mother from the same address.

25 June 1934

Affectionate Balibehn,

After long I have received your letter. I accept that you have incurred expenditure. I accept too, Manu's rebuke. I am still in Hydrabad. Every four to six days I get high fever. I cannot eat anything. There is no one to give me succour or even to hand me a glass of water. I stretch my limits even in illness and look after myself. I have no money for medicines. If I could pay for a servant I would get one. But even that I do not have. I have no money for either milk or fruits. I feed myself with difficulty, how am I to nurture my addictions? Do forgive me now, but if you wish to save my life, send telegraphically Rs. 50 to the above address. I plead to you to even incur debt for my sake. The address has changed. Write the address in English. My hands tremble. I cannot write any more. I have a strong desire to come that side once I am better. I eat by selling my clothes and belongings. My condition is pitiable.[6]

Regards,
Harilal

We do not know whether Harilal received money from Balibehn after this letter, but he did receive help from some source.

He thought of starting a business in patent drugs but nothing came of it.

Under these circumstances there might have been a change in him, for the better—though short-lived. For a short period Gandhiji and the others were free from anxiety about Harilal.

Harilal went to Rajkot before 19 August 1934. He stayed with Narandas at the Rashtriya Shala. After which he went to Porbandar and lived with his cousin Ishwarlal.[7] From there he wrote a letter to Gandhiji at Wardha. Based on the letter Gandhiji felt that Harilal had changed for the better and was looking for some work. Gandhiji felt overjoyed. He wrote that if there

6. Ref. no. 3.
7. Grandson of Gandhiji's uncle Tulsidas.

was really a change of heart, "I will for my part completely forget your past."[8] Gandhiji wrote to Narandas and suggested that he should visit Porbandar and think about giving Harilal work—either related to khadi or Harijan upliftment. Narandas suggested that a shop selling khadi should be opened for Harilal. Gandhiji felt that before the khadi store was opened Harilal should go around selling khadi in Porbandar as travelling would not be convenient for him.

On 3 October 1934, Gandhiji wrote a letter to Harilal in which he outlined his expectations and also warned him, "It will not hurt me in the least if you do not accept my advice. But it will hurt me very much indeed if you deceive me."[9] He also wrote to Narandas that security would have to be given if Harilal wanted to borrow money to start any work. Gandhiji advised that it was not proper to have Harilal enter into such transactions at that stage. He also said that some arrangements would have to be made for his daily expenses for food, etc., and suggested that Narandas should make these arrangements from his private account if he could spare such money. Gandhiji also wrote that if Narandas was unable to spare such money he should inform him and he would think over the matter.

Narandas informed Gandhiji that his monetary condition did not allow him to spare such money and maintain Harilal on his personal account.

Harilal returned to Rajkot from Porbandar. He was able to make a good impression on Gandhiji. Gandhiji felt that Harilal should stay in Rajkot. He wrote to Narandas about arrangements to be made for Harilal's upkeep. Harilal too started learning more about khadi; he began to learn its science and his daughter Manubehn, who was also in Rajkot, taught him spinning.

Kasturba, Ramdas, Devdas and others had little hope that Harilal would be able to reform himself. But the changes in Harilal gave Gandhiji confidence. Despite that, he warned him in his letter of 11 October 1934,

8. Ref. no. 24 (unpublished). (Translator's note: See also "Letter to Harilal Gandhi, September 19, 1934", *CWMG*, vol. 59, p. 27,

9. Ref. no. 24. (Translator's note: See also "Letter to Harilal Gandhi, October 3, 1934", *CWMG*, vol. 59, p. 112.)

"I would not be pained if you could do nothing, but I would certainly be pained if you were to break your word to me or do anything which might amount to breach of trust with anybody." He further wrote, "I can't stop thinking about you all the times, though. Maybe, father's love doesn't fall away from even a devotee of Mother *Gita*, or perhaps the *Gita* teaches that I should be thus concerned with you."[10]

Gandhiji wrote to Narandas that Harilal should be given a room at the Rashtriya Shala,[11] if it was convenient. He also suggested that Harilal should be given Rs. 50 per month, at the most. Harilal had incurred some fresh debts and Gandhiji was concerned about them. But he suggested that the remedy for those debts could be worked out only after Harilal stabilised some more.

It was suggested that Harilal should stay with Gandhiji at Wardha. Gandhiji did not like this suggestion, as he himself was a guest of Jamnalalji.[12] He thought it proper that Harilal should first begin observance of all the Ashram norms. His shift to Wardha could be thought of only subsequently; till such a time Harilal should stay in Rajkot.

Thus, Harilal had to stay in Rajkot, but he was uneasy there. He expressed his desire to stay with Gandhiji. Gandhiji wrote to Narandas on 7 February 1935 that if Harilal was really willing, he should be sent to Wardha. He might have also felt that if Harilal stayed with him he would be reformed. Harilal reached Wardha before 21 February 1935 and Gandhiji felt that he mixed well with the other inmates there.

Balwant Singh, a constructive worker from Rajasthan was staying with Gandhiji at Maganwadi in Wardha. He and Harilal shared a room. Harilal told Balwant Singh "I have realised my mistake; [from] now on I will stay

---

10. Ibid. (Translator's note: See also "Letter to Harilal Gandhi, October 17, 1934", *CWMG*, vol. 59, p. 187–88. According to both *Gandhiji no Akshardeh*, vol. 59, p. 80–81, and *CWMG,* the letter was written on 17 and not 11 October. Though Gandhiji did write to Harilal on the 11th as well.)
11. This school was opened in its new building by Gandhiji on 15 February 1925. In 1934 Narandas was its administrator.
12. Before Gandhiji moved to the Sewagram Ashram on 30 April 1936, he stayed at Wardha.

with Bapuji."[13] Balwant Singh had been staying in this room before Harilal reached Wardha. Harilal wanted to have the room to himself. The two of them quarrelled and the matter reached Gandhiji. Gandhiji called Balwant Singh and said to him,

> Give the room to him because you can live even under a tree. You are not going to leave me and go away but Harilal has been running away from me. Now there has been a change of heart and he has come to me. I do not want to harass him on small matters. If he stays it would be a big achievement. Ba will be most satisfied. Ba complains that I do not pay enough attention to Harilal. But I can care for him in only my way. For me there is no difference between those who are mine and those who are not. Those who walk on my path are my own. I do not despise those who walk on other paths but I would not help them. I can expect you to make a sacrifice and not Harilal.[14]

Balwant Singh was convinced. He vacated the room and gave it to Harilal.

Perhaps Harilal wanted the room for himself so that he could smoke cigarettes. He was unable to give up smoking, therefore Gandhiji had allowed him to smoke. It was decided that he would get a tin of cigarettes every fifteen days and his son Kantibhai was asked to keep an account of it. Harilal would finish the tin before fifteen days and ask for more from Kantibhai. Kantibhai was a 'sentry' of the Ashram. He would not give Harilal cigarettes before they were due.

So long as Harilal stayed at Wardha, he worked and contributed to the ashram in keeping with his abilities. He was cordial to everyone and mixed well with the other ashramites. It seemed that he had given up drinking alcohol though he continued to smoke.

Once he told Gandhiji that he wanted to stay in a village and serve the people. Gandhiji was very happy. He said, "Then I would prefer to die in your lap."[15]

---

13. Ref. no. 34, p. 55–56.
14. Ibid.
15. Ref. no. 2.

Harilal had been a loving husband. His life was lonely after the death of his wife. Initially he longed for his wife. After her death he wrote a letter to Balibehn, dated 31 December 1918, "Don't you know my feelings for Gulab? Why would I put a blot on those feelings?...But for your solace I give you a promise that before marrying again, if at all I do so, I would certainly inform you...If there was any merit in giving up life I would have certainly given my life after your sister. But suicide is considered a sin. If not by death but by living, I have given this life to her."[16]

He was a caring father. Though his children were in Kasturba's care they had to be sent from one place to another. This unnerved Harilal. He wrote in his letter of 23 December 1922 – Gandhiji was in prison during this period – "It is quite natural for children bereft of a mother to be flung hither and thither. But I am determined not to place them in the hands of a step-mother."[17]

As time passed he grew tired of living a lonely life. In a letter dated 17 April 1933 – Gandhiji was in jail this time as well – he wrote, "I am tired of leading a lonely life. I need a life companion. I am considering marriage—that is, re-marriage."[18]

Thus seventeen years passed after the death of his wife. Harilal was forty-seven years old, and eager to remarry. While he was in Porbandar he wrote to Gandhiji about it. In his response of 19 September 1934, Gandhiji wrote, "If what you want is a companion and that must be a wife, I would not regard it as in the least blameworthy provided you find a suitable widow."[19]

Margarete Spiegel, a German Jew, was one of Gandhiji's associates. Gandhiji had given her the name 'Amala'. We do not know if Harilal and Amala had met each other, or if they did, where the meeting took place.

Amala was with Gandhiji in Poona. She left Poona on 15 May 1933 for Ahmedabad. Kasturba and Harilal reached Poona on 14 May 1933. It is possible that the two might have met for a few hours then.

---

16. Ref. no. 3.
17. Ibid.
18. Ibid.
19. Ref. no. 1. (Translator's note: See also "Letter to Harilal Gandhi, September 19, 1934", *CWMG*, vol. 59, p. 27.)

Harilal was in south Hydrabad on 25 June 1934 and had gone to Rajkot before 19 August 1934. Gandhiji had sent Amala to the Sabarmati Ashram around 5 February 1934.[20] She was in the Ashram till 20 July 1934. It is possible that the two of them came to be acquainted with each other—if Harilal had stayed in the Ashram on his way to Rajkot.

It is possible that – if they had come to know each other – they felt a certain attraction and carried on a correspondence. The letter that Harilal wrote from Porbandar might have been a result of this.

Gandhiji announced on 10 July 1934 that he would fast for seven days from 7 August 1934. At this time he was travelling through north India. Amala was at the Sabarmati Ashram. When she heard of the fast she said that she wanted to serve Gandhiji during his fasts. After ten days of the announcement of the fast, on 20 July 1934, Amala left the Sabarmati Ashram without informing anyone. She had no money, so she started walking. A search took place and she was found at the Nadiad railway station. Harijan Sevak Sangh bought her a ticket for Benaras and she was sent there. Gandhiji was informed of this by telegram. On 22 July 1934 she reached Kanpur and joined Gandhiji.[21] In a letter, Gandhiji wrote, "Amala is extremely frank, but she has no common sense at all. If I sent her to you, she would waste your money. It is better that, so long as I live at one place, I should shoulder her responsibility."[22]

It is difficult to determine the validity of the reason that she had given for leaving the Sabarmati Ashram. It is possible that she might have wanted to talk to Gandhiji about her marriage and therefore rushed towards him. Gandhiji's letter to Narandas, written from Wardha on 8 September 1934, points towards this: "Amala also does some work. But I am really afraid that she will go off her head one day. She is hardly in her senses. She is growing thinner everyday. And now she has become impatient to marry. I observe that

---

20. Ref. no. 15.
21. Ref. no. 1.
22. Ref. no. 23. (Translator's note: See also "Letter to Narandas Gandhi, August 1, 1934", *CWMG*, vol. 58, p. 269.)

she is not free from passion. In consequence of her trying to suppress it, it has become uncontrollable. She hopes to be mother of twelve children. She is 37 at present. Let us see what she does. I don't have the courage now to send her to you or somewhere else."[23]

Amala was looking for a job at that point of time. She received the news before 11 September 1934 that she had been appointed as a French teacher at Shantiniketan. She was happy and cheerful.[24] She stayed at Wardha till the final reply was received from Shantiniketan.

We do not know on which day she left Wardha for Shantiniketan. But she had reached there before 22 December 1934.

Harilal went to Wardha after she left the place, between 7 and 21 February 1935. It is possible that he placed his intention to marry Amala before Gandhiji.

Amala had come to India twice; once towards the end of 1932 and again in 1933. After her first visit to India she wrote many letters to Mahadevbhai, to which he chose not to respond. She had also brought this up with Gandhiji.

A letter from her from Shantiniketan suggests that she was willing to consider Mahadevbhai's opinion and act accordingly. All concerned must have been aware of Mahadevbhai's influence over her. It is possible therefore that Mahadevbhai's opinion was sought on Harilal's proposal and such a possibility was also discussed.

Gandhiji was engrossed with many problems and one more concern was added to the list. He had decided to observe silence for four weeks – from 22 March 1935 to 18 April 1935 – to deal with long pending tasks. During this period Harilal was at Wardha.

During his silence Gandhiji wrote a letter to Harilal on 12 April 1935.

> Mahadev had had a little talk with me. Kishorelal wrote and acquainted me with the matter.

---

23. Ref. no. 15. (Translator's note: See also "Letter to Narandas Gandhi, September 8, 1934", *CMWG,* vol. 58, p. 428.)
24. Ref. no. 15. (Translator's note: See also "Letter to Narandas Gandhi, September 11, 1934", *CMWG,* vol. 58, p. 434.)

> I understand your problem. You don't wish to deceive yourself or me. You still crave for sex pleasure. If so, you must satisfy your craving. You can suppress it only when you feel a strong aversion to worldly pleasures.
>
> My difficulty is this. How can I, who have always advocated renunciation of sex, encourage you to gratify it? How can I help you to do so? I can tolerate your remarrying. But how can you carry on your search for a wife while staying with me? If I invited you to come and stay with me, even though I knew your desire to remarry, I did so not with the intention of helping you to get married but with the hope that your staying with me might help your mind to calm down.
>
> Besides, I also wanted to understand your change of heart. I do wish to help you as much as I can. But wouldn't you on your part that I did so only within my limits? Think over this and write frankly to me now. You may say whatever you wish to.[25]

We do not know what Harilal's response was. But it appears that on the day Gandhiji wrote the letter, Harilal expressed his desire to marry Amala and sought Mahadevbhai's intervention in the matter. Gandhiji wrote his response the very same day.

> I do not want to be an obstacle if Mahadev or anyone else wants to help you. You can write to Amala yourself. If you do, you must reveal to her your previous life. Do not use my name; not even Mahadev's. I would not like if Mahadev were to write. It is not good for you either. Despite this, if Mahadev wants to write because he so desires I will not prevent him. If he asks my advice it will be contrary to what you desire. You should not go from here till I return from Indore.[26] We will think about this after my return.[27]

---

25. Ref. no. 23. (Translator's note: See also "Letter to Harilal Gandhi, April 12, 1935", *CWMG*, vol. 60, p. 410–11.)
26. Gandhiji's silence ended on 19 April. He was in Indore from 20 to 24 April.
27. Ref. no. 1.

It is likely that Harilal wrote to Amala about the possibility of marriage. Meanwhile, Amala wrote to Gandhiji. It is not clear whether the letter dealt with the subject of marriage. In his response of 19 April 1935, Gandhiji wrote, "The qualifications you have described are perfect. The shy manner in which you have announced the giving up of khaddar is characteristic."[28]

Amala's response to Harilal's letter was not to his liking. He either sent this letter to Gandhiji or sent a summary of it to him.

Gandhiji was still in Indore. He wrote to Harilal from Indore on 22 April 1935.

> There is no need at all to be in a hurry to come to a decision about Amala's letter. I think you will have to drop the idea. You should write and tell her plainly that any children that may be born will have to be brought up in a simple manner. And whatever means of livelihood the Lord provides will probably be in Wardha. If you start going to women or drinking, she should be free to leave you immediately. And even this you may write only if you are sure that you wish to marry her. Amala's letter seems a good one to me, but I didn't know her as she reveals herself in it. I am, therefore, of the view that you will not be happy unless she comes to feel strongly that she cannot live without you. It is certainly a good thing that you have not become impatient. Have patience and do only what is proper.[29]

The episode with Amala ended thus. But Harilal was still eager to get married again. Either because of this or for some other reason he left Wardha in the beginning of May 1935 and went to Rajkot. Gandhiji was displeased. He wrote to Narandas, "He definitely intends to marry, provided he finds a suitable wife. I feel that if he marries, it will not be proper for me

---

28. Ref. no. 23. (Translator's note: See also "Letter to Margarete Spiegel, April 19, 1935", *CWMG,* vol. 60, p. 438.)
29. Ref. no. 23. (Translator's note: See also "Letter to Harilal Gandhi, April 22, 1935", *CWMG,* vol. 60, p. 456–57.)

to let him stay with me. I may accept his marriage, but I can't welcome or like it."[30]

He wanted Harilal to be happy, and if marriage were to lead to happiness, Gandhiji did not wish to be an obstacle.

While in Rajkot, Harilal wanted to have the room that he had previously occupied. He also wanted to start some business. He thought of trading in watches. Gandhiji wrote to Narandas that regular monthly expenses need not be paid to Harilal, and that he should give Harilal up to Rs.100 in a lump sum or in instalments as he asked.

Harilal tried to start a business but his efforts did not yield any result. He again turned to adultery. There were some serious allegations about this. He also started drinking alcohol secretly. When Gandhiji came to know of Harilal's ways he wrote, "Even if you die of hunger do not beg, die of thirst but do not drink alcohol, become impotent but do not indulge in adultery."[31]

Harilal had made many counter-allegations but they were unfounded. Gandhiji wrote further, "I wish that you would prefer death but not allow alcohol to enter your body either through the mouth or in any other way...If you are deceiving me you would not remain pure by clinging to falsehood...I understand that you resort to falsehood to cover up your inhuman act."[32]

Gandhiji felt that Harilal could no longer be reformed. He realised that Harilal had not changed his ways at all. The apparent reform was a mere charade. Gandhiji had once written to Narandas, "I will be content even if the treasure I have got back is not lost again, and thank God for His mercy."[33]

---

30. Ref. no. 15. (Translator's note: See also "Letter to Narandas Gandhi", *CMWG,* vol. 61, p. 37.)
31. Ref. no. 1. (Translator's note: Neither the *Gandhiji no Akshardeh* nor the *CWMG* have this letter.)
32. Ibid.
33. Ref. no. 15. (Translator's note: See also "Letter to Narandas Gandhi, May 5, 1935", *CWMG,* vol. 61, p. 37.)

The situation was getting uncomfortable for Harilal. He therefore left Rajkot around 29 June 1935. Gandhiji felt that his fears were coming true. Mahadevbhai was perturbed; he felt that Gandhiji would announce a fast. But Gandhiji did not do so. It was as if he was prepared for such a reversal. Harilal's going away did not come as a shock to him. He described it as a nightmare.

Harilal went to Junagadh from Rajkot. Narandas gave him the money for the journey. Gandhiji disapproved of this and he wrote to Narandas, "What makes you think he wouldn't get liquor in Junagadh? I'm sure he won't behave well in regard to anything."[34]

Gandhiji continued to receive letters from Harilal. But he did not receive any satisfactory news about Harilal from anywhere.

Harilal returned to Rajkot and sought Gandhiji's permission to go to Wardha. He also asked for money for the fare. Gandhiji did not give in this time. He also wrote to Narandas that he should not give money to Harilal.

This experiment too ended.

Meanwhile, Manubehn became engaged to Surendra Mashruwala on 25 October 1935 at Wardha.

---

34. Ref. no. 15. (Translator's note: See also "Letter to Narandas Gandhi, August 9, 1935", *CWMG*, vol. 61, p. 319–20.)

11 Conversions

In 1935 Gandhiji's health suffered. He was ill in January 1936. He travelled from Wardha to Mumbai on 16 January 1936 to have his remaining teeth pulled out. Harilal reached Wardha the very same day and after meeting Gandhiji left Wardha.

Suddenly news arrived that on 2 February Harilal had announced in Nagpur that he was going to convert to Christianity. His reasons for conversion were published in a letter to a local newspaper, *Daily News*.

> When my father has decided to forsake me and excommunicate me completely I have no other option but to erase my relations with him as a son...During the last some years my father wrote to all those who were sympathetic to me and instructed them to not provide asylum or support and thus he tried to render me helpless. Moreover, he has created acrimony between my children and me. He has forced them to live in the Ashram and caused injury to their interests. I have knowledge of my father. On basis of that I believe firmly that by such devious means he wants to subjugate me so that I accept his ideals and principles and join him.[1]

The next day, he said:

> It is public knowledge that I have differed from my father on political, social, and economic matters since last fifteen years. Therefore wherever I go I place my grievances before scores of admirers of Gandhiji and the Congress. But none of them show any empathy for me. Hence, my life has become difficult...If the Hindu community does not desire to excommunicate me I sincerely do not wish to leave the fold of the Hindu community. I have no desire to hurt the sentiments of

1. Ref. no. 9, February 10, 1936.

> the Hindu community and I am in no haste to adopt Christianity. I have made no final decision in regard to conversion. I am carrying on a correspondence with Gandhiji in this respect.[2]

The purport of Harilal's announcement was to declare that he was willing to convert to any other religion if its supporters were willing to give him higher monetary benefits.

It achieved desired results. A Hindu councillor of the Nagpur municipality recommended him for employment in the municipality. Thereafter, Harilal declared, on 27 February 1936 in Nagpur, that he did not believe in religious conversion and that he was not going to adopt Christianity. He made this announcement through the same newspaper.

> My earlier letter was in the form of a respectful public complaint against the situation in which I have been placed; it showed that I have been forcibly excommunicated from the Hindu religion. Therein I had not declared my desire for religious conversion. I am against conversion from one's own religion to another religion. In fact, I urge all those who have converted to other religions to re-enter their original religions. It is my humble belief that each individual has a moral obligation towards the community in which one is born and raised and no individual has a right to forsake it through individual volition.[3]

The person who had secured employment for Harilal wrote a letter to Gandhiji.

In response Gandhiji wrote, "I attach no value to my son's letter of recantation, and if the job he has received is the price for his recantation, it is a premium put upon sin...Nevertheless, if he is faithful in the performance of the job given to him, it is so much to the good. I can only hope that he only

2. Ibid.
3. Ref. no. 9, February 29, 1936.

appreciates the extraordinary kindness that has been shown to him by you and others and that he makes good use of the money he is receiving."[4]

On or around 25 April 1936, Harilal met Gandhiji and Kasturba in Nagpur. He wanted money, but sensing that whatever was given to him would be spent on alcohol, no monetary assistance was provided. Harilal spoke about how preachers of competing religions were eulogising him and how it amused him. Gandhiji came back with the impression that Harilal's greed was still unsatisfied.

Harilal's mind was wavering and had become unstable.

Tabligh – religious conversions – was gathering momentum during that period. Harilal fell prey to it. Due to a sense of failure or to counter hopelessness arising out of failures and to gain monetary benefits, "one of the steps he took was the conversion to Islam."[5] He converted to Islam on 14 May 1936.

According to one reference, the conversion took place in a village – Ponnani – in Kerala; while all other sources say the conversion took place in Nagpur. Nevertheless, he announced his conversion to Islam on Friday, 29 May 1936, at the Jama Masjid in Mumbai. He changed his name to Abdullah. Those present enthusiastically cheered his announcement and there was a near stampede of people wanting to congratulate him. He was surrounded by his admirers.

Gandhiji was at the Nandi Hills and Kantibhai was with him. On hearing the news of his father's conversion, Kantibhai expressed his wish to be with Harilal. Gandhiji gave him permission, but also warned him, "The Muslims surrounding him will not let you stay."[6]

There are references to the role of Janab Zakaria in this conversion episode. On hearing the announcement, Gandhiji instructed Ramdas, who was in Mumbai at that time, to meet his brother Harilal. Accordingly Ramdas

---

4. Ref. no. 24. (Translator's note: See also "Letter to PM Naidu, March 3, 1936", *CWMG,* vol. 62, p. 221.)
5. See Appendix 2.
6. Ref. no. 2.

called upon him around 10 June.[7] Ramdas has recorded the meeting in his reminiscences.

> After 9 p.m. with money sufficient for fare I left for Janab Zakaria's house. I was made to stand in a room of his house for some time. A Muslim servant came and asked me, "Who are you? Who do you want to meet? And for what purpose?"
>
> I introduced myself and told him, "I have come to meet Janab Zakaria. I want also to meet my elder brother Harilal."
>
> He returned after a while and asked me, "Why do you want to meet your brother?"
>
> I replied, "I have come to meet Zakaria Sahib and I also want to meet him."
>
> After some time Zakaria Sahib came out. He asked about the purpose of the visit. Having satisfied himself he said, "Why do you worry? We will do for your brother what all of you have not been able to do." The purport of his saying so was, "He has adopted Islam and we will bring him to the true path. We will give him not only money but we will get him married as well and mould him towards the right path."
>
> I told him, "If your intention is to bring him to the true path, it is very good. If you were to succeed, my parents and all of us would be very pleased."
>
> After this Zakaria Sheth called Harilal and left us alone to talk.
>
> Harilal [had been] given the name 'Abdullah.' He had recently converted to Islam hence, he was not receptive to what I had to say. I bade farewell to him after some time and I wrote

7. Perhaps Bibi Amtussalaam was with him. (Translator's note: Bibi Amtussalaam, Bibiji as she was known, was an ashramite. She was born in an aristocratic family of Patiala. A devout Muslim, she never missed her Ramzan fasts, nor slept without the Holy Koran by her side. She considered Gandhiji her spiritual guide and Gandhiji thought of her as his spiritual daughter. She went through a fiery ordeal in Naokhali, where she undertook a 25-day fast from 26 December 1946 to 20 January 1947 in Sirandi village against the local Muslims.)

> to Bapu in detail about our conversation and the state in which I found him.[8]

During this period, Kantibhai and his future wife Saraswatibehn met Harilal in Mumbai.[9]

Gandhiji issued a statement to the press, which was published as "To My Numerous Muslim Friends".

> If his acceptance was from the heart and free from any worldly considerations, I should have no quarrel. For I believe Islam to be as true a religion as my own...God can work wonders. He has been known to have changed the stoniest hearts and turned sinners into saints, as it were, in a moment. Nothing will please me better than to find that during the Nagpur meeting and the Friday announcement he had repented of the past and had suddenly become a changed man having shed the drink habit and sexual lust...My views on Islam are well known to the Mussalmans who are reported to have enthused over my son's profession. A brotherhood of Islam has telegraphed to me thus: EXPECT LIKE YOUR SON YOU TRUTH-SEEKER TO EMBRACE ISLAM TRUEST RELIGION OF WORLD.
>
> I must confess that all this has hurt me. I sense no religious spirit behind this demonstration. I feel that those who are responsible for Harilal's acceptance of Islam did not take the most ordinary precautions they ought to have in a case of this kind.
>
> Harilal's apostasy is no loss to Hinduism and his admission to Islam is a source of weakness to it if, as I apprehend, he remains the same wreck that he was before.
>
> Surely conversion is a matter between man and his Maker who alone knows His creatures' hearts. And conversion without a clean heart is, in my opinion, a denial of God and religion.

---

8. Ref. no. 26, p. 188–89.
9. This meeting is discussed later.

> Conversion without cleanness of heart can only be a matter for sorrow, not joy, to a godly person.
>
> My object in addressing these lines to my numerous Muslim friends is to ask them to examine Harilal in the light of his immediate past and, if they find that his conversion is a soulless matter, to tell him so plainly and disown him and if they discover sincerity in him to see that he is protected against temptations so that his sincerity results in his becoming a godfearing member of society. Let them know that excessive indulgence has softened his brain and undermined his sense of right and wrong, truth and falsehood. I do not mind whether he is known as Abdulla or Harilal if, by adopting one name for the other, he becomes a true devotee of God which both the names mean.[10]

Harilal went first to Rander and then to Ernakulam, to spread the message of Islam, where in his speech he said, "I am no longer a Bania."[11] From there he went to Calicut and afterwards to Madras. There he was arrested in an intoxicated state and he was fined on 17 September 1936.

Kasturba was deeply troubled by Harilal's actions and this last incident distressed her greatly.

Devdas wrote about the conversion in his reminiscences of Harilal.

> After he adopted Islamic faith many unworthy facts of his life as a Muslim came to be public. The pain and suffering of this pathetic life were unbearable for Ba. One morning in Delhi Ba poured out her feelings in my presence. Ba's utterances were heart wrenching and filled with compassion. A little later, on the same day, I put her words into writing. This written text was published in almost all dailies and weeklies of the country with the title, "An Open Letter from a Mother to her Son."[12]

This letter was published around 27 September 1936.

---

10. Ref. no. 7, June 7, 1936. (Translator's note: See also "Statement to the Press, June 2, 1936", *CWMG*, vol. 63, p. 5–7.)
11. Ref. no. 9, September 3, 1936.
12. Appendix 2.

My dear son Harilal,

I have read that recently in Madras policemen found you misbehaving in a state of drunkenness at midnight in an open street and took you in custody. Next day you were produced before a bench of Magistrates and they fined you Rs. 1. They must have been very good people to treat you so leniently.

Even the Magistrates showed regard for your father in thus giving you only nominal punishment. But I have been feeling very miserable ever since I heard about this incident. I do not know whether you were alone that night or were accompanied by some of your friends, but in any case you acted very improperly.

I do not know what to say to you. I have been pleading with you all these long years to hold yourself in check. But you have been going from bad to worse. Now you are making my very existence impossible. Think of the misery you are causing to your aged parents in the evening of their lives.

Your father says nothing to anyone but I know how the shocks you are giving him are breaking his heart. You are committing a great sin in thus repeatedly hurting our feelings. Though born as our son you are indeed behaving like an enemy.

I am told that in your recent wanderings you have been criticising and ridiculing your great father. This does not behove such an intelligent boy as you. You little realise that you only disgrace yourself by speaking evil of your father. He has nothing but love in his heart for you. You know that he attaches the greatest importance to purity of conduct. But you have never paid any heed to his advice. Yet he has offered to keep you with him, to feed and clothe you and even to nurse you.

He has so many other responsibilities in this world. He cannot do more for you. He can only lament his fate. God has given him great willpower and may God grant him as long a life as he may require for fulfilling his mission on this earth. But I am a frail old woman unable to stand the mental anguish you are causing.

Your father daily gets letters from people complaining about your conduct. He has to suffer all this disgrace. But you have left no place for me anywhere. For sheer shame, I am unable to move among friends or strangers. Your father always pardons you, but God will not tolerate your conduct.

At Madras you were the guest of some prominent and respectable person. But you abused his hospitality by leaving his roof and misconducting yourself in the manner reported. It cannot but have embarrassed your host.

Every morning I rise with a shudder to think what fresh news of disgrace the newspapers will bring. I sometimes wonder where you are, where you sleep, what you eat. Perhaps you take forbidden food. That and similar other thoughts give me sleepless nights. I often feel like meeting you. But I do not know where to find you. You are my eldest son and nearly 50 years old. I am even afraid of approaching you, lest you humiliate me.

I do not know why you changed your ancestral religion; that is your affair. But I hear that you go about asking innocent and ignorant people to follow your example. Why will you not realise your limitations? What judgement can you exercise in your mental condition? People are liable to be led away by the fact that you are your father's son. You are not fit to preach religion. In time to come if you will go on like this you will be shunned by all alike. I beseech you therefore to pause and consider and turn back from your folly.

I did not like your conversion, but when I saw your statement that you had decided to improve yourself I felt secretly glad even about your conversion hoping that you would now start leading a sober life. But that hope too you dashed to pieces. In Bombay recently some of your friends and well-wishers found you in a condition much worse than before. You know how unhappy your father is on account of your behaviour.

Your daughters and son-in-law also bear with increasing difficulty the burden of sorrow your conduct has imposed upon them.[13]

---

13. Ref. no. 30, p. 80–82. (Translator's note: See also Kasturba Gandhi Memorial Number, *Indian Opinion*, March 22, 1944, for the English text that is reproduced here. Courtesy, Archives of the National Gandhi Museum, Delhi.)

She also addressed an appeal to those Muslims who were interested in Harilal's act of conversion.

> I have not been able to understand your action. I am referring to those of you who are taking an active part in my son's present activities. I know and I am glad to think that a large number of thinking Mussalmans and all our life-long Muslim friends condemn the whole of this episode.
>
> Today I very much miss the presence of that great soul Dr. Ansari who would have given sound advice both to my son and yourselves. But there are others equally noble and influential but not so well-known to me, and I hope that they will advice you properly.
>
> Instead of redeeming my son I find that this so-called change of faith has actually made matters worse in the matter of his habits. You ought to reprimand him for this and try to wean him from his ways. Some people have even gone to the length of supplying the title of "Maulvi" to my boy. Is this fair? Does your religion permit such persons as my son being called Maulvis?
>
> I do not understand what pleasure you find in lionising him like this. If you truly consider him a brother you will not do as you are doing. For what you are doing is not at all in his interest. But if your desire is merely to hold us up to ridicule I have nothing to say to you. You may do your worst.
>
> But the feeble voice of a wounded mother will perhaps quicken the conscience of those who may be in a position to influence you. But I feel it my duty to repeat to you what I am telling my son, namely that you are not doing the right thing in the eyes of God.

This letter was published in newspapers all over the country. Harilal chose to respond to Kasturba's letters indirectly. His response came in the form of a speech that he gave in a public meeting at Kanpur on 1 October 1936.

> I am Abdullah, not Harilal. I therefore refuse to acknowledge that letter. My mother is illiterate. I refuse to believe that she is capable of writing such a letter. I feel that it has been written

> by someone else...Before I converted I was under the influence of wrong friends. (They used to organise many duplicitous programmes.) I participated in such activities because I had received such education. I need not learn any more. I have only one wish and that is to die as a worker of Islam.[14]

In another meeting held at Kanpur he said, "My father could not reform me in the last twenty years. How will his followers reform me in four months? My mother Kasturbai has written a letter to me. She has urged me to give up drinking alcohol. I will give up alcohol, but when? When both my father and she accept Islam. That is my response."[15]

According to Devdas, Harilal's embracing of Islam was "a mere charade".[16] It is possible that he was enticed into conversion either with promises of money or marriage.

The Arya Samaj began attempts to bring Harilal back into the Hindu religion. Harilal might also have been repentant. Around 8 November 1936, there was talk of him re-entering the Hindu religion. Kasturba was in Mumbai at this time. She was in Mumbai on the 8th, and on the 11th she had reached Wardha. It is possible that while in Mumbai she might have met Harilal – probably she was in Mumbai to meet Harilal – and tried to persuade him. Harilal's decision might have been influenced by his affection for Kasturba.

On 10 November 1936, Harilal announced that he was seriously reconsidering his conversion to Islam. After two days he ritually and ceremonially re-entered the Hindu fold. Devdas wrote, "The handful of Muslims who were taking advantage of this incident were shown their guilt and folly by this letter. It also showed them that their actions were bringing disrepute to their own religion." He further wrote, "Those persons who assisted and abated this act, gave it wide publicity and sought to fulfil selfish ends, were finally disgraced."[17]

---

14. Ref. no. 9, October 4, 1936.
15. Ibid.
16. Appendix 2.
17. Ibid.

Thereafter on 14 November Harilal released the following statement in Mumbai explaining his recent step.

> Revered Gentlemen, Sisters and Brothers, Namaste.
>
> It will be a wonder to some men to know why I reconverted myself to Hinduism. Many Musalmans and Hindoos might be thinking in many ways but I cannot help myself opening my heart. At present what goes under the name of religion does not only consist of its Principles but it includes the principles its culture and moral and social life of those who follow that religion. I embraced Islam to experience all these. From what I saw and experienced I can say that, religious principles of ancient Vedic Religion, its culture, language, its literature and social and moral life of its followers are in no way inferior to those of Islam and other prevalent faiths and religions of our country, not only that but they are superior.
>
> If we realise and appreciate the true form of Vedic Religion as shown by Maharishi Dayanand Saraswati we can emphatically say that whatever true and Universal principles are found in Islam and other religions have all come from Vedic Religion, therefore looking Philosophically there is nothing like conversion than search after truth.
>
> As some Universal truth mixed with other sectarian principles have deformed other faiths in the same way I can say that from my associations with some Muslims of India that they have remained very far from the *firmans* of and religious principles of Mahomed Saheb.
>
> As far as I know Hazarat Khalifa Umar never ordered the destructions of religious places and institutions of the other religionists, which is burning problems of our country at present.
>
> Looking to all these circumstances and facts I have come to this conclusion that I cannot serve Islam anymore in any way.
>
> Just as a fallen man reaches his original place by ascending, similarly I am also trying to reach and realise the true principals of Vedic Religion, as shown by Maharishi Dayanand

Saraswati. These principals are true genuine original, universal and useful for whole Humanity without restrictions of country, caste or community as the rays of the Sun are. These principals have been propounded without any fear or favour by Swami Dayanand Saraswati in his well known books, *Satyarth Prakash, Rigveda adi Bhashya Bhumika* and others. I thus come to the feet of my Father Religion and Mother culture by the grace of the teachings of Swami Dayanand Saraswati and efforts of Arya Samaj. If my parents, relatives and friends have become glad by hearing this news I crave their blessings.

In the end I say that protect me, have mercy on me and forgive me. I thank heartily the workers of Bombay Arya Samaj and all those who are present here.

With Namaste to all I pray [to] God:

"Lead Kindly me to light." "Aum Shanti."[18]

On 20 November he read a similar statement in English at the Arya Samaj hall in Mumbai. In conclusion he said, "My heartfelt gratitude to the workers of the Mumbai Arya Samaj and all those who are present here today."[19]

For some time Harilal stayed in Mumbai. Kantilal and Surendra Mashruwala met him here.

Thereafter he became a Vedic missionary of the Bharatiya Shraddhanand Shuddhi Sabha of Delhi. It appears that during this phase he changed his name from Harilal Gandhi, according to the tradition of north India, to Hiralal Gandhi.

Though he returned to the Hindu fold his mind was not at ease and his heartburn still remained. While he was in Mumbai he had received a letter from Gandhiji. Harilal was in Delhi on 6 February 1937 and he sent a reply to Gandhiji on the 7th.

---

18. Ref. no. 1. (Translator's note: The text of the statement is as in the original issued by Harilal Gandhi. Courtesy, Archives of the Sabarmati Ashram Preservation and Memorial Trust, SN. 23672.)
19. Ref. no. 1.

In the service of Pujya Pitashri,

I received your letter in Mumbai. You seem to have adopted one way of writing and responding to me. I do not think that this mode is at all beneficial. But if that's what pleases you, what more do I have to say?

I have read that in olden times, at times of war while breaking the spiked gates of a fort a camel was usually placed between the spikes and the elephants trying to break the gates. The camel usually lost its life but the elephants remained unharmed from the spikes. Similarly I see Ba being used as a shield. Devdas [used] that form [in] the appeal from Ba. I see a similar method in your letter.

The question is, who is causing pain to Ba? All of you or me? Ba will see a picture as it is painted before her. I do not intend to say that Ba is incapable of comprehension. But my opinion and experience is that she has not been allowed to retain independence even as a mother. Therefore I have not written even a single letter to her in recent past. She can write only if she is allowed to write. Therefore she has not written to me either. Even then I am writing to her now.

From the letterhead you would realise that I am at present in Delhi. I came yesterday morning. I have informed Devdas about my being in Delhi, let us see if he meets me.

Write to me if any decision about Manu's marriage has been made. Surendra told me in Mumbai that both he and Manu are ready for it.

Please give the accompanying letter to Ba.

Your Obedient Son Harilal's Dandvat.[20]

He wrote to Kasturba:

In the service of Pujya Matushri,

I am writing to you after a long time. But why have you not written? When you published a public appeal in Devdas'

---

20. Ibid.

newspaper[21] on his asking, if you had true feelings for me you ought to have written a letter to me. You did not write and hence I did not write either. I had given a public response to your public appeal. Did anyone read that out to you? Since when have you started writing to newspapers that you showed this sudden fit of passion? I know your feelings. In Africa we lived with Khans. Who was there but for Muslims? I adopted a name, what was my fault in becoming a Muslim? But still, you would be happy now.

At present I am in Delhi. I came yesterday. For sometime I will tour these areas. I have informed Devdas; but he is a big man, he will meet if he pleases.

How is Manu? When are you getting her married? Kanti met me in Mumbai.

Please write of other news.

Read my letter to Bapu.

Your Obedient Son Harilal's Dandvat.[22]

Gandhiji was in Delhi between 15 and 22 March 1937. Harilal had met him during this period.

Harilal was anxious about Manubehn's marriage, as he had been about Ramibehn's marriage earlier. A suitable groom had not yet been found for her. He wrote to Balibehn on 17 April 1933 proposing the name of a man who was married to a woman who suffered from tuberculosis. He believed that "even the Shastras permit divorce from a consumptive woman".[23] He gave the name and the address of this man but he was sceptical about Manubehn agreeing to the proposal.

This suggestion did not go much further.

Manubehn then became engaged to Surendra Mashruwala and her marriage was fixed. Initially the plan was to hold her marriage at Seagon but it

21. *The Hindustan Times.*
22. Ref. no. 1.
23. Ref. no. 3.

was later fixed at Hubli.[24] The marriage took place on 18 April 1937. Harilal was unable to attend but he sent his good wishes through a letter that he wrote to Balibehn. Kantibhai was present at the marriage, though he reached there just as the Kanyadaan ritual was about to take place.

---

24. A village in Belgaon district; the congress of the Gandhi Sewa Sangh was held here at that time.

12 Later Years and Death

Like they did with Harilal's other children, Gandhiji and Kasturba also looked after Kantibhai. Amtussalaam had great affection for Kantibhai, who used to call her 'Amma'. As in case of Harilal, Gandhiji arranged for Kantibhai's education as well. Kantibhai did not like the education he received. So in 1936 he decided to appear for the matriculation examination, and therefore joined the Vakil High School of Mumbai.[1]

Gandhiji had not forgotten the acrimony that had marred his relations with Harilal as a result of their divergent views on education. He was conscious that the same should not be repeated with Harilal's son. Though he did not like Kantibhai joining the school in Mumbai he did not oppose it either.

Kantibhai met his father in Mumbai. As we have discussed earlier, when Harilal converted to Islam Kantibhai had expressed his desire to meet his father. Gandhiji was open to his wish but had also warned him that the Muslims around Harilal would not allow Kantibhai to stay for too long. Kantibhai had bowed to Gandhiji's injunctions and had not gone to meet his father.

When they met in Mumbai again, Saraswatibehn, who was soon to be married to Kantibhai, was also present. According to Saraswatibehn's reminiscenes they met in the Topiwala Building at the house of Kishorlal Mashruwala's relatives. Harilal had worn a cream jacket, coat and trousers, and had sported a red tasselled Muslim cap on his head. Possibly this meeting was arranged so that Harilal could see his future daughter-in-law. Saraswatibehn was pained because Harilal did not speak to her at all. But she recollects that he spoke to Kantibhai with much affection.[2]

---

1. The 'H.M Pupils' Own School' of Khar in Mumbai was then called 'Pupils' Own School'. A Parsi couple, the Vakils, managed it. Kantibhai might have joined this school.
2. For Saraswatibehn's reminiscences see Appendix 4.

Praising Kantibhai's decision to study independently of Gandhiji, Harilal wrote, "Bhai[3] is happy that you have taken the courageous decision to acquire education at the right time. At last you paid heed to Bhai's advice and found it to be correct."[4]

After passing his matriculation examination Kantibhai went to Mysore for further education. Harilal did not like his decision:

> Mumbai is much better compared to Mysore. You would gain more knowledge and experience in Mumbai. Your Gujarati-Kathiawadi samskar would get refined in a college, but not by staying with either the Gujaratis or the Mysorians. The only good thing about Mysore is its music. For that aren't there Maharashtrians in Mumbai? You must think over this. Moreover, everyone will meet you in Mumbai. Who will come to Mysore? But if you insist on going to Mysore I would not press otherwise. Bapu had no interest in College education. He cannot guide you in this.[5]

It appears that Harilal's economic hardships continued. He asked for money from his acquaintances. Gandhiji wrote to one of those who had given him money, "You should not have helped Harilal. He has lost all sense of shame. He begs for help from everybody, and spends the money on drink. His habit of begging could perhaps be pardoned if he used the help well."[6]

Kantibhai and Saraswatibehn were married on 26 May 1939 in Rajkot at Balibehn's house. Harilal was not present. Kasturba attended the wedding. Gandhiji was in Rajkot that day but did not remain present for the ceremony. After the wedding the newly married couple went to him and sought his blessings.

On 10 February 1940 a son was born to the couple. Kantibhai's brother Shanti had died young; so their son was named Shanti in memory of the departed brother. Gandhiji sent his blessings.

---

3. The children addressed Harilal as Bhai.
4. Ref. no. 3.
5. Ibid.
6. Ref. no. 23. (Translator's note: See also "Letter to Kishansingh Chawda, May 20, 1939", *CWMG*, vol. 69, p. 286.)

We have little information about Harilal with regard to a certain period of time. We know that he stayed at the Khadi Pratisthan in Sodpur to recuperate. During his stay there he sustained some injuries after a fall. Once he was better he wrote the following letter to Kasturba on 1 November 1940, the New Year's Day.

> In the service of Pujya Matushri,
> After long I have received your letter. I too have remembered the New Year after a long time. I have been disabled a little. What can I pray for on this New Year's Day? I pray that Ba and Bapu be with us at least for another ten years. Therein lies my self-interest. Kindly do not be anxious on my count. I do not have many desires left in me anymore. Convey my Dandvat pranam to Bapu.
>
> My health is improving. My life is contained in Satishbabu,[7] Ma and the Khadi Pratisthan. But I am not yet ready to stay with him forever.
>
> I don't know Kanti and Rami's whereabouts. Where could I have written?
>
> I will continue to write to you. I will wait for either your response or a receipt of my letter.
>
> What are Nirmala[8] and Bhabhaji[9] doing? Remembering all the dear ones.
>
> Your Obedient son Harilal's Dandvat.[10]

Gandhiji sent this letter to Kantibhai. Harilal stayed at Sodpur for sometime and then left the place. Satishbabu gave him some money. When Gandhiji came to know this he wrote to Satishbabu on 23 December 1940, "Why did you give money to Harilal and how much did you give? It has done him no good. It was all spent on drinks."[11]

---

7. Satishchandra Dasgupta, the main worker at the Sodpur Khadi Pratisthan.
8. Ramdas's wife.
9. Ramdas and Nirmala's son, Kahandas or Kanu's pet name.
10. Ref. no. 2.
11. Ref. no. 23. (Translator's note: See also "Letter to Satish Chandra Das Gupta, December 23, 1940", *CWMG*, vol. 73, p. 252.)

Kasturba was in Delhi at Devdas's house between 22 March and 23 May 1941 for piles treatment. Harilal went there before 5 May 1941 and spent some days with her.

During 'Quit India' Movement Gandhiji and Kasturba were imprisoned at the Agakhan Palace Prison at Yeravda. Kasturba experienced heart pain on 17 March 1943. After she recovered a little she wrote to Kunvarjibhai on 9 August 1943, "If you have any news of Harilal do let me know. Also tell him to write to me."[12] Harilal's whereabouts were not known.

After some time contact was established with Harilal. He wrote a letter to Kasturba. She dictated a response to him on 7 February 1944, "My health is what it was. Do not worry for me."[13] But her health worsened day by day.

On 17 February, some days before her death, Harilal finally reached the prison. "Kasturba was very happy to see him. Later she came to know that he had permission to meet her only once. Ba was displeased at this. She said, 'What is this? Devdas is allowed to come everyday and Harilal can come only once? If Bhandari[14] were to come face to face with me I would tell him, why do you discriminate among brothers? Just because he is deprived and meek, can't he meet his mother?'"[15]

Harilal did not come the next day but he arrived the following day.

> Ba everyday asked after Harilalbhai. Everyone else was also looking for him, but he could not be traced. Swami Anand[16] searched him out on the 20th. Harilalbhai told the superintendent on the phone that, "I was to come but I fell asleep in the afternoon and hence could not." Everyone understood what he meant by falling asleep. Ba was angry. Bapuji talked to her and calmed her anger. Harilal came on the afternoon of the 21st. Looking at his condition Ba beat her head in agony. Harilal was removed from her presence.[17]

---

12. Ref. no. 2.
13. Ref. no. 3.
14. The chief of prisons of the Bombay Province.
15. Ref. no. 30, p. 190.
16. An associate and follower of Gandhiji.
17. Ref. no. 30, p. 193.

Kasturba died on 22 February. Harilal was present at this time.[18] He was present when Kasturba was cremated. On the 24th the three brothers – Harilal, Ramdas and Devdas (Manilal was not in India) – had a meal with Gandhiji. Gandhiji had a conversation with Harilal. Harilal left after that. We have no information as to where he went.

Kantibhai looked for opportunities to care for his father and compared to his siblings he also succeeded in doing so more often. He and his wife desired that Harilal should stay with them in Mysore. It appears that Harilal went to their Mysore house in March 1945. Both requested him to stay with them and also wrote to Gandhiji about their wish. Gandhiji wrote in response on 19 April 1945, "God will grant you success. The victory over Harilal, which was denied me, has come to you two. You are correct in saying that if he can get rid of the two vices he can be the best of all brothers. Let us see what you people can do."[19]

He wrote again on 3 May 1945, "I would consider it a great triumph if you can win over Harilal. Do not leave him...He is so stubborn by nature that he relapses into his old ways again and again. Maybe, the love of you two or, you may say, the innocent love of the kid Shanti will hold him. I shall be happy."[20] He continued to write to them; on 30 May 1945 he wrote, "If you two can reform Harilal, I shall feel that you have accomplished a great

---

18. According to Ramdas Gandhi, (Ref. no. 30, p. 189–90),

    Shri Jugalkishorji made a plan and accordingly the organisers of the Arya Samaj centres all over the country were instructed that wherever they met Harilal they must try and reform him and ascertain whether he faced economic or any other hardships and inform Jugalkishorji immediately. Necessary help should be provided to him.

    As a result when Ba died in the Agakhan Palace Harilal was present and later when Bapu died in Delhi Harilal reached there after the cremation was over.

19. Ref. no. 1. (Translator's note: See also "Letter to Saraswati Gandhi, April 19, 1945", *CWMG*, vol. 79, p. 399.)
20. Ref. no. 1. (Translator's note: See also "Letter to Saraswati Gandhi, May 3, 1945", *CWMG*, vol. 80, p. 61.)

thing."[21] Once again he wrote to them on 18 June 1945, "Both of you have served Harilal well. I do hope that he will stay on there."[22]

Saraswatibehn's reminiscences, which were written for this book, can be found in Appendix 4. This text is full of memories of the time that Harilal spent at their house. She has described the condition in which Harilal arrived at their house and how he stayed with them, interacted with others, and the joys they shared during these three to four months. She has also described the changes that took place in Harilal. After some time he went back to his old ways and started drinking again. She has narrated in this moving account how they suffered and how Harilal, despite his remorse, found himself incapable of giving up alcohol.

Harilal was restless; he left their house after three or four months. We do not know where he went.

On 27 February 1946 he was in Bangalore and wrote the following letter to Sri Aurobindo.[23]

> 27 February '46
> Banglore
> Revered Shrijut Arbindo Ghose,
> About a fortnight back I addressed a letter to Mother. I expected an acknowledgement at least, for I know how she took care of me by sending Mr. Purani to my hotel. I was in Pondicherry when my father Gandhiji had visited Pondicherry in about 1935. Kashibhai Patel's daughters were then there. Is Mother there or not is what I am worried about. Would you permit us—Mr. Nanjappa, his wife and myself to go there, stay in the Ashram for a few days to begin with. If we have this permission, we will state our desires further.

---

21. Ref. no. 1. (Translator's note: See also "Letter to Saraswati Gandhi, May 30, 1945", *CWMG*, vol. 80, p. 216.)
22. Ref. no. 1. (Translator's note: See also "Letter to Saraswati Gandhi, June 18, 1945", *CWMG*, vol. 80, p. 347–48.)
23. Translator's note: The original letter is reproduced here. Courtesy, Archives and Research Library, Sri Aurobindo Ashram, Pondicherry.

With all reverence to yourself
I remain ever in spirit at your feet
Harilal M Gandhi

Harilal M Gandhi
c/o Sri. A. Nanjappa
417 Middle School Rd.
Visveswarpuram
Banglore City

After this we know that Gandhiji wrote to him from Noakhali on 22 January 1947 and advised him to reform himself.

Gandhiji was murdered on 30 January 1948 in Delhi. At that time Manilal was in South Africa; Ramdas was in Nagpur, but reached Delhi by a special flight; and Devdas was in Delhi. Thus Ramdas and Devdas were present during the funeral procession and Ramdas lit the funeral pyre.

Gandhiji's grandson Kantilal was in Mysore with his family. He could not go to Delhi because of his examinations, while Saraswatibehn and their son Shanti reached Delhi the next day. They could not participate in the funeral procession. But they participated in other rituals, including the immersion of Gandhiji's ashes. Ramdas and Devdas were also present. All the rituals were performed by Ramdas.

When a father is murdered, all his sons might not be present at that place and at that precise moment. Ramdas was in India; Devdas was in Delhi, but he was not with Gandhiji at the moment he was shot dead. Therefore, it is quite understandable that Harilal was not with Gandhiji at the time of his death.

There are conflicting reports about his absence.

According to Robert Payne, after the cremation on 31 January 1948, some people visited the site of cremation. Harilal was among those who went there; and he was supposed to have spent the night at Devdas Gandhi's house.[24]

According to Ramdas, Harilal reached Delhi after the cremation.[25]

---

24. Ref. no. 38, p. 599.
25. Ref. no. 26, p. 190.

Saraswatibehn recalls that she was surprised to see Harilal entering Devdas's house with a small roll of bedding in his arms.[26]

This shows that Harilal was unable to participate either in the funeral procession or in the cremation.

Devdas Gandhi has written, "I saw him last when suddenly, from who knows where, he came to our house in Delhi four days after the assassination of Bapu to share in our grief."[27]

Did Harilal go there on his own? Did someone search him out? We have no information regarding this. It is true that he rarely stayed at one place. But looking at the correspondence we realise that his family was kept informed of his whereabouts.

He had reached Delhi when Rasikbhai was ill. He was contacted at the time of Kasturba's illness and death. At that time India was under foreign rule. Gandhiji and Kasturba were in the prison. Even then it was possible to locate him and reach him there in time. India had become independent, no one was in jail, but still he could not be located immediately after Gandhiji's assassination. He was untraceable for four days after a murder that was broadcast all over the country through radio and newspaper. How very unfortunate!

Devdas has written that Harilal's intention was to not become an obstacle in a ritual in which the entire population of Delhi was participating. What does not wanting to become an obstacle really mean? It is true that Harilal had harboured resentment against his father; but was he so stonehearted that he would nurture his resentment even after his father's assassination?

No. In fact, in a letter to Kasturba written on 1 November 1941, he had expressed his wish that his parents would live for another ten years at least. Would a son who was capable of such a wish refuse to participate in the cremation of his father?

Devdas says that Harilal came to his home trying to hide his remorse. Does a repentant person harbour resentment? And even if he experienced

26. Appendix 4.
27. Appendix 2.

resentment, was it so overpowering that even if he had been contacted and brought to Delhi or if he had been able to come on his own, it would not have allowed him to perform his duties as the first-born son? And would the resentment have made him so bereft of emotion that he would have declined to participate in his father's last rites?

Or was it that he had become stonehearted and hence the second son had to perform the rituals?

Devdas has said, "he had come to bless us". Where is the scope for blessing in rage? Devdas further wrote, "He was ill and in need of careful nursing." Was it his ill health that kept him away from the rituals? According to Devdas, "He left, once he was slightly better." Do we infer from this that he did not stay even for the immersion of the ashes and set himself aside from all the rituals?

Devdas recollects their final meeting: "As he sat in his Mumbai-bound train, he said, with never before seen fatigue, 'My fate is to keep wandering.'"[28]

Saraswatibehn also recollects her last glimpses of Harilal. "My heart was filled with pain and shame watching my father-in-law leave the house. Before going he told me, 'Beta I am going.'"[29]

We do not know as to where he stayed in Mumbai or what he did.

On Friday, 18 June 1948, he died in Shivari Hospital, Mumbai.[30] Both his daughters – Ramibehn and Manubehn – and Manubehn's husband Surendra Mashruwala were with him.

---

28. Ibid.
29. Appendix 4.
30. a. Ref. no. 26 p. 190, states that he died in 1949 at the Harkisandas Hospital of Mumbai. Both the place and the year are incorrect.
    b. Gandhiji too was assassinated on a Friday.

Appendices

compiled
by
Chandulal Bhagubhai Dalal

Appendix 1 Harilal's Semi-public Letter

In the service of Pujya Pitaji,

A worm enters the body of a wasp and flies away having assumed the form of the wasp.[1] I believe something similar happened to me. I have received much from you. I have learnt much, I was formed by you and my character emerged unblemished. The only difference is that I lacked the patience and endurance of a worm and ran away even before I could become a wasp.

I separated from you with your consent. In so doing I followed the dictates of my conscience. This too I learnt from you.

It is usually not possible to distinguish the Phoenix Institution from you and hence I left that too. We spoke much. You said much; you also did all that you could. I also said all that was possible for me to say. It was destined that we be separated.

When I experienced the desire to write to you at length, the following thoughts came to my mind. "Your life has been a public one. Even your personal life is no secret. All are naturally curious to know more about your life. Many would have asked you questions about the sudden change in me. I have been unable to say all that I wished to say to you." For such reasons I considered it proper to write a public letter to you.

The thoughts expressed in this letter are my own. Our differences are not of recent origin. We have had differences for the past ten years. They stem from one subject. You are convinced that you have given me and my brothers necessary education. You are convinced that you could not have given us a

---

1. The worm fears the wasp so much that it is unable to ever forget the wasp and in the end becomes like a wasp. (Translator's note: The word for worm in the original is *kita* and for wasp *brahamara,* this refers to what is known as the *kita–brahamara nyaya.)*

better education than what you did give us. In other words, you have given us necessary and sufficient attention. I believe that with your preoccupations and engagements you have unintentionally paid us no attention at all. It affected me and that is what I shall describe in this letter. I believe that due to your overwhelming desire to provide us education and care, you have experienced the illusion of having done so.

For ten years now I have been crying and pleading with you. But, for the wasp, the worm is insignificant. That is, you have never considered my sentiments. I believe that you have always used us as weapons. 'Us' in this context means me and my brothers—Manilal, Ramdas and Devdas. I believe that to a lesser or a greater degree your conduct towards us brothers has been similar. You have dealt with us just as a ringmaster in a circus treats animals in his charge. The ringmaster may believe that he is ridding the animals of their beastly character because he has the welfare of animals in his heart.

If you have no knowledge of our sentiments, then there is no possibility of you paying any heed to what we have to say to you. You have oppressed us in a civilised way. You have never encouraged us in any way. The environment around you has became such that even a person who differs from you innocently and conscientiously is as good as dead. You have spoken to us not in love but always with anger. Whenever we tried to put across our views on any subject to you and engaged in a debate with you, with your permission, you have lost your temper quickly and told us, "You are stupid, you are in a fallen state, you lack comprehension. You think that you have attained the zenith of knowledge. You argue against me in everything. You will not know what is good. Such is your samskar." By saying such things you have shown your disdain and oppressed us. Thus oppressed I have remained melancholic, anxious and, as a result, sick. You have instilled fear in us, of you, even while we are walking, ambling, eating or drinking, sleeping or sitting, reading or writing, and working. Your heart is like vajra. Your love...[2] I have never seen; so what can I say about it?

2. As in the original.

Under such circumstances what can people expect from your sons? Naturally they are disappointed. As you yourself said, after his first meeting with us, Poet Shri Rabindranath Tagore used the term 'ignoramus' to describe us. You also said that later he changed his opinion. It must be said, despite all the reverence I have for him, that he was being kind and generous. I remember one of the Phoenix inmates reporting that even Professor Gokhale had told you that our affection for you arose from fear. It is not as if I am drawing your attention to this for the first time. I have been pointing this out for years.

Whenever someone asks you about our education you reply that we study what our samskar allows us to. Forgive me Pitaji, but it is not only our samskar which is to be blamed for the state of our education.

As your political life became full of hardships you have changed your ideas, and along with that you have also twisted our lives. I believe without any hesitation that our lives hitherto have been irregular and uncertain. You went from here to South Africa, came back, went again and came back once more. What we learnt here we forgot there. We learnt one thing for six months, something else for another six months and a third thing for another six months. Naturally, nothing came of it. We might be foolish; but allow me to add that you have kept us foolish. You have never considered our rights.

Here, I am reminded of the story of a father and his four sons. The father felt that he should initiate the sons in some profession. He called each one and gave them the necessary encouragement. Each one was shown a path that suited his capabilities. What the father identified as the right path for one, he dismissed as the wrong choice for the others.

He called the first son (the father knew that this son desired knowledge) and told him, "Son, now you have reached an age where you should think for yourself and of your future. It is my advise that you should study further. Remember the shloka, '*Vidya nama narasya rupam adhika...vidya-vihina pasu.*' People will revere you if you become knowledgeable. Only the wealth of knowledge stays with us, all the rest is false.

"Do not even think of business. You must have heard how many have become bankrupt and died in bankruptcy like Chunilal Sarriya. A businessman is worried all day long. He cannot even sleep with ease.

Moreover, those who accumulate a lot of wealth endanger their lives. We have read about the son of a wealthy man in America who had to live in a golden cage because the father was afraid that his heir might be killed.

"Do not even think of agriculture. If you were a farmer and it does not rain for two years, you would have to bear huge losses. Government taxes would push you into debt. You, your labourers, your oxen—all would suffer. If you work with oxen your intelligence would also become like theirs.

"You might have thought of service, but you know that among us service is considered most inferior among professions. One has to spend a lifetime converting fifty rupees into fifty-one rupees. Moreover, you will always have to be subservient.

"Therefore, my son, don't think of doing business, or agriculture, or taking up a service even in your dreams."

Then he called the second son (this son had the qualities of a business-man). Here, the father praised business and decried the pursuit of knowledge, "My son, I see the qualities of a Bania trader in you. I would be happy if you enter into some trade. There is immense wealth to be earned. You would also be famous. Remember the shloka by Bhartrhari, '*Yasyasti vitta sa nara kulina sa pandita...sarve guna kancanam asrayanti.*' Look at Premchand Raychand! He built Rajabai Tower and his name is immortal.

"If you are considering further studies, read *M.A. Banake Kyui meri Mitti Kharab ki?*[3] Don't you see destitute B.A.s?[4] Who is willing to pay them even thirty rupees? To be educated means to be debauched. Therefore choose trade and commerce." (He denigrates agriculture and service.)[5]

He called the third son (the father knew that this son wanted to be a farmer)[6] and told him, "Son, you have improved the condition of our farm.

---

3. A novel written by Amrut Keshav Nayak.
4. This refers to a popular nonsense rhyme, which could be loosely translated as,

   Matriculates have fallen ill, the B.A.s are destitute,
   M.A.s are on deathbed, such is the condition of education.
5. In parenthesis in the original.
6. In parenthesis in the original.

I went there earlier today. I think you are fond of agriculture. I am willing to buy you more land. Moreover, there is a saying among us that farming is the most superior of all occupations, after which comes trade, and service is the lowliest of all professions. And how simple is the life of a farmer? Have you ever heard of a farmer falling sick? His body is as strong as iron. No one prays to god as much as a farmer does. You select the land and we shall buy it." (As before, he denigrates the other occupations.)[7]

Finally, the father called the fourth son. (He knew that this son liked administrative service. He presents the lowliest of professions as the most superior.)[8] "Son, it would be good if you visit our ruler. He will give you a suitable position. Our forefathers have been administrators of this state. How can we give up our claims on it? You must have heard that one of our ancestors was a Divan. That grandeur will not come back to us without state service. We were the rulers. Son, I would like you to bring back the glory of our forefathers." (He denigrates other occupations.)[9]

Pitaji, you have not paid any attention to us even when we sought it. God grants a newborn child mother's milk. If the child is given any other food, it has indigestion and falls incurably ill.

It is necessary to narrate my life story in support of what I have said earlier. The period to which I refer is from 1906 to 1911. In the end I ran away from you in 1911. This is the second time that a similar incident has taken place.[10]

In 1906, at the age of nineteen, I implored and beseeched you, I made innumerable arguments and pleaded that I should be allowed to chart the course of my life. I wanted to study, to gain knowledge; I had no other desire. I demanded that I should be sent to England. I wept and wandered aimlessly for a year but you paid no heed. You told me that character building should precede everything else. I had respectfully submitted to you that a tree once fully grown cannot be bent in another direction. My character cannot be

7. In parenthesis in the original.
8. In parenthesis in the original.
9. In parenthesis in the original.
10. This took place in 1915.

altered now. You would remember that you had gone to England at the age of nineteen against the wishes of all. Today you consider the lawyer's profession sinful! It is doubtful that you would be able to do what you do if you were not a barrister.

Today, I do not consider my character altered. I do not think even others would claim that my character has been altered. The mistakes that I committed then, knowing them to be mistakes, were due to my weakness and I was helpless about preventing them. I cannot be held responsible for the mistakes that I did not consider to be errors and those which I did not commit. With time, having learnt and understood some things, I do not repeat the mistakes of childhood. Therefore, some may very well say that my character has altered.

In order that my character be formed, using many arguments you proved that I was incapable of studying and that I first needed to acquire that capability. You made me adopt, not in Athens, but in today's world, in Johannesburg, the paths of Plato, Xenothon and Demosthenes—not with the guidance of any teacher but on my own. You asked me to drink milk not in the house of a cowherd, but in a pub. I am sorry that I am no Plato. It was proved that though I wanted to study I was incapable of it. All saw me with condescending eyes. You proved that I was utterly foolish. I had to accept your verdict.

I was told that I should leave Johannesburg and live in Phoenix to build my character. The *Indian Opinion* is published from Phoenix. Phoenix is regarded as a place for those desiring a simple life. No one can question the objectives of Phoenix. The value of nectar cannot be measured. But who got it? Who drank it? Allow me to remind you that Phoenix caused a dear friend of yours and an excellent electrician like Mr. Kitchin to run away. Phoenix also forced a gentleman and an excellent engineer like Mr. Liens to run away. There might have been other reasons in case of Mr. Cordes, but one particular reason was sufficient to drive him away. I can give other similar names. You believed (despite our warnings to the contrary)[11] for many years that

11. In parenthesis in the original.

Murabbi Bhai Shri Chhaganlal would not leave Phoenix so long as even one tile of its roof held. You are aware that this belief has been proven false.

For the sake of Phoenix's future you decided to send Murabbi Bhai Shri Chhaganlal, as someone who had the finest understanding of the objectives of the Phoenix, to England in 1910 (this despite the fact that Dr. Mehta Saheb had requested you to send one of us to England at his expense).[12] He fell ill there and returned to India in six months. You are aware that he decried Phoenix and praised the Servants of India Society.[13] I was asked to build my character in a place like that. But who was I there? Was I of any consequence there?

So be it. But, the plight of my mother was much worse than mine at Phoenix. I saw that she was being insulted often. What I saw was like witnessing a thief admonishing the sentry. People brought complaints to you: "Mrs. Gandhi consumes too much sugar and hence expenditure has gone up." "What right does Mrs. Gandhi have to assign work to a worker of the press?" People said that Harilal does this and Harilal does that. If you had maintained records of all the complaints it would certainly fill a small notebook.

We would have preferred to be caned rather than be admonished by you everytime a complaint was made. It is beyond my capacity to describe the hardships that my mother had to undergo. All this I could not bear. If we ever

---

12. In parenthesis in the original.
13. Before he went to England Chhaganlal had praised the Servants of India Society in a letter. He said that its members were committed to redeeming India. He had also mentioned that the Society had employed servants to work for its members. On reading the letter Gandhiji commented:

    I felt sad when I read Chi. Chhaganlal's description of the Servants of India Society...Is it proper for the servants to have servants?...I do feel that the aims of Phoenix as well as the way of life there surpass those of the Society...What we are doing here is the real thing, what goes on in Poona is, leaving aside the motive, unreal...That Chhaganlal could not answer their question about Phoenix only shows his timidity...

Translator's note: See also "Letter to Maganlal Gandhi, January 27, 1910", *CWMG*, vol. 10, p. 137–40.

brought complaints to you, your response would be, "He is a good man. He desires your welfare. And such and such is a jolly fellow."

It was then the idea that you were using us as weapons took root in my mind.

In 1907 the satyagraha commenced. I joined the struggle. I had the opportunity to think freely while in jail. When I was out of prison I shared with you my ideas about how and what education we could acquire. But you deprecated my thoughts. I remained oppressed. I considered myself a lost cause. I stopped expressing my views.

Finally, after pleading with you for five years, in accordance with your teaching I obeyed my conscience and ran away after writing a personal letter to you. I thought that I would go back to India. That I would earn my livelihood and stay away from relatives and their temptations. I thought that I would live in Lahore. That I would study and manage to feed myself somehow. From Johannesburg I went to Delagoa Bay on my way to India. I requested the British Counsel there to send me back to India as a poor Indian immigrant.

I was delayed at Delagoa Bay, you came to know of my whereabouts and you caught up with me. Obeying your orders I returned. I remained steadfast in my views. Therefore, instead of giving me a patient hearing you mutilated my thoughts and clipped my wings. You made me give up the idea of going to Lahore and instead made me stay in Ahmedabad. You promised to give me thirty rupees for monthly expenditure. You did not allow me to measure my capabilities; you measured them for me.

I stayed in Ahmedabad obeying your wishes. But my original objections were proved correct—relatives and social obligations to the family surrounded me. There were deaths in the family. After the death of my uncles I took ill.[14] Only those who nursed me and the doctors of Ahmedabad could possibly give you an idea of my illness. In 1912 I failed the matriculation examination. How long could your daughter-in-law have stayed in her natal home? I was worried about this.

14. Gandhiji's elder brother Karsandas died on 22 June 1913. Lakshmidas, the eldest brother, died on 9 March 1914.

How could all the expenses be met in thirty rupees? I incurred debt. You say that my mother's ornaments and those of your daughter-in-law should be sold and thus the debt be repaid. At the same time it is quite understandable that your present circumstances do not allow you to give money.

Despite leading an unhappy life in Ahmedabad I do believe that I learnt much, I experienced much.

Now you have returned to India. I spent some days with you. My effort to rejoin the Phoenix Institution has failed. My views remain unchanged. You remain steadfast in the choice of your path and consider it to be just. When I complained to you that you did not allow me to go to Lahore and asked me to stay in Ahmedabad, you responded by saying, "Why did you not remain firm in your views then?"

Now I am firm in my views and will remain so. If I were to die doing so, I shall die a satisfied man. I know that my conscience is free of sin.

Under the circumstances that I have narrated, and with my wings clipped, I recommenced studies after seven years. I failed the matriculation examination for three years. I am not worried on that account. I consider it a sign of weakness to give up studies now. I will earn my livelihood, get through my education and become a servant of the country. Our differences on knowledge of letters are not new.

I consider it useful to study the subjects that are taught in our universities. I am aware that in the recent past the government universities have discarded some important subjects. The changes in the methods of imparting education are acceptable to me. I consider examinations to be important. I consider the awarding of degrees[15] to be a form of encouragement to students. I see nothing wrong with schooling.[16] Some reforms are required everywhere. I have no wish to claim credit by pointing them out. For me, even students living in a gurukul constitutes schooling.[17]

---

15. Translator's note: English word in the original.
16. Translator's note: English word in the original.
17. Translator's note: English word in the original.

You dismissed my desire to be a barrister by saying that it was a 'sinful activity', but you sent Bhai Sorabji to England for the very same purpose. This contradiction sows the seeds of the thought that you love us less. Bhai Sorabji is a good man. But, you would have tried to please even an ant at our expense.

Even after hearing and reading all this you would say only one thing, and that I know: "I have always loved my sons to the extent that I have not allowed them to do anything that I have considered wrong." Pitaji, the facts given above contain my response to your justification. One more thing remains to be said here. It is so subtle and delicate that it cannot be said fully, nor can it be expressed through words. Nevertheless, I consider it my duty to write about it.

You admonish me that I married 'against your wishes'. I accept that. Given my circumstances I feel that my action should be pardoned. I believe that no one could have acted differently under those conditions.

You know that I got engaged while I was still a child. This was arranged by Pujya Kala kaka[18] in your absence. Thereafter at the age of seventeen I came to Rajkot severely ill.[19] On hearing that I was on my deathbed you had written a letter of solace from South Africa. At that time I was staying with Murabbi Goki phoi. There were no men in her house. Haridasbhai took me to his house. I was nursed and cared for in his house. I recovered my health. I stayed in his house for about two months.

I was not entirely unaware of the situation at that time. Haridasbhai's family was considered reformist. I knew that I was at my in-laws' place. Naturally, I desired to see what kind of girl was destined for me. I saw a photograph. A thought entered my mind that I was not engaged to an unsuitable girl, and that the in-laws' family is also good. After some days I

---

18. Gandhiji's brother Lakshmidas Gandhi.
19. The age mentioned here appears incorrect. After this illness Gandhiji had written a letter to Haridasbhai expressing his gratitude. The letter was written on 30 June 1903. Therefore, Harilal must have been fifteen and not seventeen years old at the time of his illness.

desired to see the girl face to face. I saw her. Time did the rest. As we got more opportunities we talked and joked. The bond of love linked us.

After regaining my health fully I returned to our house. How were we to meet after that? We exchanged letters. Our affection for each other grew. It was time for me to leave for South Africa. What was I to do? It would be five or more years before I could return from South Africa. In Hindu society a girl who remains unmarried after a certain age is subjected to criticism. We decided to get married. I have the letter of 1915, which proves our reasons for the marriage. I am not reproducing the letter here. But I am willing to produce it whenever asked.

We got married in May 1906. Three months after our marriage I left India to be with you.

Please allow me to state that ever since the marriage, we have remained subject to your wishes. We have been married for nine years. We have spent six of those years pining for each other.

I dissociated myself from the Phoenix Institution which is now in Bolpur because I witnessed hypocrisy there. I consider the objectives of Phoenix to be most superior; but with respect to what I have seen, you are the only one who leads his life according to those objectives. It is my view that no one else is capable of following them. We all consider the ascetic life to be the most superior way of life, but all of us still lead the lives of householders—a practice which is inferior to the ascetic life.

No one can be made an ascetic. No one becomes an ascetic because others ask him to. A person becomes an ascetic on his own volition; only such asceticism can be and is sustained. If I recall correctly, during the time of Cromwell there was a group of puritans.[20] In those days reform was in the air. Those who did not join the puritans were considered inferior to them. Many were shamed into joining the puritans. When the winds changed direction it resulted in a 'puritan reaction'.[21] People withdrew from it with the same

20. Translator's note: English word in the original.
21. Translator's note: English word in the original.

enthusiasm with which they had joined it. It is my humble belief that the same is true for the Phoenix Institution. The norms of the Phoenix Institution are the finest; but I am not willing to accept that those who stay in it follow the Phoenix path on their own volition.

At present, the Phoenix Institution has twenty-one members, young and old. Six of them have joined recently. Therefore, I am not counting them in. Of the remaining fifteen, I have known fourteen for many years. Phoenix was established six years ago.[22] With affection for my younger brothers and respect for Murabbi Bhai, I must state that in these six years of following the ideals established by you and given their efforts, the change in them is not as much as it ought to have been. The apparent change is due to time—a man with an angry disposition does not remain the same after six years. It is extremely difficult to imbibe virtues of high morality. There should be no ill will for the Phoenix Institution. But, ill will towards the institution is quite apparent.

I cannot believe a salt-free diet, or abstinence from ghee or milk indicates strength of character and morality. If one decides to refrain from consuming such foods as a result of thoughtful consideration, the abstinence could be beneficial. It is seen that such abstinence and asceticism is possible only after one has attained a certain state. By insisting on salt-free diet and on specific abstinences, at the Phoenix institution, you are trying to cultivate self-denial. It is my belief that before self-denial certain other qualities – non-possesion, courage and simplicity – have to be cultivated. I am skeptical whether those who are devoid of such qualities, but eat salt-free food or are fruitarians for the benefits offered by such diets, should be considered self-denying. Those who consume a salt-free diet because of such motives cannot be considered self-denying, as they have no ascetic qualities. Such persons promote hypocrisy by eating salt-free food. They think they have attained self-denial. They believe that godliness is manifest in them. They consider themselves superior, if not to everyone, at least to those who do not avoid consuming salt. It is

22. This is incorrect. The Phoenix was established in 1904, while the Tolstoy Farm was established in 1909.

well-recognised that among the Hindu families thousands of women and men observe rigorous vrata round the year. They observe fasts, but barring a few exceptions, they possess no sterling virtues; and good character is found also among those who do not observe any vrata.

After observing vrata, our women and men eat the usual roti and dal in large quantities; instead, if they were to follow a diet of fruits their vrata would certainly bear results. Those whose digestion is good keep good health. It is not as if the vrata observed by those who eat roti and dal does not bear results. Because, we know of many who eat roti and dal and yet observe the strictest of vows in the Jain Upashrayas. I wish to state that after the vrata people tend to overeat. It is my experience that even the self-denying are not exempt from this. If my own experience or experiment of being a fruitarian for only twenty days has any validity, I speak with experience – I have also observed this characterestic among those who were fruitarians for six months – that people eat fruits and nuts[23] far in excess to even those who overeat roti and dal. Therefore, indigestion is bound to happen. Under such circumstances I see no benefits in adopting a fruit diet.

It is my opinion that one should get accustomed to eating less food and only thereafter consider becoming a fruitarian. Eating less means being indifferent towards food and practising abstinence. Then, issues of "I will not be able to give up this and that" do not arise. Only after attaining such a state do questions of what one should eat and what one should abstain from appear meaningful and beneficial. We are usually conscious of what we should eat and should not eat. In this age, the consumption of tea and condiments has increased greatly. No one can deny the need to be strict regarding their use. One can contend that it should be possible to eat less and be a fruitarian. I believe that this is not possible. Because while food which is considered good is being cooked and its aroma wafts up to you, and others are praising the cooking, doubts arise as to how, as a fruitarian, one could be indifferent to it. It is difficult to ascertain the precise quantity of food that one should eat. I believe that a fruitarian who eats within limits does not ever fall

23. Translator's note: English word in the original.

ill. If a fruitarian or someone who abstains from ghee, milk, etc. can show that he has not taken ill in ten years I would accept that everyone should become a fruitarian. Exceptions must not be used to illustrate the success of this diet.

It is often asked, "Where are the restrictive impositions in the Phoenix Institution?" Such a contention is unacceptable to me. Because whatever I did there, and saw others do, I felt that their conduct was enforced by fear. It was as if everything was based on one principle: "Let the groom die, let the bride die, but do as Bapu says." And it is a fact, Pitaji, that those who believed so became dear to you and those who did not were despised. This was especially true for us; and among us, it was I who was so despised.

If one joined the Phoenix Institution with awareness of this rule he should be willing to give his head when asked. If not his head, he should at least be willing to make sacrifices. The stated norm is that one should not do what appears wrong, that one should fight what is wrong, that one should be fearless. To then call those who are fearless and who oppose the wrong "ignorant" and "stupid", to withdraw affection from them, to refuse to even look at them, and to taunt them by saying "Ji" in response to their questions was unbearable for me, Pitaji. I have stated that all the members of the Phoenix Institution act out of fear. I felt that under such circumstances I would not become a servant of the country and my soul would not be enlightened. In the institution I saw everyone wanting to establish their own authority by belittling others. Generosity—I found lacking. I witnessed poisonous rivalries. I saw the sense of brotherhood decline. I found everyone lacking in public courage. I found each one covering up their views for the sake of their own interests. I wanted to learn fearlessness, but instead, I saw myself benefitting through hypocrisy.

It is said that moral restrictions – even if they are labelled as fear – are natural. No one experiences fear over moral injunctions. (If one is not immoral.)[24] If a man who drinks alcohol refrains from doing so either out of fear or shame, his behaviour may be regarded as being attentive to a moral restriction. But to experience fear while eating sugar cannot be identified as

---

24. In parenthesis in the original.

observance of a moral injunction. This fear becomes coercion. Because, a person who eats sugar would do so in presence of others, but a drunkard would not drink alcohol in the presence of others; if those around him were also drunkards that would be quite another matter.

I am required to perform an unpleasant duty; but I do believe that I can perform this duty to completion.

Pitaji, whenever we told you "We do not benefit from the Phoenix Institution" or "We have not seen others gaining from the Phoenix Institution", you told us to follow the example of Murabbi Bhai Shri Chhaganlal and Murabbi Bhai Shri Maganlal. You have not said so but have indicated through your actions that we should follow Bhai Jamnadas. We should keep them as our ideals.

I have been bewildered whenever you have said so; because, I have neither been able to bear it nor have been able to express what I have observed. They are my elder brothers and I am ready to serve them and press their feet. Bhai Jamnadas is for me like Bhai Manilal. It is my duty that I should not hide my humble thoughts from you. Such is also your wish. I am performing such a duty by informing you of what I consider necessary.

Their example teaches us to nurture our self-interest. I do not intend to say that they have adopted both right and wrong means to further their selves. I have observed that their foundation is the maxim "Honesty is the best policy."[25] I believe that for them abstinence from milk for the sake of it is secondary. I fail to see the significant sacrifices that they have made. Bhai Jamnadas who is a part of your organisation could have sacrificed two or three years and refrained from encouraging child marriage. In Rajkot (it is necessary to remember here that you were prepared to break off my engagement)[26] he created an impression that no one comprehends or practices your ideas as much as he does. You would say, "Should he not obey his parents?" If he had remained subservient to the conservative religious ideas of his parents, he could not have transgressed caste and community rules. Moreover, he got

---

25. Translator's note: Sentence in English in the original.
26. In parenthesis in the original.

married, he enjoyed the life of a householder for three months and then he joined the Phoenix Institution by taking a vow of lifelong celibacy.[27] All this appears to me very perplexing. I fail to understand what lesson I should derive from it.

If Bhai Ramdas were to follow his example, he could marry whenever he desires—perhaps immediately. Because after the son attains the age of sixteen you consider him a friend and do not insist that he should act contrary to his own desires. He can not only get married, but after marriage he can directly join your institution.

Moreover, since there is no question of seeking deferment from you, it is asked, "What should we do, if we go there, to earn for ten years?" Based on such considerations, there is the answer "One cannot join your institution."[28] Since we have touched upon the question of earning I must say that the plan of Murabbi Bhai Shri Chhaganlal, Murabbi Bhai Shri Maganlal and Bhai Jamnadas to earn a living out of you is simple and superb. They have brought with them their characters. They use this character and keep you happy and pleased. They give their character to you and trade in the capital that is your character. In this transaction you have given them everything. But they can take only what their destinies allow them. There is an additional advantage of investing capital in your firm—there is no fear of losing out on the interest; each per cent of the interest is calculated and paid.

---

27. a. Jamnadas' marriage took place either towards the end of September or early October 1914. Before his marriage, Gandhiji wrote to him on 19 July 1913, "By obstinately refusing to marry, you will cause extreme pain to your parents...You cannot say with certainty that your present state of mind will last forever...I have told you that you will have to marry. All the same, if you have no sexual union with your wife, this cannot but conduce to the welfare of both of you..." (See, "Letter to Jamnadas Gandhi, July 19, 1913", *CWMG*, vol. 12, p. 145–47.) Harilal refers to this piece of advice.
    b. In a letter written some years later, Gandhiji said, "So far as I know, Chi. Jamnadas had joined the institution, but there may have been a misunderstanding on my part. Jamnadas thinks that he had taken no vow." See, "Letter to Narandas Gandhi, May 4, 1915", *CWMG*, vol. 13, p. 73.
28. This sentence was crossed out in the original.

But, you have given us no capital. That is my quarrel with you. If you had given us some capital we could have traded with some firm. What are the consequences of this? We trade without capital. In business the norm that one must remember is that accounts must be calculated to the last paisa even with a brother. Therefore, people mock us. "Go away, you free-loaders. You are eating out of your father's earnings. Why are you putting on airs?" (What airs? That I am a son of M.K. Gandhi.)[29] What do you, with whom we could have traded, say? "Go away, stupid fool. I feed you but you don't even know how to eat?"

How can we feed off you? How could we possess a trader's cleverness? From where could we have gained the experience of such transactions that we could have become adept at them?

A dog that roams the farms belongs neither to the road nor to the village. Clever—it cannot be. Pitaji, you have kept us in such a condition. What example should we follow?

If Bhai Manilal were to follow the example of Bhai Jamnadas – he would not do so because I think the worm has become a wasp, but still – he could escape from the work that he now does at Shantiniketan—of cleaning the sleeping quarters of Mr. Andrews, making tea for him, etc. You have made all of us do such work. I have seen Bhai Jamnadas escaping from such work as he considers it lowly.

Bhai Manilal addresses me by my name because Bhai Jamnadas does that. Bhai Manilal is elder to Bhai Jamnadas both in age and relationship. But still, Bhai Jamnadas calls him Manilal. Vashisthaji used to address Vishwamitraji as "Rajarshi". I do not know if such is the case with them. I have no objection to it. But in our family and among us it is considered discourteous and insulting.

People wonder that if not much, something should have happened at the Phoenix Institution, some training in literacy should have been imparted. It is my view that no training in literacy has been imparted whatsoever. You admit that such training has not been imparted, but you also insist that such

29. In parenthesis in the original.

a sacrifice had to be made. We began making sacrifices around 1907. But many of us belong to the Phoenix from long before. All of us, and especially we brothers, have expressed our deep desire to acquire education, but you have never paid any heed to us. It is doubtful if Bhai Manilal, Ramdas and Devdas at the age of twenty-three[30] have the knowledge of a fourth grader.

Pitaji, I have not been able to say even one-fourth of what I have to say. The letter has become very long. Printing is expensive. From where will I find the money to pay for it?

Before I conclude, Pitaji, if I have unknowingly expressed rash and immature ideas I seek your forgiveness from the depths of my conscience. At the age of twenty-eight I have been forced to write to you like a young child; this pains me, but I had no other choice. My conscience dictated the letter and I merely wrote it. Whatever I have said about the Phoenix Institution I have said because of my blood relations with it. Therefore, I have pointed out only its shortcomings. The virtues of the Phoenix Institution are known to the world.

My entire letter stresses one point—you have never been generous and patient with our failings. You have never considered our rights and capabilities, you have never seen the person in us. Your life and actions are very harsh. I consider myself unsuitable for a life such as yours. To you a son and others are equal. If there be two accused – one of your sons and someone else – you have considered it unjust to regard the other as guilty. It is justice that a son must suffer, but unfortunately I have not been able to bear such suffering.

Moreover, whether it is right or wrong, I am married. God has granted me four children. I am caught in the web of worldly relations, in its delusions and enchantments; I cannot acquire the detachment of an ascetic and renounce the world like others. Therefore, I had to separate from you with your consent. I feel that I must earn my own livelihood. Even after this I am willing to join the Phoenix Institution at your command. You know that I have not disobeyed you on purpose. It is possible that my views are wrong.

30. Only Manilal was twenty-three years of age.

I hope that they prove to be wrong—if I realise that they are wrong I shall not hesitate to reform myself. In the deep recesses of my conscience, my only desire is that I be your son—that is, if I am good enough be your son.

Your obedient son Harilal's Sashtang Dandvat Chaitra Sud Purnima
Samvat 1971
31 March 1915
Mumbai

Appendix 2 My Brother

by Devadas Gandhi[1]

The hand of death has brought deliverance to a restless soul. My elder brother, Harilal (not Hiralal) never knew mental or physical peace in his sixty years of life.

The last time I saw him was four days after the Assassination when in one of his penitent moods he turned up from somewhere at our house in Delhi to mourn with us. He was ill and had to be carefully nursed. His face was drawn and emaciated, and as my wife remarked and our little Gopu showed by his behaviour, it resembled Bapu's a lot. When he felt better, he went away, for he had come to bless us, not to interfere in the ceremonies in which the whole of Delhi was then occupied. As he boarded the train for Bombay he said with a weariness not noticed in him before, "It is always my lot to be on the move!" That was his last long journey on earth. The news of his death in Bombay reached us in London on our return from the Continent.

Although he had forsaken the family—as the family had forsaken him—and wandered under conditions of great discomfort throughout the length and breadth of the country, at times of distress, he would always make a point of putting in an appearance. He was there when Ba died at Poona in the Aga

1. Translator's note: The first edition carried a translation of this essay, based on the version given by Neelam Parikh. Shri Gopalkrishna Gandhi gave from his collection the essay that Shri Devadas Gandhi wrote in his moving English, which was published in *The Hindustan Times* on 22 July 1948. The same is published here in full. I am grateful to Shri Gopalkrishna Gandhi for his generosity.

Khan Palace prison, during many of Bapu's perilous fasts and when his son Rasik died in my arms in the Jamia Millia Islamia in Delhi where I was in 1928.[2] He grieved bitterly, but with no complaint against any one over his son's death. In the prime of his life the boy was studying under my care and fell victim to typhoid. It is dangerous to have typhoid at or about the age of 17. He used to teach spinning to the boys in Jamia and was himself adept in the art. He would himself turn out more than his own quota and had kept on spinning even after the onset of fever.

A Bitter Lesson

I had taken his lassitude lightly, a fact I have always regretted and which taught me a bitter but simple lesson. When he had taken to bed, Rasik pleaded that he be sent back to the Ashram at Sabarmati, remarking: "There I shall get well." These things are controlled by a hidden hand, and it does not help to be wise after the event. But I feel sure he would have been saved had I taken him back to the Ashram.

Right from his South African days Bapu had performed marvels of cure. The personal care he gave to patients could not be easily rivalled. His very presence made for confidence and a complete sense of security. That, however, applied to healthy people as well. No matter how many assistants he had to look after sick people he would visit the "ward" himself morning and evening and in the course of the day if necessary. His method of treatment was, in cases of ordinary fever particularly, nature cure, which consisted, among other things, of open air, wet-sheet pack, Kuhne bath, sunshine, fruit juice for diet, constant attendance, and little medication. He was himself a first class nurse and could give a sponge-bath satisfying the most meticulous test. One thing that he insisted on was a superlative standard of hygiene.

2. Translator's note: Rasik's death occurred in 1929. The anomalies in dates were pointed out by Chandulal Dalal.

Shock For Ba

Dr Ansari, who was also Chancellor of the Jamia, wore himself down for Rasik. But the toxins were too strong and the heart gave way just when the corner was about to be turned. A factor against us was the December cold of Delhi. My brother was located and contacted with difficulty and came just in time to see life ebbing away. It was his wont to quarrel with his brothers, but not on an occasion like this. He reproached himself, was gentle with us all, thanked the good doctor and his friends, and left for one of his unknown destinations. To Ba, who was there, the episode was a major shock. My pride was humbled. Bapu consoled me in his touching telegrams and letters. He was more convinced than I that the boy could have been saved had be been sent to Sabarmati. But he did not stress the point beyond its academic significance.

A scene during my childhood which I vividly remember was that of my brother carrying on his shoulder a huge leather bag and engaged in deep conversation with Bapu as they walked together from Phoenix railway station, near Durban, to our home. I walked behind. For me it was just one of those innumerable walks I enjoyed having with Bapu between station and home. I hardly followed the conversations. My brother had rebelled against Bapu's life of "experiments" and fled in secrecy with only a few personal belongings. His disappearance caused alarm, but before things became unbearable, particularly for Ba, a friend in whom he had confided informed Bapu that he was on his way to India. Bapu sent a telegram at the port in East Africa where he was to embark, asking him to come back to talk the matter over in person and promising him full ultimate liberty of action.

His Ambitions

He had on several occasions wished to go to Europe and to study for the Bar. Bapu had a little money to spare, even after he had renounced worldly life in South Africa, but he had decided to spend it for the community and not on his family. When a young Parsi lad, Sorabji Adajania, was chosen to be sent to London for higher education, my brother's sense of injury was complete. (It made little difference to my brother that Sorabji Adajania was to dedicate)[3] his future service to the cause of Indians in South Africa. It was the final signal for departure. The talk during the walk, as I learnt years later, was infructuous and my brother kept to his programme. This must have been near about 1910.[4] He never returned to Bapu after that in any sense of the term. He has now followed him in death.

In his youth he was one of Bapu's best subalterns in the early phase of the struggle in South Africa. He cheerfully underwent every kind of suffering and was always in the front line. Prison life in South Africa was more arduous than prison life as it has been known to most gaol-birds in India. Two weeks with hard labour was like three months in India. A month was regarded as a stiff sentence. Ring leaders and habituals got three months, and six months was a barbarous punishment, reserved for the select. Conditions inside the prison were terrible and ruined the most stubborn constitutions, worse definitely than our "C Class." There was no mercy and the environmental advantage we had in India was completely lacking but it was not worse perhaps than what the early revolutionaries endured in India.

Ba's Gaol Term

When Ba had done three months she was no longer the Ba we knew. She used to be chubby and always looked much younger than Bapu. Three months of life in a South African prison changed her totally. There is on record the story that a prominent South African when he saw Bapu and Ba at a railway station shortly after her release greeted him with, "How do you do, Mr Gandhi? Is this your mother?"

My brother had done two terms of six months, and even as a child the separation to me was exceedingly long and painful. All little Indian children

3. Translator's note: Words in brackets reconstructed as they are missing in the available reproductions of the article. I am grateful to Shri Gopalkrishna Gandhi for the reconstruction.
4. Translator's note: This incident took place in 1911.

in South Africa knew how hard their elders suffered in imprisonment. I was nearly the same age as his elder daughter and we had common toys.[5] The last I remember of his days of valour and charm in South Africa was a touching farewell at Phoenix just as he was going off to serve one of his many prison sentences as a Satyagrahi. He used to be handsome and parted his hair in the middle with beautiful curls over the forehead. As he walked away he waved to me and said: "Yes Devadas, I will send you your top from Durban." I forget the top. But I remember sharing sweets with my niece the next day, while my sister-in-law shed tears over a letter.

When we met years later in India he was a changed man. He had broken completely, both physically and mentally, from Bapu. Upon his return to India, after Bapu had failed to persuade him to stay in South Africa, he had written a long Open Letter to Bapu which he had intended but could never summon the necessary hardihood to publish. He had, however, circulated it privately among a fairly wide circle and Bapu had received his copy. It was an indictment of sorts centring round Bapu's supposed neglect of his own children to the benefit of the sons and daughters of relatives and friends. It, however, gave his case away in many respects and I am sure that it was a sense of the weakness of his thesis that prevailed with my brother in the decision not to proceed any further with the "Letter." But it was a landmark in his life and in his connection with the family.

Respect For Bapu

He always obstinately clung to his own ideas. He respected Bapu and defended him vigorously outside the circle of family and friends. He had tender regard for Ba and liked his brothers. But he enjoyed remaining in perpetual opposition. We, his brothers and cousins and others we moved with, were affectionately termed "hypocrites" who pretended to but did not really serve or follow Bapu.

---

5. Translator's note: Harilal's eldest daughter Ramibehn was born in 1908 while Devadas Gandhi was born in 1900.

When his wife died in the influenza epidemic of 1920[6] he became even more thoroughly independent and irresponsible. It was a perfectly nomadic life he led from then onwards. His alcoholism had by now became chronic. He co-operated honestly when on numerous occasions Bapu tried to cure him. But the results were always disappointing. The effort of others never had any chance. He had a strong mind and could never bring himself to suffer those who talked virtue to him. He repelled all precept as sanctimonious and generally saw motives of personal gain behind the good conduct of others. My chances with him were nil. But only for the sake of Ba, I, like my brothers, tried my hand at reclamation. Our one misfortune in this case was that he was the eldest. He was therefore naturally superior and had even brought us up or watched us grow. Once he had caught me stealing groundnuts in South Africa. Bapu encouraged the eating of groundnuts. I often used to have my pockets full. Once he lay in siege for me. As I dipped my hand in the sack a door opened and he took me by the arm feigning anger. The rattle of the nuts was what he had waited behind the door to hear. So when twenty-five years later the groundnut thief of yours proffered to him a copy of Zola's *Drink* he said with contempt: "My boy, don't try such things on me. I can write one like that."

The Conversion Stunt

But others also failed with him equally miserably. His stock retort was: "Mind your business, as I mind mine." The last twenty years of his life were the most tragic. Excessive drink had dulled his conscience, if not the intellect, and he would give his parents, brothers and children and friends shock after shock. One of his well-known escapades was the mock conversion to Islam. He meant it as a stunt. But it had its inevitable complications and brought great discredit to those who sponsored and glorified the event and sought to make all manner of capital out of it. Simultaneously came unseemly stories of his life as a "Muslim." The strain and agony of humiliation of it all was too much for

---

6. Translator's note: Gulabbehn died in 1918.

Ba. She gave vent to her feelings one morning in Delhi as she soliloquised in my presence. It was so pathetic and piercing that later in the day, I reduced it to writing and the result was the famous "Open Letter from a Mother to her Son," which found publicity in nearly every daily and weekly in the country. As a spontaneous expression of the heart it was the most telling of anything of the kind I have ever known. To the handful of Muslims who were exploiting the situation it brought a consciousness of their folly and guilt and the contempt they were bringing their own religion into. My brother quickly retracted his step.

In the number of miles travelled by railway train in India, his record could touch Bapu's. He kept fleeting from place to place and everywhere was looked after by friends. The number of those of all creeds and communities to whom we are indebted for the friendly care they bestowed on him is legion. In spite of his familiar vagaries they never ceased to love him. He had that something which drew people to him and enabled them to overlook his failings. He always held his head high and never sought seriously to injure anyone.

Courage to Suffer

But a remarkable trait in him was his audacious readiness to suffer the consequences of his ways and what he called his free thinking. For few people can survive even a few years of the shelterless and foodless existence that was his self-chosen lot. He would be penniless and in tatters for days together and would live literally like a beggar in the streets. And although it is true that evil people sought him out and used him for their own ends, it was while he lived as a perfect destitute that he found some of the best specimens of humanity on the lowest rungs of the social ladder, who succoured and comforted him. He would at times spend a few days with his relatives and old friends, but only as a concession and perhaps to recuperate. His son Kanti who has a part of Bapu in him and is a doctor, always sought opportunities to look after his father and succeeded better than most others. Last year he managed to keep him with him for several months and with his wife, he served him with the true devotion of a son. He is a sensitive boy and has always carried, in silence and with dignity, his burden of sorrow.

My brother used to read little, but always chose what he read with fastidious care. One book he always spoke of with reverence and great satisfaction was Lokmanya Tilak's famous treatise on the Bhagawat Gita. He carried a copy with him everywhere and even when he did not have a shirt to wear he would still have with him that copy of the *Gita Rahasya.* If I can at all find the particular copy which he used, I shall keep it with other treasures of the kind.

Appendix 3 My Experiences with Harilalbhai
by Kunvarji Parikh

In January 1924, Harilalbhai Gandhi came to his sister-in-law Balibehn's house in Rajkot, from Calcutta, for the betrothal of his elder daughter Ramibehn. At that time I was called from Morbi to Rajkot. I was acquainted with Balibehn, Gulabbehn and Kamubehn. I grew up in my mother's natal home in Morbi. My elder mami, Raliyatbehn, was a phoi of Balibehn and Gulabbehn. Therefore, we met often in Morbi and Rajkot. When Gulabbehn died at a young age in 1918, Rami was the eldest of the four children of Harilalbhai. She was ten at that time. All the children lived with Pujya Ba–Bapu at Sabarmati Ashram and often visited their aunt in Rajkot. During that time Rami and I came to know each other. Balibehn was widowed at a young age and she raised all the four children of Gulabbehn with love and care.

I stayed with Harilalbhai in Rajkot for two or three days. During this stay he introduced me to some members of the Gandhi family. He decided on Rami's engagement with me. He obtained the consent of my mama and mami. He had a photograph of mine taken in Rajkot, which he kept with him. Pujya Ba–Bapu were in the Sassoon Hospital in Poona (after the appendicitis operation). Harilalbhai went there, showed my photograph to Pujya Ba–Bapu, talked over all the matters with them and obtained their consent. After reaching Mumbai he sent a telegram to Rajkot, as a result Bhai Kanti, accompanied by Balibehn's old servant Jhina Patel, came to Morbi with the coconut and our engagement was made public (on Vasant Panchami of Samvat 1980).

A few days after our engagement, Pujya Ba sent me a letter written by the hand of Prabhudasbhai Gandhi from the Sassoon Hospital. This fifty-year-old letter was recently published by Prabhudasbhai Gandhi in the monthly, *Lokjivan* (June 1974).

On Harilalbhai's wish and insistence, Pujya Ba–Bapu got us married at the Sabarmati Ashram in a simple ceremony conducted at the Lal Bungalow on

24 February 1925. They gave their blessings to us. At that time, Harilalbhai was in Calcutta and had sent us a telegram with his blessings.

When he had come to Rajkot in 1924 for our engagement, he had borrowed Rs. 10,000 from the Thakore Saheb of Rajkot as a personal loan for his business in Calcutta. Questions were raised about this outstanding loan in the Praja Pratinidhi Sabha of the State of Rajkot. At that point of time, the Thakore Saheb had instructed the treasury to account the amount as his personal debt. It so happened that after some time, the heirs of Gandhiji's elder brothers – Lakshmidas Gandhi and Karsandas Gandhi – decided to sell the ancestral house, Kaba Gandhi no Dahelo. Gandhiji had already given up his claim on the house. Lakshmidas' son, Samaldas Gandhi, and Karsandas' son, Jethalal Gandhi, had sold the house to someone. The Thakore Saheb decided to take the amount of Rs. 10,000 that he had loaned to Harilal. He stopped the sale of the house from being completed till the amount was recovered.

Harilalbhai was in Mumbai. Samaldas Gandhi cabled him one hundred rupees and asked for his presence in Rajkot. Harilalbhai came immediately. He met the Thakore Saheb and persuaded him, "Bapuji has forfeited his claims from the Kaba Gandhi no Dahelo. My younger brothers too make no claim on the property; hence I too can have no claim on the house. I owe you ten thousand rupees and it is my responsibility to repay the entire amount. I promise to repay the amount with interest in instalments." Harilalbhai convinced the Thakore Saheb and obtained his permission for Samaldas Gandhi and Jethalal Gandhi to complete the sale of the house. Both the brothers expressed their gratitude to Harilalbhai after which he went back to Mumbai.

Harilalbhai possessed a clever, sharp intelligence and was hardworking. Despite these qualities, he had to face many shocks and downturns. After Gulabbehn's demise, he had no one to care for him and provide support, and at the same time he had no responsibilities. Therefore, with each day he increasingly disregarded all limits and exercised absolute free will.

Harilalbhai's desire for higher studies was not fulfilled, and for this reason he always had differences with Bapuji. Many a time he voiced his resentment in public. In 1927 he wrote a series of articles in the daily, *Hindustan*

Prajamitra, titled "Amaro Balvo yane Mahatma no Buddhavtar", wherein he expressed his own and his brothers' grievances.

He started many business ventures in Calcutta under different names, but he did not succeed in them. Moreover, after Gulabbehn's demise he took the wrong path. But he did have a knack for business. He had canvassed, by travelling around India, for the toilet soap of the famous company of Mumbai, Godrej, and increased their sales substantially. This had pleased Godrej a great deal. After three or four years of work, Godrej gave him a monthly sum without his doing any work for a long time. He used to stay at Mumbai's Kashmir Hotel situated at Dhobi Talav. During this period I had gone to Mumbai to visit him. There, I met A.B. Godrej. He had told me, "Your father-in-law Mr. Gandhi has on his own ability – not as Gandhi's son – done very good canvassing work for our toilet soap. Therefore we give him money every month even though he stays in the hotel and no longer works for us. But he is addicted to drinking alcohol. We Parsis also drink, but never lose our senses. He drinks continuously. Someone like you should stay with him and reform his ways. If you stay with him we will give you the money for your expenses."

I made an attempt to stay with him for some time in the hotel, but could not reform him. I had to leave him and inform Godrej that his money was being wasted. After sometime Godrej stopped giving him money; Harilalbhai was angry with me for this.

After a while he left Mumbai, but did not settle down anywhere. We, both his sons-in-law, used to live in Mumbai. At times he would come to our houses and stay for short periods. But he could not stay permanently with anyone. The reason was that he had no responsibilities. Now, we feel that when he was widowed at the age of thirty, if the elders had persuaded him to marry again and had also placed the responsibility of raising the children on him, the situation might have been very different. But destiny plays its own games. His Will is supreme!

Kunvarji Parikh
October 1974

Appendix 4 Memories of My Father-in-law Shri Harilal Gandhi

by Saraswati K. Gandhi[1]

It is with great enthusiasm that I venture to write a few things about my father-in-law, whom the world has proclaimed a bad character, while to me and my husband he was a very dear person. The world may say that Harilalbhai was the most unworthy son of his great father Mahatma Gandhi. But it is not so. He had many many good qualities, and I found him to be a dear father. Only, you have to search a little and you can see all the good qualities of a human being in him.

I had very little opportunity to be very close to him, but the little time I spent with him convinced me that he was not at all a bad man. I regard him to be the most intelligent of the four sons of Bapuji. He was very humorous, very generous and very hospitable; yet he was given to drinking. Why? Who is to be blamed?

Well, I am not a good writer, still, I am going to put here all efforts to picture my father-in-law as I knew him. Believe me, I won't add a word of exaggeration. I had seen him (then he was my would be father-in-law) for the first time when he had become Abdulla Gandhi. That was about three years before my marriage. I met him at the Topiwala building in Bombay. He was in a cream suit with a cream waistcoat inside, and he also had a Muslim's cap—a red Muslim cap with a tail at the top. He looked like a Muslim completely. I presume he did not like me to be his son's wife, and he did not notice my existence. He might have had his reasons. But I was scared in my mind because he was a Muslim, and I feared all Muslims. I do not know why. I felt sad about my being unnoticed; but at the same time he was talking very affectionately to his son.

1. The original English text is reproduced here.

After that we parted and we did not know anything about him for a very long time. Years rolled on. I got married to Kantilal Gandhi who was a medical student at Mysore Medical College.

Before I proceed further, let me introduce myself to you as an individual. I hail from Kerala and I am the niece of the present chairman of the Khadi and Village Industries Commission, Dr. G. Ramachandran. My marriage with Kantilalji was due to him. It was through him that Kantilalji came to our place and stayed with us to learn shorthand and typewriting, and to learn English from my uncle. At that time I was a girl of ten years and schooling. There was quite a strong opposition from my grandparents to this alliance, the reason being that I was too young for Kantilalji and I did not know any language other than Malayalam. But my mother was firm [about getting] me married to Kantilalji…She said, by the time I grew up to be a young woman I would be worthy of him, and that girls grow up very fast and everything would be adjustable. That is how I became the granddaughter-in-law of Bapuji.

After our marriage we stayed at Mysore where my husband was doing his medical course. Very soon I became a mother. We named our son 'Shanti' for the reason that my husband had had a younger brother by that name whom he had loved very much. That brother died at a very early age. In his memory we named our son 'Shanti'. At present my son Shantikumar is a cardiac surgeon, in the U.S.A. and has married an American girl by name Susan. When this son was round about 3–4 years old, my father-in-law came to Mysore to see his son and family! Now starts my close association with him, and it is interesting to narrate the incident. I remember it very clearly though it happened years ago.

It was one fine evening, when my husband was returning home from his college, I saw along with him an old man of thin structure, fatigued and looking weak, arriving at the gate. I was waiting for my husband. So when I saw a stranger with him, that too a person wearing dirty clothes and with a worn-out look, I thought he must be some Gandhian worker or something of that sort. My husband used to have prayers, spinning and all other Gandhian activities at our home, along with his studies. So naturally I thought that some

Gandhian had come to see him. I did not give much importance to the new comer and opened the door, and they came inside. My husband asked me to do pranam to the elderly person by his side. I said a hurried "Namaste", not knowing who he was. How could I ever dream of such a thing? The person gave me a broad smile, and said, "You don't know me, I guess. I am Kanti's father." I felt a real shock. "My husband's father in such a condition!" I thought, but immediately my conscience guided me. I bowed down and touched his feet. All these things happened in a fraction of a second. Though this incident occurred many years ago I remember as if it happened yesterday.

From here starts my close contact with my father-in-law, upon whom the world looked down with contempt.

Harilalbhai had in him all the required human qualities. He was very gentle, very generous, and very humorous and hospitable. He used to bring his good friends to our place, and he used to ask me to cook nice dishes for the guests. He was very particular about that. He never once behaved with the authority of a father-in-law. He loved me like his own daughter; and I too began loving him like my own father.

During those days my father too had come to Mysore to spend his vacation, as he used to do often. So there were two fathers and they liked each other very much. And my father could not believe that he was talking to the Harilal whom he had pictured in a different angle—as a pervert and a drunkard.

Really, it was an unbelievable incident for six months.

During those days I used to get letters from Bapuji. Once I received a postcard from him. Unfortunately I lost it during our shifting to some other place; but I well remember the contents of it. It said, "Chi. Saru, the victory over Harilal, which was denied to me, has come to you. My blessings for a complete victory. Bapu."

But my efforts to win him failed completely.

One day he called me and asked me to bring pen and paper. I thought, perhaps he wanted to dictate a letter to someone. But it was for something else. He began dictating. The heading was "My Grievances against My

Father". He dictated a few lines and then cancelled it. I did not have the guts to ask why he did not complete it or for what reason he cancelled it. I just obeyed him implicitly. At the same time, I could see his mental conflict. He never spoke anything about his father to me. He always used to talk about his wife whom he had lost at a very early age. He used to tell me about her high intelligence, her calm nature, her beauty, etc., and that revealed his intense love for her. He actually adored her. That is what I guessed from his talk.

He used to talk about his dear mother Kasturba. I used to watch his emotions when he talked about his mother.

In between he used to call Shanti, my son, and ask him to go to the nearby shop and get one Gold Flake cigarette, and he used to give the required money too. In a day he used to have six cigarettes.

Days passed very nicely and Bhai regained his originality; and when he laughed and cut jokes he resembled Bapuji very much.

When the vacation started we decided to go to Kerala. My parents stayed at Trivandrum. So we started for Trivandrum via Calicut. We broke our journey at Calicut and stayed at Balybehn's place. She was an old ashramite and married to P.L. Ashar who is a good friend of Kantilalji. Balybehn treated me as her younger sister. She used to shower love on me always. Even today it is so. Bhai fell sick there and Balybehn looked after him like he was her own father. She did everything for him. When Bhai became alright we continued our journey. In Trivandrum we had a nice time. Bhai was happy all the time. We stayed very happily. My father-in-law by this time had become a very normal man. When the vacation was over we returned to Mysore.

At this juncture the story takes a different shape.

One day my father-in-law inquired of me as to what cosmetics I used. At that time I was a very simple girl. Our circumstances also did not permit an expensive life. I said, "I use only Pond's cream and powder." He said that I should buy Hazeline snow and some other powder—I forgot the name. He said he would get those things for me. As he had no money I could not believe it. I kept mum. Even for the daily cigarettes Kantilalji used to give him money. I did not know how he was going to get me cosmetics. Nearly six months had passed and Bhai had not touched alcohol.

Next day he went out. While going he said he was going to meet Shri Mirza Ismail, the former Dewan of Mysore. He came back after sometime and gave me a packet which contained one thousand rupees. Mirza had given the amount to him. I did not accept it fearing my husband's wrath. But Bhai forced me to keep it, and said that it was for me, to buy all that I needed. He also reminded me to buy Hazeline snow. I felt very upset, I could guess what was coming. He did not use it to buy any alcohol. That also surprised me. But before Kantibhai returned home he went out.

Kantibhai came within a short time after Bhai left. I narrated the whole incident. He got wild with me for accepting the money. He said that we had no right to keep it, and asked me to give it back to Bhai when he returned. He also told me that he feared that Bhai would soon take to his old habits. "This money is the indication of it," he said.

We waited for him for dinner. He did not come. So we had our dinner. Late in the night he came fully drunk, slowly got into his room and lay down on his bed. As he had consumed too much alcohol he lost control of himself. He began talking loudly. That was the first time I saw a drunkard—that too someone dear to me. I was terribly frightened. Kantibhai went to his bedside and began talking to him. He told Bhai that he was very unhappy about what Bhai had done; and if Bhai behaved in that manner he won't tolerate it. Bhai in his intoxication went on talking in a high pitch. I heard him saying, "Look my son, what is Bapu going to do for you? I am going to make you an eye-surgeon. I will send you to a foreign country," and so on. Then Bhai vomited and soiled the room, the bed and everything. I ran away to my room with my son, closed the door from inside fearing Bhai might come and beat me or kill me.

Next day when I woke up Bhai was sleeping soundly. Kantibhai told me, "Now Bhai may not stick to us," and that I should not worry. He left for college. I was terribly scared. When Bhai woke up he called me. I would not go near him and stood at a distance from him. He asked me to give him Rs.100, but I gave all the money without speaking a word and went to my room. My son Shanti thought that his grandfather was very sick. Bhai called me again and I went to him. He had tears in his eyes. He was crying.

He said, "Look Beta, I hurt you and my son. I am very sorry. Today I won't do it. I will go out and come back soon. Do not cry, my child." Then he vanished. That evening too he came home drunk, but not like the previous day. Kantibhai told him that he would daily give him a peg of it if he would stay with him calmly. Bhai did not agree. He shouted so many things at the loudest pitch of his voice. Kantibhai said if Bhai was going to continue in that manner it would hamper his career and his Gandhian work. He requested him repeatedly to stay calm. He said the students and teachers who came to our house for prayers and spinning were shocked to see the condition of his father. What answer should he give, he asked Bhai.

We wanted our Bhai to stay with us as the head of our family. We were prepared to do anything for him. But he did not pay any attention. This continued for a day or two; and after that he did not come home for two days. On the third day I saw a tonga arriving at our gate. I saw Bhai inside the tonga. He got down from it. He was carrying a big basket in his hands. He came inside and called me. I was afraid and I stayed away from him. Bhai was not drunk at this time; but his condition was bad. He did not have his long shirt on, and was wearing only his banian and dhoti. These also looked dirty. I did not go near him when he called me. He said in a pleading voice that he had not drunk and would not behave like a drunkard. So I went to him with tears in my eyes. He put the basket near me saying that it contained very good vegetables and costly fruits. He folded his hands in an apologetic manner and tears came in his eyes. I also started crying. I did not know what to tell him. I was too young to give him any advice. His tears made me very sad. I knew he was shedding the tears of helplessness, repentance and affection. I could visualise the terrible conflict in his mind. But what could I do?

I wished my husband would come back early. Bhai said I should cook nice vegetables from the basket for Kanti, for Kanti liked them. Then he placed his hands on my head and said, "Look my child, I am a very bad man, I am unworthy of your selfless service. I know my son loves me and he will keep me with him till the end. But I am much too addicted to this vice; I am helpless. I cannot be corrected. My child, do not cry. Pardon this old man. Tell

Kanti also to pardon me. Beta forgive me."[2] Then he put both his hands on my head and said, "May God bless you. You are my Manu."

It was really heartbreaking.

After he went I sat and cried and prayed for him. Though he was a drunkard he possessed a golden heart. I was prepared to do any service for him, provided he stayed with us.

But the question did not arise. Bhai left us. We did not hear from him for a long time. As time would heal the wound, the memory of my father-in-law became a faint remembrance. We shifted to another home in another locality.

Suddenly and surprisingly, one evening he came to our new home. I was surprised as to how he found out our new address. He came, of course, in a drunk condition. He had a big packet-like thing in his hands. He talked to his son for a while. Then he asked me to bring a pen. He opened that packet. There was my mother-in-law's enlarged photograph. He was going to present it to me. He wanted to write something below the photo. He took the pen, but his hands trembled. He scribbled, "To my daughter-in-law", and gave the photo to me. He told me to treasure it. Then he asked me to look into the eyes of my mother-in-law. He said, "Don't the eyes look beautiful? Doesn't she look very kind and dignified? And pretty?" He laughed loudly and after sometime went away. Again the same silence prevailed in the house and we had no knowledge about his whereabouts. I felt too much for him. I loved him as my father. I worried about him being alone and uncared for. But we were helpless. How much I wished that he had stayed with us till the end.

The news of the assassination of Bapuji flashed in every corner and India was plunged into grief and everyone was shocked. As we were his nearest relations, Minister Dasappa took sympathy on us, and he sent a message to us that he would arrange to send us to Delhi in a military aircraft. But he could not send us on the very same day of the assassination for want of seats. My husband's final M.B.B.S. examination was to take place very soon, so he could not go. However, my son Shanti and I flew to Delhi.

---

2. Translator's note: Gujarati phrase *"Mane maf karjo"* in the original.

So we could reach only on 31 January and I could not take part in the funeral procession, but I and my son were there for the rest of the rites. And our seats were booked in the cistern special.

We stayed at Devdaskaka's place at Hindustan Times. To my great surprise, I saw my father-in-law entering Devdaskaka's home with a small bedding in his hands. I got up and did pranam to him. He seemed to be in a very bad mood. He did not talk to me or ask anything of me. He entered Kaka's room. He looked very tired and sick. After sometime he called me and gave me his kerchief and banian to wash. I did the job.

Bhai came to Delhi to do the sacred performance of Asthivisarjan of his father. But, with a heart full of grief and shame, I saw my father-in-law leaving the house. Before he left he said, "Beta I am leaving." That is all. The end of the story.

Who is responsible for Bhai's ruin? Let the reader draw his own conclusions; but I, his daughter-in-law who had the little privilege of his fatherly affection, tell you, though he was a drunkard, he possessed a lot of good qualities which I have not seen in others—not even in 'Gandhians'. If the circumstances were different and favourable to him, he would have excelled everyone and would have shown his intelligence and worthiness beyond expectations. Whatever the world may say he was not at all a bad man.

May God give peace to the soul of my father-in-law. Amen.

Saraswati K. Gandhi
October 1974
Mumbai

Appendix 5 Affection for Ba
by Vanmala Parikh

Once Ba and Bapu were travelling by train. As the Jabalpur Mail reached the Katni station, a call, different from those heard at other stations, reached their ears: "Kasturba Mata ki Jai." Ba was surprised. She stretched her neck out of the train window and looked out—she found Harilal standing on the platform.

The once-strong physique was now feeble and weak. All the front teeth were missing. His clothes were torn. He came to the window and took out an orange from his pocket. "Ba, I have brought this for you."

Before Ba could respond, Bapu came to the window. He asked, "Haven't you brought anything for me?"

"No. This is for Ba. I want to tell you that you have achieved greatness because of Ba," replied Harilalbhai.

"There is no doubt about that. Would you like to come with us?"

"No. I have come to meet Ba."

Bapu went back to his seat. Mother and son continued talking.

"Ba, take this orange."

"Where did you get it from?"

"Does it matter from where I got it? I have got it for you with love. I begged for it."

Ba took the orange in her hand. But Harilal was not satisfied. He said, "Ba, you have to eat this orange. If you are not going to eat it, give it back."

"Give it to me. I will eat the orange." She looked at him for a while and said, "Look at the state you are in. At least consider whose son you are. Come, come with us."

But he knew how to bring this part of the conversation to an end. "Don't even mention it. There is no redemption from my condition."

Tears filled her eyes. The guard blew his whistle. The train moved. Harilal said, "Ba, only you must eat the orange."

As the train moved Ba realised that she had given him nothing. "I couldn't even give him fruits! He must be starving. Let me see if I can still give him something."

She took out some fruits from the basket and looked out. The train had moved ahead leaving the platform behind.

They heard a feeble voice, "Mata Kasturba ki Jai."[1]

Vanmala Parikh
Amara Ba

---

1. Excerpt from Vanmala Parikh's *Amara Ba.* It has not been possible to ascertain a precise date for this incident.

Translator's Appendices

compiled
by
Tridip Suhrud

A Note on the Translator's Appendices

I have added twelve new appendices to the work of Chandulal Dalal. This requires an explanation. I was moved by the same impulse that informs the works of Chandulal Dalal and Neelam Parikh. Chandulal Dalal was an archivist and his intimate knowledge of the archives of the Sabarmati Ashram Preservation and Memorial Trust is evident in his writing. He included five documents as appendices to the book, two of which were written at his request for the book.

Neelam Parikh's biography of Harilal is significant for the new letters that she published for the first time. Twenty-nine of these letters from Gandhiji to Harilal were not included even in the *Collected Works of Mahatma Gandhi (CWMG)*. She also published Harilal's letters to Gulabbehn and his sister-in-law Balibehn, apart from several other letters.

The twelve appendices presented here contain 110 items—98 letters, 6 articles, 4 tables and 2 family trees.

Appendices 1, 2 and 3 contain material from the *CWMG*, it represents all of Gandhiji's published letters to Harilal, Gulabbehn and his public statements concerning Harilal.

Appendices 4, 6, 7, 8, 9 and 10 have been taken from Neelam Parikh's book, albeit in my translation. Appendix 4 has twenty-eight letters from Gandhiji to Harilal, and one to Gulabbehn. Many of these letters are undated, but an attempt has been made to ascertain the possible date(s) from the evidence contained within the letter. Appendix 6 has one letter from Harilal to Gulabbehn. Appendix 7 has thirteen letters from Harilal to Balibehn, his sister-in-law. They contain the most intimate account of his life after the death of Gulabbehn. Appendix 8 has two letters of Gulabbehn to Balibehn, they give an account of her life with Harilal. These are the only two of her letters available, apart from her letter in verse to Harilal which has been published in the book. Appendix 9 has two letters that Harilal wrote to his daughter Manubehn Mashruwala. These are the only published letters of Harilal to his children. Appendix 10 contains Kasturba's letter to Harilal.

Appendix 5 has two letters that Harilal wrote to Mrs. and Rev. Joseph Doke. These letters have been taken from Eric Itzkin's compilation *Gandhi's Johannesburg: Birth Place of Satyagraha.*[1]

Appendix 11 contains four tables giving details of the imprisonments of Gandhiji, Kasturba, Harilal and Manilal during the satyagraha in South Africa. The arrests, imprisonments and their impact on the lives of the Gandhi family are recurring themes in the early part of the book and the letters of this period.

The two family trees – one of the extended Gandhi family and one of Harilal and Gulabbehn's family – are included as Appendix 12 to give an idea of the interrelatedness of the various members of the Gandhi family mentioned in the book. The Gandhi family tree is not updated, on purpose. It includes only those generations that are mentioned in the book.

These appendices are intended to supplement the biography of Harilal written by Chandulal Dalal and they bring together at one place all available source material for future scholars.

Tridip Suhrud

1. Eric Itzkin, *Gandhi's Johannesburg: Birth Place of Satyagraha* (Johannesburg: Witwatersrand University Press and Museum Africa, 2000).

Translator's Appendix 1

Wednesday [27 January 1909][1]

Chi. Harilal,

Your letter to hand. I can see that you are unhappy. I have got to accept your opinion as to whether you would be happy or not on account of separation. However, I see that you will have to undergo imprisonment for a long period. I would like to know what you think about it. Please write to me in detail. The struggle is likely to be a prolonged one. There are some indications of its being a short one also. There is a likelihood of Lord Curzon interceding. Let me know what arrangement should be made in regard to Chanchal during your absence. More when I have time.

I have not been able to follow what you say about taking a stone in exchange for a pie. In what context have you written that?

You may not have to come here before the 5th.

Blessings from Mohandas

[P.S.] Was the Bhagwat read?

Fagan Sud 5 [5 March 1911][2]

Chi. Harilal,

I had your letter when it was least expected. We are all surprised whenever a letter comes from you. The general expectation is to have no letter from you.

What you write about Ba is not true. Had she intended to go she would hardly have been scared by my stipulation. And my condition also was meaningless. If she had wanted to return she could have borrowed money

1. *CWMG*, vol. 9, p. 173.
2. *CWMG*, vol. 10, p. 428–29.

from anybody and done so. The fact is that Ba does not know her own mind. However I have nothing to say against your pleading for her.

There is nothing to be ashamed of in your being weak in mathematics and general literary education. You could have learnt them had I given you the necessary opportunity. The practical knowledge boys in India possess is not due to the education they receive in schools, but is due to the unique Indian way of life. It is due to the meritorious deeds of our ancestors that we find healthy standards of behaviour, thrift, etc., around us, in spite of the repeated inroads of modern education, the immorality that we see among the people and their growing selfishness. This I am writing to you to give you courage and ask you to go deeper into the matter and observe things for yourself. It is not right to attribute the relation of cause and effect between things after just a superficial glance.

I will not stand in the way of your studies or other ambitions that you may have, provided there is nothing positively immoral about them. You may therefore cast off all fear and pursue your studies as long as you like. I may not like some of your views, but having no suspicion about your character I do not have any anxiety on your account.

Sorabjee is sitting by me as I am writing this letter. Shelat also has come to the Farm.

The Bill has not yet had its second reading.

Blessings from Bapu

3 July 1911[3]

7.30 p.m.

Chi. Harilal,

I got your letter from Zanzibar at Phoenix. There could not have been any subsequent to that. I am expecting one again in a few days. As regards the

3. *CWMG*, vol. 11, p. 117–19.

reception you were given at Zanzibar, I was happy that most of those who took part were Khojas and secondly, that they were not put off by the mention of satyagraha. Your reply was good. I thought it proper to insert a short paragraph about it in *Indian Opinion* and you must have seen it. *The Star* publishes every week a biographical sketch of some well known person and they have published mine, too. I send you a cutting [herewith]. Please pass it on to Sorabji after reading it. He must have reached there by now.

Our people in Durban put up a fine show indeed. On Coronation Day I had been to Phoenix. The credit for the demonstrations on that day should, therefore, go to the local fighters.

Here, registration has not yet begun. I expect to send the first list to Mr. Chamney tomorrow.

I had a talk about a good many things with Manilal. He is thinking of going to England next year if the campaign is not resumed. His work in the press is good.

I have probably written to you about the vow Medh has taken.

I have now taken up school work on the Farm. I wonder how long I can keep it up. Pillay's children have all left and he himself is not here either.

Thambi Naidoo now lives in Johannesburg all the time. P.K. Naidoo is here.

Ba went to Phoenix with me. It was found necessary to take her. I have had no letter from Chanchi for a long time now.

Your brothers are all happy. They are sitting beside me reading while I write this. It is 7.30 p.m.

Messrs Ritch and Pragji arrived at the Farm today (Sunday). I propose to spend five days [of the week] at the Farm and the remaining two at Johannesburg.

Blessings from Bapu

Tolstoy Farm[4]

Vaisakh Vad 14 [27 May 1911]

Chi. Harilal,

I have the letter you wrote before leaving Delagoa Bay. It is desirable that Rami grows up under the influence of strictly Indian ideas. Accordingly, I think you have done right in deciding not to send her chocolates. However, I should caution you against taking the line that 'this must be done because Bapu wants it so.' From among the ideas I suggest, you should put only those into practice that appeal to you. I should like you to grow up in freedom. I know your motives are good. Whenever your ideas are mistaken, they will therefore get corrected automatically.

The prisoners have not been released so far but they will soon be.

It appears that the cable I sent you about [the need for] your applying for registration has not reached you. I sent it care of Nanji Dulabhdas.

Keep reading *Indian Opinion* carefully while you are there.

The following Gujarati books are eminently worth reading:

Kavyadohan, Panchikaran, Maniratnamala, Dasbodh, Chapter VI of *Yogavasishtha*—Hindi translation available—Poet Narmadashanker's *Dharma vishe Vichar*, two volumes of Raychandbhai's writings. And, of course, there are *Karanghelo* and other books. *Karanghelo* evidences the maturity of the Gujarati language. Taylor's grammar and his introduction to it are both very good. I have forgotten whether it is a preface or a separate essay on the Gujarati language.

I should advise you to make it a regular practice to read Tulsidasa's *Ramayana*. Most of the books I have listed at the end of *Indian Home Rule* are worth going through. In order to learn Sanskrit well, I would advise you always to start your reading with it. Only then will you remember and understand it all. You won't find it difficult after the first book is properly done. Do not take up the second book before you have mastered the first.

---

4. *CWMG*, vol. 11, p. 94–95.

Whenever you come across a Sanskrit verse, you should immediately try to understand its meaning in Gujarati.

Please write to me in detail and regularly.

Blessings from Mohandas

[Lawley][5]

Ashadh Vad O [25 July 1911]

Chi. Harilal,

There should have been a letter from you from India. You met Chi. Chhaganlal there, and he is now already here. I do hope there will be one by next mail.

Chhaganlal has brought news that Revashankerbhai advised you to join some commercial class in Bombay, deprecating [the idea of your going to] Ahmedabad. Chhaganlal also told me that you, on the other hand, continued to prefer Ahmedabad, up to the time he left. I still consider Ahmedabad to be better. It serves our purpose better. Though English may be less easy to learn in Ahmedabad, Gujarati, Sanskrit, etc., can certainly be done well there. I personally do not like Bombay at all. You may, however, do what you think best.

I see from Chanchi's letter that Manilal is suffering from a serious illness. Please try if you can to persuade him to come here. Let him and Bali both come. Open air and nutritious but simple food is the only remedy for a tuberculosis patient. Please write to Chanchi not to expect regular letters from me. The burden on me at present is especially heavy, I go to Johannesburg only on Mondays. This is how things go on: physical labour on the farm up to 10 a.m.; teaching work at the school from 1.00 to 4.30 p.m.; meal at 5.30 p.m. and office and other correspondence at night. As I do everything single-handed, I have no time left and I do writing work till late at night. It is 9.45 p.m. now as I write this and I have more letters to write yet.

5. *CWMG*, vol. 11, p. 129–31.

Mr. & Mrs. John, Rambhabhai, Mrs. Phillips, Mr. K. Naidoo and his wife are at the Farm. There are five boys and two girls in my school. But as they all belong to different standards, even these few are too many.

I am still on saltless diet. I personally feel better for it and as for Ba, it appears her very life has been saved. So far as I can see, she is a new woman altogether. Even the children take saltless diet on alternate weeks. It is possible they might, by and by, adopt it for good. Mr. Kallenbach has also started the experiment of saltless diet. I have a feeling that it purifies the blood to a very high degree.

Manilal is at Phoenix. It seems to me his mind is quite at peace there.

I saw Mr. Smuts again as Mr. Quinn's comrades have not yet been released. I still hope that they will be. Only two persons remain now. Smuts talked about the new Bill also. I found him quite amenable, in conversation at least. Perhaps he might even repeal the tax on women in Natal. I took occasion to raise this issue as well.

Let me know how Chanchi and Rami are doing. You may send both here whenever you feel inclined to. Take the money required from Revashankerbhai. Ba simply longs for them. I told her that as you were in India the decision regarding their coming here should be left to you.

Could you read anything while on board ship? Was your luggage inspected on your landing at Bombay? Give me all such details.

Blessings from Mohandas

[About 7 October 1911][6]

...Manilal Adalaja has expired. This is a cruel blow. You should take a lesson from it. I wish that in your infatuation for modern education you would not sacrifice your health. I shall write no more, since I have already told you of my views on the subject.

I have received what looks like an invitation to be President of the Congress. I have accepted it on condition that I have the utmost freedom

6. *CWMG*, vol. 11, p. 165.

[to express my views]. I do not covet the position but, in case I do have to come, we shall have occasion to meet.

[Lawley][7]
Maha Vad 0 [18 February 1912]

Chi. Harilal,

I have had a letter from you after many months. You say you try to be regular, but you seem to have failed in your effort, and the fresh hope you held out to me has not been fulfilled. Since you wrote last, there have been two posts without a letter from you.

Chanchi has expressed a desire to stay on with you and asked for my opinion. I have replied to her, and given her other news as well. She will send the letter on to you. If she does not, ask for it. I do not therefore repeat [its contents]. I have no objection to your living together. Do what you like and live as you deem proper.

Your staying with Sheth Miankhan is all right. Press him once again to accept some rent. I shall speak to Chandabhai when I meet him.

Why Chanchi [should have] the same disease as Ba...[8]

[Lawley][9]
Shravan Vad 2 [29 August 1912]

Chi. Harilal,

It would seem you have made up your mind not to write.

I enclose a letter from uncle Karsandas. I just do not understand this debt. I do not know how the expenditure on Gokuldas's marriage came to be incurred, and by whom. If you remember anything, however, let me know

---

7. *CWMG*, vol. 11, p. 238.
8. Rest of the pages of this letter are missing.
9. *CWMG*, vol. 11, p. 312–13.

what expenditure I had agreed to. It is unlikely that I agreed to so large an amount. All the same, tell me what you know.

At present, preparations for Professor Gokhale's visit are going on. Mr. Kotwal has been working hard on the Farm. Jekibehn has also been helping. Manilal is occupied with his studies. Ramdas and Devdas, too, study regularly, and work on the farm as well.

Anibehn is also on the Farm.

I shall be going to Durban in a day or two to receive Mr. Polak. Ba and Devdas will go with me and stay in Phoenix for some time.

Chanchi can come over here whenever she feels like it. I should like you to send me some news from your end.

Blessings from Bapu

[Phoenix][10]

Shravan Vad 9 [5 September 1912]

Chi. Harilal,

I have your letter. I am surprised. I cannot recall a single month during which I did not write to you. I am certain that my letters to you have miscarried. You complain that there has been no letter from me and say you are sad on that account. We, in the absence of letters from you...[11] let us see what happens at the address. Ba, Devdas and I have come over to Phoenix. I brought Ba over because she was very ill. Devdas [too] was very keen [to come here]. The understanding with him is that he should continue at Phoenix till my next visit, learn composing while still attending to studies and live on a salt-free diet for 28 days in the month. For the present at least, he does all this.

---

10. *CWMG*, vol. 11, 315–16.
11. A page missing here.

I have made further changes in my way of life, which I hope to describe when I have the time.

Mr. and Mrs. Polak will stay in Durban for the present. I have advised Mr. Polak to start practice. Let us see what happens.

Since the Immigration Officer here is strict nowadays, Mr. Pragji has not landed as yet. He will probably do so tomorrow.

Mr. Sorabji continues to write.

Manilal is busy with his studies. Ramdas, Mr. Kotwal, Jekibehn, Ani, etc., are on the Farm.

Mr. Kotwal and I also live on one meal a day. After hearing from Chanchi about your one-meal practice, I, too, felt strongly inclined to adopt it. Mr. Kotwal offering to join me, the idea was immediately put into practice. Follow any course that you like, so long as you are mindful of your health. I shall not forgive you if you ruin your health. I cannot help feeling that the time and money spent on French are being wasted. I can give you no idea of how much better it would have been if you had spent this valuable time on Sanskrit. The atmosphere, however, in which you move nowadays being corrupt, you thought of French. What a good thing it would have been if you had taken up Sanskrit! Though that might have delayed your passing the examination by a year. Knowledge of Sanskrit opens the doors to all the Indian languages. These doors, you went out of your way to shut. I make these observations, since you opened the subject of French again. I should be happier if you would reconsider the matter even now and start on Sanskrit, sacrificing a year and spending Rs. 8 instead of Rs. 7 on private coaching. Do as you will, however; I do not wish to stand in the way of your joining any standard you choose. Treat my advice as no more than that of a close friend.

Blessings from Mohandas

[P.S.] I have not been able to understand why Chanchi did not come.

Cable when you send her so that I can arrange for her landing. It was Chanchi who gave the news about Rami.

[Lawley][12]

Aso Sud 6 [16 October 1912]

Chi. Harilal,

I have your letter after so many months. My letters to you seem to have gone astray.

I have written to Revashankerbhai about your attending the Congress.

You have not understood the step I have taken regarding Sorabji. The chief thing is that he is a Parsi, and it befits a Hindu to encourage him. If Sorabji succeeds in becoming a barrister, his responsibilities will increase. Sorabji's services cannot be used beyond a certain point, but this is not true of Medh. That is why I would not encourage Medh to be a barrister. How then could I ever encourage you [to become one]? If I did, all my ideas would go by the board; though, at present, you will not appreciate them. We shall discuss them if and when we meet. Just now you should only attend to the strengthening of your character in your own way—that is all I want. I am sure you will change your ideas in future. You have again succumbed to passion in regard to Chanchal. I can well understand it. The fault does not lie with the Ahmedabad [atmosphere]. The thing itself is so difficult that you cannot attain it without great effort and careful and sustained thought. If you, however, continue in your endeavour you may some day overcome the weakening passion. You will be a different man altogether when you have succeeded in overcoming it. You will have a new strength. From your letter I gather that Chanchi will not now be able to come here for a couple of years.

Blessings from Bapu

[Phoenix][13]

Posh Vad 4 [26 January 1913]

Chi. Harilal,

Medh has had a letter in which his father gives news of your failure. You should have written to me.

---

12. *CWMG*, vol. 11, p. 33–34.
13. *CWMG*, vol. 11, pp. 449–50.

I have not felt disappointed over your failure. Since you have resolved to pass that examination, go on working for it again. Send me your question-papers. You must have preserved them. Let me know in which subject you failed.

I read in *Mumbai Samachar* that you were present at the Gokhale meeting. Give me your impressions of it.

I am arranging to go there in six months. I should certainly be able to go if a law satisfying to our demands is passed; so it appears. I have therefore settled in Phoenix. I don't wish to stir out from here for five months.

There are in all 30 children to be taught, including those in Phoenix. Jekibehn, Miss West, one Patel named Maganbhai, Kashi and I do the teaching. I get up at 4.45 in the morning and wake up the children at five. The press hands, the schoolchildren and I do farming from 6 to 8. Between 8 and 8.30, the students and the press hands have breakfast. At 8.30, all the press hands return to the land and work there until 11. I take the children to the school, where they are taught to read and write from 8.30 to 10.30. From 10.30 to 11, again, they learn farm-work.

Between 11 and 12.30, people bathe and eat. From 12.30 to 4.30, work in the press where the older boys train for two hours; the last two hours [are spent] reading and writing in the school. I cannot at all look after the school in the afternoons. I may be able to do so, I think, when things settle down a bit.

At 5.30 the boys have dinner. After katha kirtan from 7 to 7.30, the boys go to sleep. From 7.30 to 9, I go over Manilal's lessons. Das wants to start a press in Durban. Perhaps Virji, too, will go there.

Send this letter for Chanchi to read. I have no time to write her another.

Blessings from Bapu

Phagan Sud 6 [14 March 1913][14]

Chi. Harilal,

After many months I have had a letter from you. Every time you express regret and say you are sorry for not writing regularly. Your repentance has no

---

14. *CWMG*, vol. 11, p. 484–85.

meaning either for you or for me. Repentance will bear fruit only when it relates to one's failure to do a thing despite one's best effort and when it is followed by greater vigilance in guarding against further failure. Your regret amounts to mere formality. Do children have to be formal with parents?

As soon as I knew of your examination [result] from another source, I wrote you a letter. But it could not be posted until now, because the diary containing your address had been misplaced. You will therefore get that letter as well as this one about the same time.

I am not the only one to wait anxiously for a letter from you. Ba keeps on inquiring, and so do Miss Schlesin and the others.

Your mind has not become calm even there. I do not understand what it is that you want. All that I can make out is that you want to live in Ahmedabad and with Chanchi. Perhaps you wrote to the Doctor too, about this. You may live as suits you best.

In reply to the second portion of your letter, I shall say only this: "Live in any way that suits you, [but] strive to realise God anyhow." I shall not argue.

Our paths may well be different. If our destination is the same, we shall meet there. What would it matter even if we should follow contrary paths? I am not so arrogant as to believe that I am wholly right and others, in the wrong. Of course, I hold on to the idea that I must do what seems to be my duty. Though I know that we do not become equal even if I give you this freedom, because, in following a course opposed to my ideas, you have to depend on me for money. I wish I could release you even from this situation [of dependence] and then argue with you as an equal. But how is this possible? If, impelled by my sense of duty, I have erred in giving up the source of my income, I shall of course have to repent for that. Have I not, however, done an injustice because in doing this I failed to take my sons' interests into account? My answer is "No." I did consider their interests, too, accordingly to my own lights. Whether my judgement was right or wrong time alone will show to us both.

I observe that England is still on your lips. Please overcome the desire. Your time is not yet.

Send me the question-papers of your examination if you have preserved them.

Manilal is deep in his studies. He is interested in them. I give him an hour and a half every day. Let me know what books you read—for your examination, I mean. Send me some samples of your English composition.

Blessings from Bapu

P.S. Ramdas and Devdas also study fairly well, but they have developed no interest in their studies. Ba is well, more or less. Anandlal has left Phoenix that he may be able to look after Abhechand's business.

[Durban][15]

Bhadarva Vad 3 [18 September 1913]

Chi. Harilal,

You have not kept your promise about writing to me. You gave such a promise more than once and you have broken it every time.

I am very unhappy that your health has gone down. I always thought it would. I even warned you. You know that, though you went with my consent, I did not want you to go. Even now, your way of life and your ideas do not appeal to me. Personally, I feel that the education you are having is of the wrong kind. You have harmed Chanchi's interests and now you are harming those of the children. Still, I regard you as friend, with due affection, so that I do not wish to order you. I want to bring you round only by appealing to you. I do not wish to exploit your filial piety to make you do anything. There is no anger in this. I do this as a matter of duty. Still I must advise you to shake off this craze for examinations. If you pass, it won't impress me much. If you fail, you will feel very unhappy. However, take the course you think is best. If you give up the thought of examinations and if, when you get this letter, the struggle here is continuing, come over here along with Chanchi, both of you prepared for imprisonment. Chanchi has

15. *CWMG*, vol. 12, p. 189–91.

otherwise no right to come now. If the struggle ends soon, I shall go there immediately and we shall have a good hug and a talk.

There is only one remedy for your dyspepsia—a daily walk of 15 miles. By way of diet, you should have solid food, according to appetite, which you can chew. If you have read the chapters on health, the experiments described there will help you to get rid of [the complaint] altogether. It is not surprising that you have lost your mental powers. The education there is useless because it is ill-conceived. Since you have never reflected over the mental vacuity of thousands of educated people, what can I say and to whom am I to say it? What have your studies been that you should acquire strength of mind through them? Where the aim is merely to pass an examination, the result is bound to be unhappy. As far back as thirty years ago, Mr. Ranade used to discuss this problem. Just think of the condition of the ordinary B.A. What can you do if, after passing a big examination, you find yourself a physical or mental wreck? Have you had a careful look at things round you?

Ba, Ramdas, Kashi, Santok, Chhaganlal, Kuppu, Govindoo, Revashankar, Shivpujan, Raojibhai, Maganbhai, Sam, Rustomjee Sheth, Solomon and others have set out to get imprisoned. They were arrested at Volksrust on Tuesday. I am writing this letter on the morning of Thursday. There has been no telegram yet about what happened yesterday. Devdas is in Phoenix. He has acquired great efficiency. I get up at 3.30 a.m. and Devdas at 4.30 a.m. At 5, studies and other activities begin. He has filled out a little. Of course, changes do occur in this schedule. For the present, the boys who have remained behind go without salt on all days except Sunday. They propose to continue the practice as long as the satyagraha lasts. Maganlal and Miss West will look after the children. I shall leave for Johannesburg on Saturday. People at Johannesburg will then try to get arrested. I shall get arrested last. I have thought out a way of getting arrested, one which will require a little especial courage. I am constantly praying to God to grant me that. Manilal is in Johannesburg. He has now subjected himself to strict vows and is going through a course of penitence. He will court arrest in Johannesburg. Jeki has accompanied Ba to get arrested. She, too, has changed her way of life altogether. Medh and Desai are also in Johannesburg. Jamnadas is impatient to be in gaol. I shall most probably wire to him to come over. I have not made up my mind, though. Please remember that you have not sent me your examination papers, which I had asked for. I am trying to make arrangements for the maintenance of Gangabhabhi. For the present, my desire to go over there has come to nothing.

Blessings from Bapu

[P.S.] My wish is that whatever steps you take should be without reference to me or my views.

[Durban][16]

Aso Vad 2 [17 October 1913]

Chi. Harilal,

It hurts me to have no letters from you. Your lethargy in this matter makes you doubly guilty. The first guilt is that you neglect the duty which you owe to your father, and the second that you break your promise to me that you would write regularly. There have been three mails [from India] and no letter from you. Mr. Sorabji and Ratanshi left after you did, but I have had more letters from them than from you. Chanchi writes more often than you do. Ba, too, is unhappy because there are no letters from you.

Both of you may come over here and get arrested. Chanchi may come while the fight is on only if she has the courage to go to gaol. I have already written to you to say that you should not wait for the examination. If you yourself wish otherwise, I do not want to come in your way. Ask for money from Doctor Saheb. It is likely that I shall be in gaol when you arrive. I think I shall succeed in getting myself arrested somehow or other. I have been making efforts to this end. If, before this letter reaches you, you hear that there has been a settlement, there will be no need for you to come over.

I want you to be fit and at peace with yourself.

Blessings from Bapu

---

16. *CWMG*, vol. 12, p. 242.

[Cape Town][17]

Phagan Sud 5 [2 March 1914]

Chi. Harilal,

I have your letter. You apologize in every letter of yours and put up a defence as well. It all seems to me sheer hypocrisy now. For years, you have been slack in writing letters, and then coming forward with apologies. Will this go on till death, I forgiving every time? And what is the point of my forgiving? Forgiving has a meaning only to the extent that the person who has apologized does not err again. My forgiving you all the time means that I should go on doing my duty as father though you may not do yours as son. My duty, of course, I shall continue to do according to my judgment. I don't believe that you are impatient to see us both; equally, this idea that you were to come here sounds insincere to me. Does one who really means to come trumpet it aloud? Now, of course, your coming is pointless, as you say. I see that your ideas and mine differ very much. Your conception of your duty as son differs from mine, but I have no right to enquire what your duty is. If you go on doing your duty as you in all sincerity conceive it to be, I shall be perfectly satisfied. Whether your idea of duty is sincere or not, I and others will be able to judge from your actions. It seems you have also applied your mind to what my duty is, and in this respect, too, our ideas differ. It should be for me to consider what my duty is. You may, nevertheless, continue to tell me what you think.

I did not reply to your letter. I got it after my release from gaol. Your suggestions, however, were carried out; that is, I wrote to Revashankerbhai that he should have a talk with you and give you more [money] as may seem necessary.

You want my advice regarding Chanchi, and also about your studies. You violate all the conditions I had made and you promised to fulfil. You were asked never to go in for studies at the cost of your health. You have failed to take care of it. No wonder that Ramdas and Manilal have outdone you.

---

17. *CWMG*, vol. 12, p. 367–69.

And Ramdas has put in a fine effort, indeed, and grown in size as well. Manilal, too, has plenty of strength and would have been stronger yet if he had not taken to the evil ways of pleasure. Even their studies I take to be sounder than yours. Your mind is now running after Bombay. You say you have Revashankerbhai's consent for that. What weight can that consent carry with me? I would submit in all humility to Revashankerbhai's judgment of a diamond. How could I listen to him in the matter of studies? You are, so it seems to me, in a state of stupefaction. What, then, am I to say? You can only think of Davar's classes. That simply stuns me. Do you think it will be much of an achievement to pass the matriculation examination? I do not even understand what it is that you want to do. I would only advise you to do nothing. Wait till my return. Meanwhile, read as you like. Do not, however, start a new venture. Later, you may talk things over with me, but only if you want to.

If, indeed, you wish to go ahead with your plan for studies, you should have Chanchi stay with me and should yourself stay away from me. I shall supply your needs. Think of Chanchi when you turn your mind to earning. If you wish to live as I want you to, stay with me and be my right hand. Use your own judgment in all these matters, taking no thought of my personal inclinations. Weighing my advice against that of others, do what you think best. I am a father who is prejudiced against you. I do not approve of your ways at all. I doubt whether you have any love for us. This statement sounds very harsh, but I see extreme insincerity in your letters. If I am mistaken in this, consider that I am in Kurukshetra and so forgive me, showing me the generosity that Shravana did to his parents. Even worldly children show some marks of love for their parents. You have shown none. Nevertheless, I am so proud a father that I attribute perfection to my children. This is an error. It is spiritual darkness. But, apart from this...[18] have not fulfilled...[19] Despite your promise, you did not send me the papers of the last year's examination. You have not taken the trouble to remember to send this year's either. I become

18. A few words are missing in the original.
19. A few words are missing in the original.

angry when writing to you and also feel like crying. This is my ignorant state, my lack of enlightenment. I ought not to be so much attached to you. I will free myself from this. Be patient with me till I succeed.

Now I have given you too long a lesson. I will write no more. I shall be satisfied if you treat me as a friend and show me the regard due to a friend. I want you to improve your character and train your inner self.

I will probably go there in April. Just now I am in Cape Town. Ba is with me. She lies hanging between life and death. Till yesterday, she was very bad indeed. There is again a little improvement. She is a mere skeleton. She gives me no trouble, but, not having succeeded yet in disciplining the palate, she suffers and pines. I am by her side the whole day. Between yesterday and today, she must have consumed the juice of two tomatoes and a teaspoonful of oil.

Blessings from Bapu

Motihari[20]

14 November 1917

Chi. Harilal,

Today is *Diwali* day. May the New Year bring you prosperity. I wish that all your aspirations are fulfilled and that all of you increase in your wealth of character, and pray that you realize more and more that this is the only real Lakshmi and our highest good lies in the worship of this alone.

Blessings from Bapu

[On the train][21]

1 May 1918

I got your letter in Delhi. What shall I write to you? Everyone acts according to his nature. The true end of all effort in life is to gain control over the

20. *CWMG*, vol. 14, p. 89–90.
21. *CWMG*, vol. 14, p. 385.

impulses of one's nature; that is dharma. Your faults will be forgotten if you make this effort. Since you are emphatic that you did not commit the theft, I may believe you but the world will not. Bear the world's censure and be more careful in future. You should give up your notion of what the world means. Your world is your employer. Have no fear if you are tried in a court of law. If you take my advice, do not engage a lawyer. Explain everything to the advocate on the other side.

You had in your hand a diamond which you have thrown away, thanks to your rash and impatient nature. You are no child. Not a little have you tasted of the good things of life. If you have had enough of that, turn back. Don't lose heart. If you are speaking the truth, don't lose your faith in it. There is no God but Truth. One's virtues are no dead matter but are all life. It is a thoughtless and self-willed life you have lived so far. I should like you to bring wisdom and discipline into it.

As things happened, I have done something very big in Delhi. You will find some account of it in the papers. I have no time to write about it. Mahadev will find some time to do so. He was an eyewitness to it all. He has taken your place, but the wish that it had been you refuses still to die. I would have died broken-hearted if I had no other sons. Even now, if you wish to be an understanding son without displacing anyone who has made himself such to me, your place is assured.

Blessings from Bapu

[Nadiad][22]

9 July 1918

I have your letter. If it was cruel to say what I felt was true, then certainly my letter was cruel. I repeat that the world will most emphatically not consider you innocent. Whatever you may have said in your sincerity, Narottam Sheth could have had no idea about your speculation. You have followed one wrong thing with another. It was not enough for you that you had lost ten thousand

22. *CWMG*, vol. 14, p. 480.

rupees. But there is no use arguing with you. May God give you wisdom. If I have made a mistake, I will set it right. If you think you can point out any, do so even now.

I understand what you say about your enlisting. I made the suggestion at a time when I did not doubt your truthfulness. I do not think I have any interest in it now. I can give you no idea of what my condition has been since I began to doubt your truthfulness.

May God bless you, I pray, and show you the right path.

Blessings from Bapu

29 August 1918[23]

Chi. Harilal,

I have your letter. My health is improving. There is no cause for anxiety. I shall have to be in bed for some days more. The nursing leaves nothing to be desired. I cannot imagine even an emperor being better looked after. I was very pleased to learn that you cook your own food and that you enjoy doing so. Maybe you will find this an instructive experience; understand through it the secret of life and, repairing past mistakes, bring light into your life. I wish you do so. I shall be happy if you keep writing regularly.

Blessings from Bapu

9 September 1918[24]

It is true that cooking takes some time but I believe that this time is not wasted. It is also generally not true that some more important work could be done during that time. Ninety-five per cent of the people waste more time every day than is taken up in cooking. I am being rather liberal in my estimate in saying ninety-five per cent. You will be surprised in how short a time

---

23. *CWMG*, vol. 15, p. 36.
24. *CWMG*, vol. 15, p. 46–47.

a person doing his own cooking finishes it when he is very busy. If I give my own example, when I was very busy with studies in England I did not take more than half an hour in the morning and in the evening for cooking. In the morning, I used to prepare porridge, and this took exactly twenty minutes; if I cooked in the evening, I prepared soup. As it did not require stirring, the only time spent was in getting the materials ready. After putting the thing on the fire, I would sit by and read. Occasionally, students come to me from Benares. I ask all of them what they do. Most Brahmins cook their own food. One of them told me that he only prepared *khichdi* and ate it with milk and pickles. While he was eating the meal, the *bhakhri* would be getting baked. This *bhakhri* he would eat with milk in the evening. In this, he spent three-quarters of an hour in all. This is an extreme case I have cited. I do not want you to be all that particular. This is only to illustrate that it is possible to do one's cooking in a very short time. That student was quite healthy and strong, because *khichdi*, milk or curds and pickles gave him all the nourishment he needed. Anyone who can get good milk or curds will care little for other things. Do not imagine that I write this to suggest that you should always cook yourself. I have said all this only in order that, on occasion, you should not hesitate in the least to do your own cooking and [when you have to do it] be so unhappy, all without reason, that you were wasting your time. Otherwise, when you have mended your ways, I can have no objection to your calling Chanchi, having good things to eat and enjoying life, within limits. Only see that you do not repeat your mistakes. I want you not to be too eager to get rich quickly.

Think of Sorabji's death, of Dr. Jivraj's being on his death-bed, of the passing away of Sir Ratan Tata. When life is so transitory, why all this restlessness? Why this running after money? Get whatever money you can earn by ordinary but steady efforts. Resolve in mind, though, that you will not forsake the path of truth in pursuit of wealth. Make your mind as firm as you can and then go ahead making money.

Blessings from Bapu

2 October 1918[25]

Chi. Harilal,

I have a feeling that I am now going. I have very little time left. The body is becoming weaker and weaker. I am not able to eat anything. But my heart is at peace and so I do not find the going at all difficult. I think whatever inheritance I am leaving to you brothers is appropriate. What would you have gained if I had left money? But the inheritance of character which I am leaving to you is invaluable in my view. I wish you to cherish it. Follow the path of religion. I have written a letter to Devdas. Ask for a copy of it. If you think you can apply that letter to yourself, do so.

[Ahmedabad][26]
31 October 1918

I got your postcard. There is nothing particular to write about today. I am always thinking how you may come to be at peace with yourself, and remain so. If I could help you by any word of mine and if I knew that word, I would write it at once. I do not know whether you have understood what this world means, but I have the clearest vision of it every moment and I see it exactly as it has been described by the sages, and that so vividly that I feel no interest in it. Activity is inescapable so long as there is this body and, therefore, the only thing that pleases me is to be ever occupied with activity of the utmost purity. It is no exaggeration to say that I experience wave after wave of joy from the practice of self-restraint which such work requires. One will find true happiness in the measure that one understands this and lives accordingly. If this calamity puts you in a frame of mind in which such happiness will be yours, we may even regard it as welcome. If your mind can ever disengage itself from its concerns, ponder over all this. We are all well. Those who were ill are all on the way to recovery—I too am doing well. I take it that you show all the letters to Ba and hence I do not write separately to her.

---

25. *CWMG*, vol. 91, supplementary vol. 1, p. 170.
26. *CWMG*, vol. 15, p. 60.

[Ahmedabad][27]

26 November 1918

Chi. Harilal,

I gave you some news about myself yesterday. I give you more today. My health is both good and bad. I feel that the improvement which should have taken place in some respects has not come about. I cannot complain about food now. Everyone says that it would be better for me to go out for some time, and I also think I should. I have been, therefore, thinking of doing so, and am making arrangements. It will be good if you come over before I leave. Whatever you wish to say, you may pour out before me without any hesitation. If you cannot give vent to your feelings before me, before whom else can you do so? I shall be a true friend to you. What would it matter if there should be any difference of opinion between us about any scheme of yours? We shall have a quiet talk. The final decision will rest with you. I fully realize that your state at present is like that of a man dreaming. Your responsibilities have increased, your trials have increased and your temptations will increase likewise. To a man with a family, the fact of being such, that is, having a wife, is a great check. This check over you has disappeared. Two paths branch out from where you stand now. You have to decide which you will take. There is a bhajan we often sing in the Ashram; its first line runs: *Nirbal ke bala Rama.*

One cannot pray to God for help in a spirit of pride but only if one confesses oneself as helpless. As I lie in bed, every day I realize how insignificant we are, how very full of attachments and aversions, and what evil desires sway us. Often I am filled with shame by the unworthiness of my mind. Many a time I fall into despair because of the attention my body craves and wish that it should perish. From my condition, I can very well judge that of others. I shall give you the full benefit of my experience; you may accept what you can. All this after you come.

Blessings from Bapu

27. *CWMG*, vol. 15, p. 65–66.

23 February 1919[28]

TO

THE MOST WORTHY FIRM OF SATYAGRAHIS

Just as I was about to start this letter, I had to hold a court. The accused was Rasik, and the complainant an innocent dog. The latter declared by his wailing that he had been assaulted by someone. I discovered that the guilty party was Rasik. The accused admitted his guilt and confessed previous offences as well. I thought of Lord Krishna and Shishupal. Shri Krishnachandra had forgiven a hundred offences, of the latter. And so the court had compassion and forgave the accused, Rasik, five offences, warning him at the same time that, if he repeated the offence again, it would not be forgiven and that he would be made to realize, in his own person, the dog's suffering when stoned.

As I write this, Kantilal is holding the inkstand. He and Ramibehn read the letter as I proceed and correct me. The accused, too, is here, meekly standing by the bed. Manubai interrupts now and then to give us the benefit of her laughter. And now she has started crying, wanting to climb up the bed. The scene reminds me of your childhood, of that of Jadibehn and others.

Though I am confined to bed, you will see from the foregoing that my health can pass as good.

Satyagraha is in the air here. Mahadev will write to you about it all—or I, if I can.

Blessings from Bapu

5 May 1919[29]

I got your letter of *Chaitra Vad* 10. My health has begun to feel the strain now. There is much too heavy a pressure on the brain. God will keep this body going as long as He wants work from it. I have not read *The Englishman*

28. *CWMG*, vol. 15, p. 100–01.
29. *CWMG*, vol. 15, p. 277–78.

and I do not read it generally. Yes, I think it will be good if you keep sending me cuttings from there.

Mrs. Besant is in a pitiable condition. She is completely at a loss what course to adopt.

How could you ask whether the Government would really disallow the Rowlatt Bill? How can the Bill remain [on the Statute-book] while satyagrahis are alive? Personally, I believe that, if no violence breaks out, the Bills will be repealed in no more than a few months. I do not say this from inside knowledge, but from my unshakable faith in satyagraha.

I did not stop Pragji. I have left him to himself entirely. It seems he has now decided on going to Madras. He is taking Parvati with him. I did not stand in his way in this either.

I do not like your idea of going to South Africa. My own wish is that all of you, having called yourselves satyagrahis, should content yourselves with lower profits and do business only in swadeshi goods.

The children are quite happy. I did not notice that they were particularly homesick for Rajkot or Calcutta. The thing to be most happy about is that the climate has suited them. Rami seems to be improving gradually. I have sent some *jeevan* of the best quality for her from here.

Madhavdas told me of your financial difficulties. He has accepted my advice. It was that you should go forward without monetary help from anyone, that is what I would have you do. Medh, a man of sudden impulses that he is, is naturally apt to do things without thinking and enter into too many forward deals; you think nothing of risks and want to get rich quickly. Pragji cannot resist the temptation of joining a public movement. In these circumstances, you will find yourself in trouble before you know where you are. Hence it would always be my wish that you did not depend on other people's money for your ventures. Moreover, they may send me out of the country or imprison me at any time and I take it that you will not be able to continue in business then. How can you, in this situation, invest others' money? In a country where injustice prevails, there is no dignity except in poverty. It is impossible, in the prevailing condition, to amass wealth without being a party, directly or indirectly, to injustice.

Blessings from Bapu

Telegram to Harilal Gandhi[30]

[On or after 11 December 1921]

WELL DONE GOD BLESS YOU. RAMDAS, DEVDAS AND OTHERS WILL FOLLOW YOU.

The Ashram, Sabarmati[31]

Sunday, 30 May 1926

Bhai Harilal,

It is certainly not possible to reply to your letter through *Navajivan*. I am sure that the educational and other reforms which you advocate will not come about at the present time. All of them may be indications of an attitude of tolerance, but they cannot create such an attitude. At present it will be more than enough if though going our separate ways, we live in peace with each other. I cannot think just now how inter-marriages will ever become possible. How can we have a family in which one member is a vegetarian and another a non-vegetarian? In which tradition will the children of such a couple be brought up? Problem alliances of this kind will raise many other issues besides these. Any attempt at this time to persuade people to act upon your suggestions will furnish one more ground for opposition or make the achievement of political unity impossible. How unwise it is to imagine a connection between political unity and other issues where none exists!

30. *CWMG*, vol. 21, p. 567. The telegram was sent after Harilal courted arrest in Calcutta as civil resister.

31. *CWMG*, vol. 30, p. 512.

27 April 1932[32]

I will still not give up hope of your reformation, for I have not given up hope about myself. I have always believed that I was a bad man when Ba carried you in her body, but after your birth I have been doing greater and greater penance for my former life. How can I, therefore, give up all hope? I will continue to hope as long as you and I are alive. And hence, contrary to my usual practice, I am preserving your letter so that, when you have awakened, you may see the insolence of your letter and weep over it and laugh at your folly. I am not preserving this letter to throw it in your face then, but only that I may laugh at it, if God wills that I should see that day. All of us are full of short-comings. But it is our dharma to overcome them. I pray that you do so.

6 May 1933[33]

HARILAL
NIZAMIAH HOTEL
225/26 HARBOUR BUILDING,
FRERE ROAD, BOMBAY

YOUR LETTER TOUCHES ME. IF THIS FAST MEANS YOUR RETURN TO PURE LIFE IT WOULD BE DOUBLY BLESSED. SEE ME. I SHALL TRY GUIDE YOU. GOD BLESS YOU.

BAPU

19 September 1934[34]

Chi. Harilal,

I got your letter. If there has really been a change of heart in you such as you describe, my hope has been realized. In that case, I will for my part completely forget your past.

32. *CWMG*, vol. 49, p. 374–75. (Fragment in the original.)
33. *CWMG*, vol. 55, p. 128.
34. *CWMG*, vol. 59, p. 27–28.

...[35] I understand about marrying. If what you want is a companion and that must be a wife, I would not regard it as in the least blameworthy provided you find a suitable widow. There was a widow of 60 who married a man of nearly the same age. I knew her. Her only motive was desire for companionship. But perhaps there is no need to think about this just now.

Harilal Gandhi

Porbandar

3 October 1934[36]

Chi. Harilal,

I have your letter. Narandas has been a little hasty. I am sending a wire to you today as follows:

"Delay spending money received from Narandas. Await letter. Bapu"[37]

I woke up at 2.30 and started thinking about my dharma towards you. I couldn't go to sleep again and left the bed at 2.45. After cleaning my teeth and drinking warm water with honey, I have set down to write this.

I want the loan which Narandas may give you to be debited to his private account. Till I am quite sure, I do not wish to draw your expenses from a public fund or secure them from friends in public life. It would be compromising dharma to do so.

I do not yet believe in your regeneration. I must have independent proof of that. I, therefore, do not wish to ask you for an assurance to that effect. However, I wish to assure myself through your conduct. If you have produced a good impression on Ishvarlal with whom you are staying, ask him to write to me. And let me have your own replies to the following questions.

1. Have you touched liquor any time after you wrote your first letter to me from there?

---

35. Omission as in the source.
36. *CWMG*, vol. 59, p. 110–12.
37. The wire message is in English.

2. Have you indulged in sexual pleasure through mind, speech or body?
3. Do you smoke?
4. Have you any other addiction?

Let there be this understanding between you and me. If at any time you break your word to me or if it is proved that you have deceived me, I should fast for at least seven days. I may fast even longer, if I wish and have the strength to do so, in case your breach of promise or misdeed pains me very much. Though I was still hopeful about you, I had hardened my heart to stone and did not give you any monetary help. But I felt from the letter which you wrote to me from Porbandar that there had been a change of heart in you and wanted to give you whatever help I could.

If you have come to have trust in my way of life and my understanding of dharma, you will be convinced of the correctness of whatever demands I make or advice I give. Please do not ask me to discuss and explain, but carry out my suggestions as a patient does those of a vaid as so many orders. Do not do anything through a feeling that because I am your father you have a special dharma towards me. You may have such dharma to help me when I am completely disabled. But in this matter treat me as a friend, a vaid and a co-worker. Why are you so keen on staying in Porbandar? It would be convenient for me to help you if you stayed in Rajkot.

If, however, you decide to stay in Porbandar, I will have no objection to your staying in our ancestral house. Is any part of it vacant? Does it get good air?

Till I am satisfied, and Ramjibhai also is satisfied, that you have become steady, please give up the idea of starting a store. With the help of khadi samples, you may secure what orders you can in Porbandar.

If you have come to have the same faith in the spinning-wheel and khadi that I have, you should enthusiastically start learning spinning on the *takli* and the spinning-wheel, and spin daily on the former. Learn all the antecedent processes also. You can do all this more easily in Rajkot. Are you ready to live with me and under my eyes? I may like you to do that after the Congress session is over.

Kakasaheb and Kishorelalbhai are here with me. And Vinoba also, of course.

Whatever you do, do after full deliberation. Do not do anything that is beyond your strength, nor anything that does not appeal to your heart or reason. Do not try to establish good relations with me merely in order that you may be able to live. You have been able to do that somehow all these years. Doesn't God provide for everybody, good or bad, in some manner or other? But imperfect man must continue to discriminate between good and evil till the end of his life. Nobody living in the flesh has become perfect or will ever become, for the marriage of the *atman* with the material body is in itself a limitation of its perfection. Marriage by its very nature is a limitation. When the *atman* becomes a perfect *brahmachari*, it will no longer create new bodies for itself. But why need I take you into all this?

May you attain the highest good. May God dwell in you. He alone is your true Guru. "Friends of the body but care for their own interests; they will keep away at the end." You should, therefore, do as the self within bids you, with God as witness. It will not hurt me in the least if you do not accept my advice. But it will hurt me very much indeed if you deceive me. I am an old man now, and you are not a child.

Blessings from Bapu

4 October 1934[38]

Chi. Harilal,

I got your letter. I liked it. I am glad that you have gone to Rajkot. If you continue to accept my advice with more and more conviction, your good will be assured and I shall feel supremely happy. God has given you sufficient ability. It is not too late yet. If the heart has become pure, the body also will regain its light. I will write more in the next letter.

I think Bali should be repaid the money that you have spent.

Blessings from Bapu

38. *CWMG*, vol. 59, p. 122.

6 October 1934[39]

Chi. Harilal,

I wrote a brief reply to your last letter. I said in it that I would write more and here it is.

The nine implications of khadi work which you have explained are correct. We can add some more, but these nine are enough. Let us immediately start putting into practice whichever of them apply to you and me. It was for this reason that I suggested to you to learn khadi work. That means learning all the operations from the sowing of cotton in the fields to the manufacture of khadi and mastering the processes involved in the latter, as also learning the ways and means of selling the khadi produced. All these things should be studied scientifically.

I am making arrangements for sending the books.

I am glad to learn that you are tired of travelling. I shall prefer your staying at Rajkot instead of at Porbandar, as I think that you will be safer there. Narandas's being in Rajkot is one more reason why I should like you to stay there. Moreover, Bali, Manu, etc., are also there. In your awakened state, you can serve Bali, Phuli and Manu in a great many ways. But all this will have meaning only if you can find peace of mind in that way.

Harilal

Rajkot

~

11 October 1934[40]

Chi. Harilal,

I liked your letter very much. I hope the changes in you will endure. You should have patience. Since you have come to trust me, there will be no difficulty.

We shall think before asking Nanalalbhai for help.

Blessings from Bapu

~

---

39. *CWMG*, vol. 59, p. 141–42.
40. *CWMG*, vol. 59, p. 162.

17 October 1934[41]

Chi. Harilal,

You are constantly in my thoughts. If I had time, I would go on inflicting long letters on you. If the change that you have described endures, a painful episode in my life would end and I would be extremely happy in this last stage of my life.

I do not wish that you should do anything beyond your strength. Only as much as your reason and heart accept will endure and seem natural. I am sure that if you followed rules of diet, etc., you would be completely all right. Do not regard yourself as an old man.

I would not be pained if you could do nothing, but I would certainly be pained if you were to break your word to me or do anything which might amount to breach of trust with anybody.

At the moment, it is I who trust you most. Others, that is Ba, Ramdas, Devdas, Kanti, etc., are less hopeful for they have memories of bitter experiences. I have them, too, but I had never given up hope about you, and always believed that one day you would be reformed. I believe that that day has come now. May God help you.

Write to me and give me exact details of your debts and the names of the parties to whom you owe them. I wish to help you as much as I can consistently with my dharma. Do you have to pay interest on the loans?

I see that you have not been able to give up smoking. So long as you find it absolutely necessary to smoke, you may do so as if you were taking medicine. Perhaps you do not know that it is not in the least difficult to give up smoking. It can be done by adopting a simple diet. What do you eat? Are you ready to make changes in your diet?

I had a long letter from Maneklal. He says that you are afraid of temptations in Rajkot. If there is the slightest truth in that, let me know. Have no hesitation at all in telling me the exact truth. Write to me frankly and open out your heart as you would do to a very intimate friend. You made many

41. *CWMG*, vol. 59, p. 187–88.

friends in the past. Forget now the harm that those friendships did you. Now regard me as your only friend. That will certainly do you no harm. And, moreover, there is a Supreme Friend between you and me, who dwells in our hearts and, therefore, knows our thoughts.

I very much wish to send for you here and keep you with me. But my condition is quite peculiar just now. I don't enjoy a moment's leisure. I rise up at 2.30 every morning. Today I rose at 1.45. It is nearing 3.30 now. If I called you, I would feel tempted to talk with you, which, however, I cannot afford to do. I can't stop thinking about you all the times, though. Maybe, father's love doesn't fall away from even a devotee of Mother *Gita*, or perhaps the *Gita* teaches that I should be thus concerned with you. Be that as it may. If you have no fear just now of being overcome by temptations, remain there for the time being and learn spinning on the *takli*, etc., thoroughly. If you are not keeping a diary, start doing so. A letter for Manu is enclosed. Ramdas is fairly well. He is still in hospital, though. There is no fever, but he has not regained strength.

14 February 1935[42]

Chi. Harilal,

I have received your letter. It is my earnest desire to have you with me if you can come willingly. I think of you every day. If you have come to have the same faith about the truthfulness of my life, your place from now on is with me. What you hope to get in Amreli can be had here and in the neighbourhood. And if you are in a position to do some work, I have plenty of it. Moreover you will have an unlimited number of good companions here. The most weighty argument is that there is no certainty about me. One cannot say when I may get the invitation to go to the temple.[43] I would therefore like you to be with me. Now you do whatever you deem proper. Kanti will write to you about the other part of the letter. Maybe we shall meet very soon.

Blessings from Bapu

---

42. *CWMG*, vol. 60, p. 226
43. Jail.

Ramanawami, 12 April 1935[44]

Chi. Harilal,

I have been wanting to write to you all these days, but for one thing and another I never got the time. I have snatched a little time somehow today.

Mahadev had had a little talk with me. Kishorelal wrote and acquainted me with the matter.

I understand your problem. You don't wish to deceive yourself or me. You still crave for sex pleasure. If so, you must satisfy your craving. You can suppress it only when you feel a strong aversion to worldly pleasures.

My difficulty is this. How can I, who have always advocated renunciation of sex, encourage you to gratify it? How can I help you to do so? I can tolerate your remarrying. But how can you carry on your search for a wife while staying with me? If I invited you to come and stay with me, even though I knew your desire to remarry, I did so not with the intention of helping you to get married but with the hope that your staying with me might help your mind to calm down. Besides, I also wanted to understand your change of heart.

I do wish to help you as much as I can. But wouldn't you on your part that I did so only within my limits? Think over this and write frankly to me now. You may say whatever you wish to.

Are your efforts to give up smoking nearing success, or do you think you will never be able to give it up?

Do not employ Mirabehn's labourers in cleaning those buildings or washing the baths. Clean whatever you can with your own hands. I am not happy about the labourers being employed even in the orchard. I tolerate that being done because of my helplessness.

Avadhesh has informed me of his final decision not to accept the sum of Rs. 15. I felt that day that you were unnecessarily hurting him. He had already yielded. Where was the need, then, to go on lecturing?

Blessings from Bapu

---

44. *CWMG*, vol. 60, p. 410–11.

22 April 1935[45]

Chi. Harilal,

There is no need at all to be in a hurry to come to a decision about Amala's[46] letter. I think you will have to drop the idea. You should write and tell her plainly that any children that may be born will have to be brought up in a simple manner. And whatever means of livelihood the Lord provides will probably be in Wardha. If you start going to women or drinking, she should be free to leave you immediately. And even this you may write only if you are sure that you wish to marry her. Amala's letter seems a good one to me, but I didn't know her as she reveals herself in it. I am, therefore, of the view that you will not be happy unless she comes to feel strongly that she cannot live without you.

It is certainly a good thing that you have not become impatient. Have patience and do only what is proper.

Blessings from Bapu

Faizpur Congress[47]

21 December 1936

Chi. Harilal,

If you can give up drinking for eight months for my sake and for nine months for the sake of Vijayshankerji, then for how long will you do so for your own sake and for the sake of God?

Bapu

14 June 1945[48]

Chi. Harilal,

I got your letter. I do get news of you from time to time. I would not at all like your going away from there. Kanti and Saraswati serve you so well, keep you

45. *CWMG*, vol. 60, p. 456–57.
46. Margarete Spiegel.
47. *CWMG*, vol. 64, p. 160.
48. *CWMG*, vol. 80, p. 321.

with them so lovingly. It is, therefore, your duty to stay with them. How can you be a burden on them? Moreover, you are able to keep yourself in control there. You should not, therefore, think just now of going away anywhere else. The climate of the place also is good. And certainly there are facilities. You may even help them while you are lounging about. Your health is not good enough to permit you to run about. The rains have started here. Do not trust any rumours that may appear in the newspapers.

Blessings from Bapu

22 January 1947[49]

How delighted I shall be to find that you have turned over a new leaf! Just think of the affection I have lavished upon you! Mine is an arduous pilgrimage. I invite you to join in it if you can...If you purify yourself, no matter where you are, you will have fully shared it. Take it on the authority of the *Bhagavata* that you will then also cease to look prematurely old as at present.

Chi. Harilal,[50]

Received your letter. If you are really repenting, if you have seen your bad habits, God will certainly help you. If you find peace, the help rendered by generous people like Mukundlalji would have served its purpose. Be firm and get rid of the filth of many years. Be calm. Do not run to the newspapers.

Keep writing to me. Your task is difficult, no doubt. However, nothing is difficult for God. Everything would be well if you seek His protection.

49. *CWMG*, vol. 86, p. 376.
50. *CWMG*, vol. 95, supplementary vol. 5, p. 218, undated.

Translator's Appendix 2

Thursday [28 January 1909][1]

Chi. Chanchal,

Your letter received after a long time. I am pained to see that your mind is restless. However, I would always want to know your inner feelings. Do not hide them thinking that I shall be unhappy. It is not right that you should think you are away from your father's house. I consider you to be my daughter, not a daughter-in-law. Had I considered you as my daughter-in-law, I would have looked upon you as a child. I take you to be my daughter, and hence I do not want to accept that you are a child. You have not been able to understand that. Just as I do not consider Manilal a child, so also I would not consider you one. Had I kept up our relations as between father-in-law and daughter-in-law, that is, had I kept up such a distance between us, I would have, in accordance with my usual nature, first tried to win you over and would have taken work from you freely only when a sense of oneness with the family had developed in you.

But I had taken it for granted that you would forget our relationship of father-in-law and daughter-in-law as I have fondled you in my lap as a daughter long before your marriage to Harilal. You have not forgotten that. Try to forget it now. I must on no account behave in a way that may cause any harm to you or make you unhappy. There have been innumerable women in India who saw their ultimate good in separation from their husbands. Damayanti became immortal on account of her separation from Nala. Taramati separated from Harishchandra and that separation led to the good of both. Draupadi's separation from the Pandavas proved a blessing to them and the entire Hindu nation sings the praises of her resoluteness. Do not think that these instances have not taken place. Lord Buddha left his

1. *CWMG*, vol. 9, p. 174–75.

wife and became immortal and so did his wife. This is an extreme case. By these examples I only want to show you that your separation is not going to do you any harm. That it would cause you mental agony is quite natural. That is a sign of love. But that does not necessarily mean that it will do you harm. Weal and woe depend on the purpose behind separation. My separation from Ba was almost involuntary; that is, it was not of my choice and yet it proved to be a blessing to us both. By giving these examples, I do not want to impress upon your mind that you have to live in separation for ever. I write this so that you are not unhappy over your separation during the struggle. I shall hardly be a cause of your separation after the struggle is over. My effort, however, is to change your mental attitude. That also will be effected after you understand and get used to it.

Preserve this letter. Read it again and again. Ask me whatever you do not understand. Do both of you read it. My object in writing this is your welfare. I am always eager to promote it. But I do not insist that you should accept my ideas. My only desire is that both of you should grow with your own effort.

Blessings from Mohandas

Volksrust[2]

Saturday [16 January 1909]

Chi. Chanchal,

I was arrested, deported, again arrested and am now released on bail. I shall now proceed to Johannesburg. You will know more from Manilal.

I feel unhappy that I was not able to have much talk, rather any talk, with you. But such is my plight. I purposely dictated to you that day. I want to make you adept in such work. I would even keep you with me when Rami is grown up. Be sure that if you give up the idea of staying with Harilal for the present, it will do good to both of you. Harilal will grow by staying apart and will perform his other duties. Love for you does not consist only in staying

2. *CWMG,* vol. 9, p. 150.

with you. At times one has to live apart just for the sake of love. This is true in your case. From every side, I see that your separation is for your benefit. But it can be a source of happiness only if you do not become restless owing to separation. I think Harilal will have to stay at Johannesburg till the struggle is over.

Considering your stage of life, I do not intend to treat you as a child. I wish you and Manilal take charge of the household. You two have to look after everything in the house, keep Rama and Deva in proper form, take care of their belongings, and teach them to do so themselves, see that they are clean and their nails are well trimmed.

None can say when Ba will completely recover. Even when she is fully restored, your role will not be affected. You have to behave as mistress of the house. Do not forget that we are very poor.

Blessings from Mohandas

Volksrust Prison[3]

Transvaal

26 February 1909

Chi. Chanchal,

I am sorry not to have any letter from you. I see that Ba is getting better. Please read good writings and poems to her. Always write to me after consulting her and let the letters be signed by both Manilal and you. You may ask Ba what she has to say and let me know that also.

Let me know about your own health as well as the condition of your right ear, feet and cough. The change that I made in your diet is to be adhered to as an order from me. Take sago and milk regularly. Feed Rami at the breast for a few days more. Take sufficient food after feeding her also. Your health will not improve so long as you do not get open air. I need not write more.

3. *CWMG*, vol. 9, p. 200.

Ask Willie not to do any mischief at all. If Ramdas has a sore throat, apply an earth bandage.

Blessings from Mohandas

[P.S.] Harilal and I are quite well. Be sure that we are happier here than you.

Please read out this letter to Ba.

Tolstoy Farm[4]

Sunday, Posh Sud 7 [8 January 1911]

Chi. Chanchal,

I was very glad to read your long and interesting letter. Ba also read it with interest. Harilal will read it on his release tomorrow. I hasten to write this today as I have no time at the office. I am at the Farm just now. It is 9 p.m. You must be getting *Indian Opinion* regularly. Do you ever go out for a walk? It is good that you have kept up the habit of reading.

I wish you not to wear jewellery for fear of being criticized if you don't. There is no beauty in jewellery. The first and real ornament for both man and woman is purity of character. That you possess such character is in itself a precious ornament. Our custom of wearing ornaments on the nose and the ears seems to me barbarous. I mean barbarous, not in comparison with the whites, but according to our own ideas [of civilized life]. That the poets have described Ramachandraji, Sitaji, and others as wearing jewels seems to me to be suggestive of the custom prevailing at the time [they wrote]. Otherwise I cannot imagine the benevolent Ramachandraji or the deeply devout Sitaji carrying even a particle of gold on their bodies. Whatever that may be, we can easily understand that there is no beauty in perforating the nose and the ears and inserting something there or in wearing ornaments round the neck or the arms. However, I say nothing about putting on bangles round the wrists, as their absence would suggest something inauspicious.

4. *CWMG*, vol. 10, p. 397–98.

It would be enough if we put on these things to prevent talk. These are my views. Think over them and do as you deem proper. You need not be embarrassed and do anything because of me.

Ramdas and Devdas are quite cheerful. There are twenty boys here, so they feel quite at home. I find Ba also happy as she has the company of other women. She has given up tea at least for the present and is now habituated to bathing in cold water.

There is talk that the struggle might come to an end within this month or in February. Let us see what happens. Harilal will remain free, as the Government do not make arrests nowadays. I know his health was excellent in the Johannesburg Gaol.

Purshottamdas is also here after his release from gaol. A kiss to Ramibai. My regards to Chhabalbhabhi. I shall await Bali's letter. What can I expect from Kumi when she does not write at all?

Blessings from Bapu

[Lawley][5]

Maha Vad 0 [18 February 1912]

Chi. Chanchal,

I had a letter from you after many months. I should like you to be less lazy about writing letters.

I can very well understand your natural desire to be with Chi. Harilal. I do not at all wish to come in your way in this. Live, both of you, as you wish and do what you like. I can have but one wish: you should be happy and remain so.

Personally, I do not like your giving Kanti Mellin's Food. I think it a sin to use any foreign goods in India, and the use of food products is all the more distasteful to me now. I cannot help feeling that all such products are polluted. Even when they do not contain animal fat, alcohol, etc., I have

5. *CWMG*, vol. 11, p. 237–38.

noticed that they are not entirely free from contamination by them, since foreigners do not object to the use of these. We should know that our children grew well enough in the olden days without these foreign foods; hence my advice is that we too should do without them. Wheat, well roasted, ground fine and mixed with a little *gur* and water will serve the same purpose as Mellin's Food. We can prepare a number of things to replace it.

It is easy to see that your presence there and that of Rami and Kanti must be a great comfort to Chhabalbhabhi.

Personally I don't see how Ba or I can get away from here just now.

Manilal is here at present. He will leave in the middle of Phagan. Jamnadas, too, is here. I am busy at present with the affairs of the school. There are 25 pupils, eight of them Muslims, two Parsis and the rest Hindus. Among the last, five are from Madras and one from Calcutta, and the rest are Gujaratis. Jamnadas and others help with the teaching.

My loving kisses to Ramibai and Kantibhai. Ask Bali to write to me.

Blessings from Bapu

[After 3 August 1912][6]

Chi. Bali and Chanchi,

I have letters from you both.

A part of the blame at least for Rami's fractured hand should, I think, go to you. But such accidents always occur. If we are destined to survive, God saves us even from these.

Chi. Veni writes to me to say that Chanchi now wants to come over here. She should know that she is free to come whenever she likes. I allowed her to go, believing as I did, and as I still do, that she would feel she was happier there and that Harilal too would feel likewise. That is why she is there. As to when I shall be able to go there, it is impossible at present to say. I do not think I can leave before the Act is passed at any rate.

---

6. *CWMG*, vol. 11, p. 296–97.

It is good news that Kanti is growing stronger. My advice is that no foreign foods be brought into the house. My experience of them has been bad. I am more convinced each day that almost all these foods are objectionable.

Bali has done well in taking up the study of Sanskrit. If ever it is my good fortune to go to India and I have to take up my work there, I intend to use Bali's services fully.

Manilal, Ramdas and Devdas are on the farm. Jayakunvar, Dr. Mehta's daughter, is also with me. She is a great help to me in teaching the children. You must have read in *Indian Opinion* that her husband has gone to Fiji. Chi. Jamnadas, too, is with me. Ani is likewise on the Farm. Devibehn...[7]

7. Missing in the source.

Translator's Appendix 3

Trial of Harilal Gandhi and Others

[Johannesburg, 28 July 1908][1]

Six more Indian hawkers[2] appeared in D Court before Mr. P. C. Dalmahoy yesterday [28 July], charged with hawking without licences. These included Thambi Naidoo, who went to prison in January last with Mr. Gandhi, and who was sentenced to four days' imprisonment on Tuesday of last week for hawking without a licence, and Harilal Gandhi, eldest son of Mr. M. K. Gandhi, who was arrested some days ago at Volksrust [for failing to register] and warned to appear at Pretoria to apply for a registration certificate. Young Gandhi came to Johannesburg, and immediately commenced hawking fruit, when he was arrested. Mr. Cramer prosecuted, Mr. Gandhi appearing for the defence. The first to be charged was an Indian named Hera Mariji.

Formal evidence as to accused's having been hawking within the municipality without a licence was given, and the accused, who pleaded guilty, was fined £1, with the alternative of seven days' imprisonment with hard labour. The next to be placed in the dock were Harilal Mohandas Gandhi (son of Mr. M. K. Gandhi), Thambi Naidoo and Govindasamy Kistnasamy, who were all described as Indian hawkers. They pleaded guilty.

A sergeant of police gave evidence that he had arrested the accused, who were hawking fruit in Bellevue East without licence. Mr. Gandhi said he did not propose to call witnesses, but wished to make a few remarks. He had been weak enough on the previous day to protest against the increase of penalty, but in this instance he had a long conference with the prisoners at the gaol, and he had been requested to ask for the severest penalty. The accused had

---

1. *CWMG*, vol. 8, p. 405–06.
2. According to the *CWMG*, the six hawkers were P.K. Naidoo, Harilal Gandhi, Hera Mariji, Kistnasamy, Pillay and Naiker.

acted as they had done with deliberation. Naidoo had been in gaol last week, having been sentenced to four days' imprisonment for hawking without a licence.

THE MAGISTRATE: There is a previous conviction against Naidoo.

MR. GANDHI: Two previous convictions under this Act; one for hawking without a licence.

Continuing, Mr. Gandhi said that the two others had also asked him to ask for a severe sentence. If a light sentence was imposed, as soon as they came out, they intended to repeat the action. It would be a saving of time to give them a long sentence, and it would be better for the sake of their health if they had a sustained term.

Naidoo was fined £2, with the alternative of 14 days' imprisonment with hard labour, and Gandhi and Kistnasamy were fined £l [each], or seven days' imprisonment, with hard labour. Two other British Indians, named Sinnappa Rangasamy Pillay and Soopa Veerasamy Naiker, were then charged. They pleaded guilty, and were fined £l, or seven days' imprisonment, with hard labour.

In each case the accused elected to go to prison.

The Transvaal Leader, 29 July 1908

Trial of Harilal Gandhi[3]

[Johannesburg, 10 August 1908]

An unusually large crowd of Indians assembled in B Court yesterday afternoon [10 August] to hear the case of Harilal Mohandas Gandhi, a son of Mr. M. K. Gandhi, aged 20, and described as a student, who was brought before Mr. H. H. Jordan on a charge of contravening the Asiatic Amendment Act by failing to be in possession of a registration certificate.

The accused pleaded guilty, and was defended by his father. Mr. A. Cramer prosecuted. Superintendent Vernon, of B Division, gave evidence of arrest,

3. *CWMG*, vol. 8, p. 436.

and further stated that he called upon the accused to produce his certificate of registration, who, however, failed to do so, saying that he did not possess one.

Mr. Gandhi, on behalf of the accused, said that the latter had no desire to leave the Colony, but nevertheless he was desirous that the Court should make an order for the accused to leave the Colony within 24 hours. He made the request because two other Indians whose time under the Act would expire on Wednesday would be ready to go to gaol. He (Mr. Gandhi) hoped His Worship would adopt this course, as the accused's affairs were in his hands.

Mr. Jordan ordered the accused to leave the Colony within seven days.

The Transvaal Leader, 11 August 1908

Why he Sent his Son to Gaol: Mr. Gandhi's Explanation

The Editor
Indian Opinion[4]

SIR,

I have received inquiries from many quarters as to why I sent Harilal, my son, to gaol. I give some reasons below:

1. I have advised every Indian to take up hawking. I am afraid I cannot join myself since I am enrolled as an attorney. I therefore thought it right to advise my son to make his rounds as a hawker. I hesitate to ask others to do things which I cannot do myself. I think whatever my son does at my instance can be taken to have been done by me.
2. It will be a part of Harilal's education to go to gaol for the sake of the country.
3. I have always been telling people that satyagraha is easy for those who can understand it well. When I go to defend those who have been arrested, I do not, strictly speaking, defend them but only send them to gaol. If we have acquired real courage, there should be no need for me to present myself in Court. I thought it only proper that I should make this

4. *CWMG*, vol. 8, p. 432–33.

experiment in the first instance with my son. Accordingly, no arrangements were made for him at Volksrust, and he was left to fall back on his own strength. Since there were others with him in Johannesburg, I attended the Court, but asked for the maximum penalty for him and for his associates. It was their misfortune that they did not get it.

4. I have often advised that no one should give his thumb-impression on arriving at Volksrust. People have not followed this advice. I have not insisted on the point, but the time has now come for me to insist on it. Thumb-impressions are now asked for at Volksrust under the obnoxious law, and they should not, therefore, be given. This [objective] also, I thought, I could easily achieve through Harilal.

I want every Indian to do what Harilal has done. Harilal is only a child. He may have merely deferred to his father's wishes in acting in this manner. It is essential that every Indian should act on his own as Harilal did [at my instance] and I wish everyone would do so. Satyagraha can be claimed to have been perfectly successful only if we do so. I repeat that

(1) those who are prepared for imprisonment should go to gaol without depending upon a lawyer or myself. That is not to say that I go back on my promise of defending Indian satyagrahis arrested in connection with the campaign against the law. I shall go wherever I find my presence is needed. But the best way is to have no lawyer and go to gaol straight away and undergo whatever sentence is passed;

(2) every Indian, whatever his status, must go to gaol for the sake of his country without giving much thought to what the others do;

(3) no Indian should give his thumb-impression or fingerprints on entering the Transvaal. Not doing so will mean imprisonment for Indians. They must accept it rather than give thumb-impressions or finger-prints or even signatures as signifying [compliance with the provisions of] the law.

I remain,

Satyagrahi

Mohandas Karamchand Gandhi

A Domestic Chapter[5]

A *vakil* from Layallpur sends the following letter addressed to the Editor, *Young India*:

> About three or four years ago, a company, "All-India Stores Ltd.", was started at Calcutta with Mr. H. M. Gandhi, son of our Mahatmaji, as one of the directors, as advertised by a representative of the said company at Rawalpindi. A client of mine was persuaded to pay certain sums to the said representative and also to the company in pursuance of his having been so persuaded to become a shareholder. I have written to the known and notified address, 22 Amratalla Street, Calcutta, of the company and so has my client. My client fears that perhaps it was a bogus affair and he has been done out of his money. In the interests of your (Mahatma's) good name and the economic welfare of this poor country, I fondly hope and wish and even pray, my client's fears may be unfounded. The post office has returned all our letters back through the Dead Letter Office. So, some ground at least exists for my client's suspecting that the company is no more. Is it a fact that Mahatmaji's son was a Director in it, and is it a fact that such a company came into being and is still existing, and where?
>
> Please excuse my writing to you about it. My client who is a Mohammedan gentleman and whose respect for Mahatmaji led him to become a shareholder in the company, wants to verify these facts. Hence the query.

But for some important principles involved in the letter, I would have satisfied myself with a private reply, though the letter is meant for publication. It was necessary to publish it also, because it is highly likely that many shareholders feel like the *vakil's* client. They too should have such satisfaction as I could render to them. I do indeed happen to be the father of Harilal M. Gandhi. He is my eldest boy, is over 36 years old and is father of four children, the eldest being 19 years old. His ideals and mine having been

5. *CWMG*, "*Young India*, June 18, 1925", vol. 27, p. 259–62.

discovered over fifteen years ago to be different, he has been living separately from me and, since 1915 has not been supported by or through me. It has been my invariable rule to regard my boys as my friends and equals as soon as they completed their sixteen years. The tremendous changes that my outer life has undergone from time to time were bound to leave their impress on my immediate surroundings—especially on my children. Harilal who was witness to all the changes, being old enough to understand them, was naturally influenced by the Western veneer that my life at one time did have. His commercial undertakings were totally independent of me. Could I have influenced him, he would have been found associated with me in my several public activities and earning, at the same time, a decent livelihood. But he chose, as he had every right to do, a different and independent path. He was and is still ambitious. He wants to become rich and that too, easily. Possibly he has a grievance against me that, when it was open to me to do so, I did not equip him and my other children for careers that lead to wealth and fame that wealth brings. He started the Stores in question without the least assistance of any kind whatsoever from me. I did not lend my name to them. I never recommended his enterprise to anybody either privately or openly. Those who helped him did so on the merits of the enterprise. No doubt his sonship must have helped him. As long as the world lasts, and in spite of its protest against *varnashrama*, it will give credit to heredity. Being my son, he must be good and straight, cautious in his pecuniary affairs and as reliable as his father. So must many have argued. They have my sympathy, but beyond that nothing more. I must disclaim all responsibility, moral or otherwise, for the doings of even those who are nearest and dearest to me except those wherein they act with me or, I permit them to act in my name or with my certificate. I have enough to be responsible for myself. I alone know my sorrows and my troubles in the course of the eternal duel going on within me and which admits of no truce. I ask the reader to believe me when I say that it taxes all my energy, and if I feel as a rule stronger for the combat, it is only because I remain wide awake. I make the reader a present of the thought that even my swaraj activity has a bearing on that duel. It is for the supreme satisfaction of my soul that I engage in it. "This is selfishness double distilled," said a friend once to me. I quickly agreed with him.

I do not know Harilal's affairs. He meets me occasionally, but I never pry into his affairs. I do not know that he is a Director in his Company. I do not know how his affairs stand at present, except that they are in a bad way. If he is honest, limited or unlimited though his Stores were, he will not rest till he has paid all the creditors in full. That is my view of honest trade. But he may hold different views and seek shelter under the law of insolvency. Sufficient for me to assure the public that nothing crooked will have countenance from me. For me, the law of satyagraha, the law of love, is an eternal principle. I co-operate with all that is good. I desire to non-co-operate with all that is evil—whether it is associated with my wife, son or myself. I have no desire to shield any of the two. I would like the world to know the whole of the evil in us. And in so far as I can, with decency, I let the world into all the domestic secrets so-called. I never make the slightest attempt to hide them, for I know that concealment can only hurt us.

There is much in Harilal's life that I dislike. He knows that. But I love him in spite of his faults. The bosom of a father will take him in as soon as he seeks entrance. For the present, he has shut the door against himself. He must still wander in the wilderness. The protection of a human father has its decided limitations. That of the Divine Father is ever open to him. Let him seek it and he will find it.

Let the *vakil* and his client know that my good name is not worth keeping, if it suffers because of the errors of a grown-up boy who has no encouragement from me in them. "The economic welfare of this poor country" will be fairly safe in spite of failures of private firms, if the President for the time being of the Congress and the members of the various organizations remain true to their trust and never mishandle a single pice. I pity the client who, out of respect for me, became a share-holder in a concern whose constitution he evidently never cared to study. Let the client's example be a warning against people being guided by big names in their transactions. Men may be good, not necessarily their children. Men may be good in some respects, not necessarily, therefore, in all. A man who is an authority on one matter is not, therefore, an authority on all matters. *Caveat emptor.*

To My Numerous Muslim Friends

Bangalore[6]

2 June 1936

The newspapers report that about a fortnight ago my eldest son Harilal, now nearing fifty years, accepted Islam and that on Friday last 29th May in the midst of a large congregation in the Jumma Musjid at Bombay, he was permitted to announce his acceptance amid great acclamation and that, after his speech was finished, he was besieged by his admirers who vied with one another to shake hands with him. If his acceptance was from the heart and free from any worldly considerations, I should have no quarrel. For I believe Islam to be as true a religion as my own.

But I have the gravest doubt about this acceptance being from the heart or free from selfish considerations. Everyone who knows my son Harilal, knows that he has been for years addicted to the drink evil and has been in the habit of visiting houses of ill-fame. For some years he has been living on the charity of friends who have helped him unstintingly. He is indebted to some Pathans from whom he had borrowed on heavy interest. Up to only recently he was in dread of his life from his Pathan creditors in Bombay. Now he is the hero of the hour in that city. He had a most devoted wife who always forgave his many sins including his unfaithfulness. He has three grown-up children, two daughters and one son, whom he ceased to support long ago.

Not many weeks ago he wrote to the Press complaining against Hindus—not Hinduism—and threatening to go over to Christianity or Islam. The language of the letter showed quite clearly that he would go over to the highest bidder. That letter had the desired effect. Through the good offices of a Hindu councillor he got a job in Nagpur Municipality. And he came out with another letter to the Press recalling the first and declaring emphatic adherence to his ancestral faith.

---

6. The statement, published in the *Harijan* under the title "To My Numerous Muslim Friends", was issued to the press on 2 June 1936. *CWMG*, vol. 63, p. 5–7.

But, as events have proved, his pecuniary ambition was not satisfied and in order to satisfy that ambition, he has embraced Islam. There are other facts which are known to me and which strengthen my inference.

When I was in Nagpur, in April last, he had come to see me and his mother and he told me how he was amused by the attentions that were being paid to him by the missionaries of rival faiths. God can work wonders. He has been known to have changed the stoniest hearts and turned sinners into saints, as it were, in a moment. Nothing will please me better than to find that during the Nagpur meeting and the Friday announcement he had repented of the past and had suddenly become a changed man having shed the drink habit and sexual lust.

But the Press reports give no such evidence. He still delights in sensation and in good living. If he had changed, he would have written to me to gladden my heart. All my children have had the greatest freedom of thought and action. They have been taught to regard all religions with the same respect that they paid to their own. Harilal knew that if he had told me that he had found the key to a right life and peace in Islam, I would have put no obstacle in his path. But no one of us, including his son now twenty-four years old and who is with me, knew anything about the event till we saw the announcement in the Press.

My views on Islam are well known to the Mussalmans who are reported to have enthused over my son's profession. A brotherhood of Islam has telegraphed to me thus:

> EXPECT LIKE YOUR SON YOU TRUTH-SEEKER TO EMBRACE ISLAM TRUEST RELIGION OF WORLD.

I must confess that all this has hurt me. I sense no religious spirit behind this demonstration. I feel that those who are responsible for Harilal's acceptance of Islam did not take the most ordinary precautions they ought to have in a case of this kind.

Harilal's apostasy is no loss to Hinduism and his admission to Islam is a source of weakness to it if, as I apprehend, he remains the same wreck that he was before.

Surely conversion is a matter between man and his Maker who alone knows His creatures' hearts. And conversion without a clean heart is, in my opinion, a denial of God and religion. Conversion without cleanness of heart can only be a matter for sorrow, not joy, to a godly person.

My object in addressing these lines to my numerous Muslim friends is to ask them to examine Harilal in the light of his immediate past and, if they find that his conversion is a soulless matter, to tell him so plainly and disown him and if they discover sincerity in him to see that he is protected against temptations so that his sincerity results in his becoming a god fearing member of society. Let them know that excessive indulgence has softened his brain and undermined his sense of right and wrong, truth and falsehood. I do not mind whether he is known as Abdulla or Harilal if, by adopting one name for the other, he becomes a true devotee of God which both the names mean.

The Case of My First Son[7]

Q: You have failed to take even your own son with you, and he has gone astray. May it not, therefore, be well for you to rest content with putting your own house in order?

A: This may be taken to be a taunt, but I do not take it so. For the question had occurred to me before it did to anyone else. I am a believer in previous births and rebirths. All our relationships are the result of the *samskars* we carry from our previous births. God's laws are inscrutable and are the subject of endless search. No one will fathom them.

This is how I regard the case of my son. I regard the birth of a bad son to me as the result of my evil past whether of this life or previous. My first son was born when I was in a state of infatuation. Besides, he grew up whilst I was myself growing and whilst I knew myself very little. I do not claim to know myself fully even today, but I certainly know myself better than I did then. For years he remained away from me, and his upbringing was not

7. The Gujarati original of this appeared in the *Harijanbandhu*, 10 August 1940. The English translation here is reproduced from the *Harijan*, where it appears under the heading "Question Box". "The Case of My First Son, *Harijan*, 18 August 1940", *CWMG*, vol. 72, p. 354–55.

entirely in my hands. That is why he has always been at a loose end. His grievance against me has always been that I sacrificed him and his brothers at the altar of what I wrongly believed to be public good. My other sons have laid more or less the same blame at my door, but with a good deal of hesitation, and they have generously forgiven me. My eldest son was the direct victim of my experiments—radical changes in my life—and so he cannot forget what he regards as my blunders. Under the circumstances I believe I am myself the cause of the loss of my son, and have therefore learnt patiently to bear it. And yet it is not quite correct to say that I have lost him. For it is my constant prayer that God may make him see the error of his ways and forgive me my shortcomings, if any, in serving him. It is my firm faith that man is by nature going higher, and so I have not at all lost hope that some day he will wake up from his slumber of ignorance. Thus he is part of my field of experiments in ahimsa. When or whether I shall succeed I have never bothered to know. It is enough for my own satisfaction that I do not slacken my efforts in doing, what I know to be my duty. 'To work thou hast the right, never to the fruit thereof' is one of the golden precepts of the *Gita.*

Sevagram

5 August 1940

Translator's Appendix 4

21–24 Court Chambers
Johannesburg
28 December 1905

M.K. Gandhi,

Attorney

Chi. Harilal,

I am happy that I have your letter after many months. I hope you will pass the examinations. It would have been good if you had sent all the questions. You can send them even now.

I am glad that you have decided to come with Chi. Maganlal.

There is no doubt that I am dissatisfied with you. Do not think that my love for you is any less for this reason. I have, in the past, written to you about the reasons for my dissatisfaction. I write them again.

1. It is your duty to write a weekly letter. You have neglected this duty.
2. You give no news about yourself even when you write a letter.
3. Whenever I receive news about you, they contain criticism regarding your conduct.
4. You asked me to send you a cable but you did not come in response to that.
5. Naturally, your mother awaits your letters more eagerly. But you have not written even a chit to her. Children writing a few lines to their parents do not make letters. Letters are not written for the sake of formality. Children pour their hearts out to their parents. Only stonehearted children neglect writing letters or write short letters.
6. Your general conduct towards your parents betrays no love for them.

I will take back my words if I am mistaken in saying them. I consider it my duty to make you aware of my views. Now that you are an adult, what more can I write? I have natural curiosity to know about each aspect of your life, all your thoughts and your aspirations. You have not fulfilled this curiosity. Even your present letter is lacking in interest. You have failed to understand the love of your parents. It is not an insignificant shortcoming. When I was your age, I lost my father. Bapa was like a father to me.[1] I used to write ten-page letters to him from England, but even this left me dissatisfied.

Blessings from Mohandas

[P.S.] Chi. Gokuldas is at Phoenix.

21–24 Court Chambers
Corner Rissik
Anderson Street
PO Box: 6522
Johannesburg
9 February 1906

Chi. Harilal,

I have your letter. I was pleased to read it. I have replied to the doubt you raised in my previous letter. It is not a problem that you did not go to Banaras. You will learn much from observation once your intellect matures.

You must do as your Mota Bapa[2] suggests, that is, if he does not grant you permission to come over now, come after the marriage takes place.

Your handwriting is not good. I am not worried that you failed. I had not nurtured any hope either. I only want you to have qualities of simplicity, poverty, truthfulness, humility, etc. If you possess these qualities knowledge will increase effortlessly.

Chi. Gokuldas works in the press these days. He works well. If you continue to write a letter every week, I would be very satisfied. Do not think that if I cannot come, it is due to any sin of yours.

---

1. Bapa is a term often employed for father's elder brother in Saurashtra. Here, it probably refers to Gandhiji's elder brother Lakshmidas.
2. Father's elder brother.

Blessings from Mohandas

[P.S.] I believe that even Ba would not be able to come if the wedding is in Vaisakh. You must not be unhappy because of that. There are many elders there.

Chi. Harilal,[3]

Do not worry about me. The machinations of Shahji and others are not evident at present. All others are very cooperative.

Make sure that your letters to me are descriptive. If you use every minute, all work will get completed. Look after the garden and all matters pertaining to the household.

I live with Mr. Kallenbach. I do not go home with Mr. Pollack. I come to the office regularly at nine and leave at five thirty sharp. I use the bicycle both ways. I get down from it while climbing the hill. Mr. Kallenbach accompanies me. I get up between six thirty and seven. I take a Kuhne bath. I have continued with the poultice on the eyes. I drink milk in the morning. I eat fruits for lunch and eat milk, cherries, etc. in the evening. I have all three meals with Mr. Kallenbach.

I have sent some pages of the Ramayana yesterday. I wish you would do this work with speed. The more I think about it, I feel that it is of considerable importance. Whatever is completed should be printed. Give it the title *Ramayana Sar*. Make corrections with care. Send me copies of the printed pages. Please remind Chi. Chhaganlal that it cannot be like what we had done with the life of Prophet Mohammad. It should not be a problem if the size of the book is a bit larger. Use the time at night with care. Set aside half an hour to forty-five minutes for studying the Gita and the rest for other reading.

3. This was probably written after 11 July 1907. In his letter to Chhaganlal Gandhi of 11 July 1907 (*CWMG*, vol. 7, p. 96–97), Gandhiji makes a mention of the printing of the Ramayana, which is also referred to in this letter.

Do write to me about the visitors...[4] All should read the letter. Even Chi. Chhaganlal and others, so that I need not repeat the same details.

Blessings from Mohandas

Government Lodge[5]

Tuesday

Chi. Harilal,

I just received a cable from Mr. Polak. I see that the charge against me is not severe. That is disappointing. Such is Hari iccha.[6] 'Hari' could include even you. But, that will be when you acquire the qualities of your name. I see seeds of it in you. It is my wish that it grows into a vast tree. That is my blessing. Your samskar are good. It is possible therefore that you would better me in terms of service. It should be so. You partake of even my samskar, because you are a part of me. If you and I are joined by this thread, the fruits of it in the form of your character should be more vigorous. Ask me why so, when we meet. Are you attending to all aspects of I[ndian] O[pionion]?

Blessings from Mohandas

---

4. As in the source.
5. This letter was written in prison. Gandhiji mentions that the charges against him were light, therefore the punishment too would have been light. Gandhiji was awarded simple imprisonment for two months on 10 January 1908, the lightest punishment that he received in South Africa. He was in Johannesburg jail from 11 to 30 January 1908, after which he was released following an agreement with the government. The letter was written on a Tuesday; in January 1908 there were four Tuesdays—7, 14, 21 and 28. The letter could have been written on one of these days.
6. Literally, 'God's will'. The next sentence becomes meaningful only when the 'Hari iccha' is retained.

Chi. Harilal,[7]

If Ba comes here, the accompanying letter would be useless. In that case, destroy it after reading. Or else, seal it in a blank cover[8] and hand it to Ba so that she is assured.

I have already sent Mr. Andrew's address.[9]

I can write about my future to you. But I cannot write to Ba because she would not be able to comprehend and would be deeply troubled.

Consider all that I have written to you and make your body like that of others. Suffering will be limitless. I will explain when we meet; consider misery a means to happiness. Truth does not have a golden bed, remember that. Inner joy is true happiness. Enjoy it as much as you can. The shortcomings that I have pointed out to you may not appear to be shortcomings. But do not harbour anger in your mind towards me because of that. Keep my words in mind and remove the shortcomings that you see. Write to me about all your feelings.

Your thought of coming here...[10]

Your duty is to stay there. You may not be of much assistance to me, but if you come, Chanchi left to be on her own would wilt. This requires some arrangement. How can it be that I do not come there, yet drag even you away? Whatever happens to me, it is your duty to stay there till I call for you.

I write this to you in the presence of many others, therefore I will stop.

Read my writings in I[ndian] O[pionion] again and again with feeling. I hope to go to office from...[11]

Blessings from Mohandas

---

7. This letter was probably written between 10 and 20 February 1908, while Gandhiji was recovering from Mir Alam's assault at Rev. Doke's house.
8. English word in the original.
9. Most probably Mr. David Andrews, an Indian born in South Africa, who was a clerk and an interpreter, and an active satyagrahi. Gandhiji and C.F. Andrews met for the first time on 2 January 1914.
10. As in the source.
11. As in the source.

Chi. Harilal,[12]

There has been no letter from you for the past two days. Today I return home. Detectives follow me for my protection. The real protector is our Maker. You need not worry.

Mr. Doke read your letter to me. 'Heartifully'[13] is not an English word. 'Heartily'[14] is the proper word.

Friday night[15]

Chi. Harilal,

I have got two letters from you. Even now I find it difficult to understand some parts of your letters. Do you wish to go soon after Chanchi delivers? That is, after a month? I do not believe that you cannot stay away from Chanchi. But consider if it would be proper for you to leave while she is in confinement. She would be scared. Ba would be afraid and my mind would be restless. It is necessary, therefore, for you to give me answers to the following questions.

1. How soon after Chanchi delivers do you wish to leave?
2. What is Chanchi's opinion?
3. Will Ba and Chanchi get along after you leave?
4. Is Chanchi's permission the result of fear? (If she concurs.)[16] Or is it lack of comprehension? Is it to honour you, or is it with the readiness to bear the pain that would come her way?

---

12. This letter was probably written on 20 February 1908, the day on which Gandhiji left the home of Rev. Joseph Doke where he had been recovering from Mir Alam's attack on 10 February 1908. There is a reference to Harilal's letter of 14 February 1908 (see Letter 2, Translator's Appendix 5) to Rev. Joseph Doke in this letter.
13. English word in original.
14. English word in original.
15. This letter was probably written on either 6 March 1908 or 13 March 1908—both were Fridays. Chanchalbehn delivered her daughter on 10 April 1908.
16. Within parenthesis in the original.

5. What do you intend to study in England?
6. Would a life of extreme poverty be enriching for you?
7. Do you feel capable of caring for your body?

I deserve to know the answers to these and similar questions. Please clarify.

A time would come when I will no longer be at the Phoenix. Would Chanchi be able to live in Phoenix patiently even if I were wandering around or if I were dead? Do not tell...[17] about my possible death if you do not deem it fit. But you must explain regarding the other situation I have mentioned.

I am very happy to know that you will be doing household work in the farm. It is a good habit not to waste a single minute.

You write that you have been free of mental debauchery. I am overjoyed. If you have reached such a state I have nothing to say. At your age, and even later, I have not been free of mental desires, especially towards Ba. If you are free from such desires, I consider that a matter of honour for you and see that as a result of my piety and your meritorious acts in the last birth. I suspect that you are mistaken in your belief that you have been freed from mental desires. Great yogis have been able to attain such a state after years of self-practice; I do not say that you cannot achieve the same with childlike naturalness. Lakshmanji remained celibate from childhood. It is indeed grand if the same is true for you. Therefore, I remain in doubt and urge you to nurture such a doubt. If you attain pure truth and pure celibacy (of body, speech and thought), there is no limit to the heights you can attain. You will never be diseased. If you attain such a state at this age, even though you are my son, you would be worthy of my worship. This is no exaggeration. I write my true utterances. For King Dasharatha, Ramchandraji was worthy of worship. Sitaji (though a Vaidehi)[18] was worshipped by King Janaka.

Blessings from Mohandas

---

17. As in the original.
18. Within parenthesis in the original.

Chi. Harilal,[19]

I have your letter. You write about going to England, but I am yet to receive the letter regarding sending you there.

You write about 'running away'. This is a sign of your cowardice. Your mind is still unsteady and undecided. Different situations affect you very quickly. How can you go to England in such a situation? The condition of England is so strange that you cannot say what impact it would have on you. It is good that you went to Phoenix. That is your test.

Till such time even the thought of going away appears meaningless to me. I do not want to disappoint you by writing this. I am pointing out to you the dangerous rocks that you must steer clear from.

What you write about Ba is not correct. It is good that you appear innocent before her. When your heart is filled with devotion to your mother, she will melt. You need not play act with her, rather express your natural feelings.

You need to use a dictionary more often. Inform me as to the arrangements regarding mid-wife, etc., for Chanchi. Did Ba observe superstitions of *kholo bharvo*[20] and other similar things or not? Write to me about it.

Blessings from Mohandas

Monday[21]

Chi. Harilal,

I have your letter. I have difficulty understanding the letter. You have written it without a thought. What is it that you want? Do you want to go even before Chanchi has delivered the baby? You should stay for a month or two

---

19. This letter was written before 10 April 1908. The letter mentions some rituals that are performed before the birth of the first child.
20. Literally, 'filling the lap', a fertility ritual observed before the birth of the first child.
21. This letter was written *before* 10 April 1908 (2, 9, 16, 23 and 30 March 1908 and 6 April 1908 were Mondays).

even after she gives birth. If Ba and Chanchi do not get along, what would be Chanchi's plight? Do you not think that if Ba is displeased the fault must also lie with you somewhere? I have confidence in you and have given you freedom without any reservation now. I have allowed you to do as you wished. Before going to England many issues need consideration. Despite that I am making arrangements. It would suffice, if you work hard on the Ramayana.

I cannot understand your having control over your mind on the question of celibacy. Celibacy with respect to whom? If it is in regard to Chanchi, I cannot believe that you desired intercourse with her during a full-term pregnancy. If you have remained chaste[22] with respect to other women and consider that as control over mind, it indeed would make me sorry. Because you, with respect to other women...[23] have taken it.

You have not improved your handwriting even while here. You have not been able to satisfy either Mr. West or Mr. Cordes. They...[24] I am not willing to believe...[25]

This does not mean that I am not willing to send you to England. I am merely showing you how immature you are.

Do let me know clearly as to what you desire. Remove the apprehensions you have caused. Ensure that I am not required to pose questions again.

Where does Chanchi sleep now? If she is to deliver in the room where Ba sleeps, she should as well sleep in that room. You will realise that she should not be made to walk once the labour commences. This problem came to me at night in a dream, hence I place it before you. You would know that a woman must stay completely away from a man for a month and a half after giving birth.

---

22. The description in the original is *bandh kaccha*, literally 'one whose loin-cloth or lower garment is fastened to the girdle or the waistband'. In colloquial usage, the opposite of *bandh kaccha* is *lisi nadi*, literally 'one with smooth drawstrings', hence debauched.
23. As in the source.
24. As in the source.
25. As in the source.

You can call upon Virji for help with the Ramayana by meeting Mr. West. But where is your capacity? How can that be found in an unsteady mind?

There can be no composure in an unsteady mind.

Blessings from Mohandas

Chi. Harilal,[26]

So long as I am alive you must ask the questions that you need to. You must remember my words, involve yourself in all aspects of the household and think about each penny spent.

I do not see much danger here. I am certain that milk and rice, or milk and roti are the best diet for Chanchi.

Put a fistful of salt in the bathwater and examine the results. Take care to boil the drinking water.

Do not ever forsake the Gita*ji* or the Ramayana. Your pronunciation must be correct. Ensure that all recite in one voice and rhythm. Learn English well.

Be in regular touch with Mr. West and Mr. Cordes. Perform each task with skill and intelligence. Write long letters to me. Make sure that I get an exact picture of the happenings there.

Blessings from Mohandas

[P.S.] Why did you not write to Mr. Isanmama?

Thursday[27]

Chi. Harilal,

Today, I have come to Pretoria. I am pained by your letter. Please tell me the deeper reason for Ba's taunt. Duty is never easy. You should calm her with deep love. Ask her in all humility the reasons for this taunt.

---

26. This letter was probably written soon after Chanchalbehn gave birth to her first daughter Ramibehn on 10 April 1908. The advice about her diet is indicative of that.
27. This letter was probably written on 27 August 1908, which was a Thursday, when Gandhiji was in Pretoria to negotiate with General Smuts. The reference to the possible attack by the Pathans also supports this.

Ba's health does not appear to be good. I do not tell Ba all about myself. I wish that you too would not do so. Keep I[ndian] O[pionion] in such a place that she does not find and read it. Warn Manilal too, if he is likely to meet Ba.

There can be no cause of concern regarding me. The Pathans do not appear to comprehend all the intricacies. So what if they take my life? The body has often been sacrificed while securing the progress of the country and imparting true education to people. It has been so before as well. If you study the examples with care you would realise that often this is true of teachers. It ought to be so. Those who preach that the body and the soul are separate cannot be frightened by pain of the body. Even they have to show their face to others. This appears to be the easiest method of making an impact on the minds of people. It is natural that the Pathans should attack my body. It is not as if all people are weakened. Weakness there is, which will prolong the struggle; but, it will not do much else.

Keep your mind steady amidst all troubles and Ba's illness. Having done your duty, do not think of the fruits of duty. The appeal...[28] will be on the fourth, leaving you with a lot of time. If you feel that by staying with Ba, both of you are ill at ease, stay at Phoenix leaving Manilal with her. I will say nothing about the matter. Do what is appropriate according to you.

Blessings from Mohandas

[P.S.] Please tell Dr. Nanji[29] that I have not written anything that would cause Ba anxiety. I have written two lines for her satisfaction. Ask Ba and write for her whatever she wants to convey to me.

Chi. Harilal,[30]

I have your letter. I am not satisfied with either your handwriting or what you write. You give me no information.

---

28. As in the original.
29. Dr. Nanji operated on Kasturba Gandhi on 10 January 1909 in Durban.
30. This letter was probably written either in July or August 1908, when Harilal courted imprisonment.

1. What work will you do in the prison?
2. When are...you?[31]
3. Has your health improved there or is it what it used to be here?
4. What impact has the climate had on you?
5. How does Chanchi like Phoenix?
6. Does she go for walks?
7. How is Ba doing?
8. What is the diet that all of you take?
9. What is the condition of your mind?
10. How do you find the people there?
11. What are your brothers doing? How is their conduct? Do they pay heed to you? Do they study well?
12. Have you resolved your differences with Maganlal?
13. You...[32]
14. ...[33]
15. Hasan has written a far more detailed letter. Your letter is not in the least like a letter written by an obedient son to a father who is pining for the son. Either your feelings are not pure or else your condition is that of a stupefied person. Do not misunderstand the term 'stupefied person'. I cannot believe that your feelings are not pure. Therefore, I think that to an extent you are unable to understand my feelings and also that you are in stupefied condition. I infer from your writing that you have given up studying the Gita. I shall be happy, if you give complete answers to all the questions I have asked.

I shall hold you guilty if you have not replied to the letters received by Ba. A truthful man naturally recognises his duties.

Blessings from Mohandas

---

31. As in the source.
32. As in the source.
33. As in the source.

Chi. Harilal,[34]

You will understand that I do not have even a minute anymore. I cannot say when I will be deported...[35]

I do not say that we should seek unhappiness, but by believing that we are unhappy, we even appear to be unhappy. In fact, we are happy. Those among us whose minds are not yet steady consider ourselves to be unhappy. Ba believes that she is unhappy and that I am the one who causes her to be unhappy. The changes that we seek are not yet firm and natural to us. During this period apprehensions misguide you and cause illusions. The one who remains with me and takes my colour will be happy. Those who forsake me will appear to be happy but would in fact be unhappy. Those who overindulge are not happy, they appear happy...[36] I am ignorant of any other meaning for the term. Who do you call 'Bhadyo'?[37]

Babuji is required to write an application in English addressed to the immigration officer, Charlestown. If you were to write it with a good hand, I would forward it.

It was not my intention to suggest that the two of you should forever live apart from each other, but it was and remains desirable till such time that your intellect attains maturity. In my estimation you still...[38]

Celibacy may be observed easily when the minds of both become steadfast.

---

34. This letter was probably written between 18 and 27 September 1908. Gandhiji refers to his imminent arrest. He was arrested on 7 October 1908. Prior to this Harilal was arrested and imprisoned twice—once on 27 July 1908, to be released on 3 August 1908, and the second time on 10 August 1908. He was released on 17 September 1908. Gandhiji was in Phoenix from 27 to 29 September 1908 and again from 1 to 5 October 1908. The letter should have most probably been written on the dates mentioned earlier.
35. As in the source.
36. As in the source.
37. The context and meaning of this term remains unclear. It appears to be a nickname.
38. As in the source.

Chanchi needs the exercise of slow walking. She should sit and sleep in a place with ample air. Moreover, instead of sitting cross-legged it is better to sit and work from a chair.

If you believe that reading my letters is not detrimental to Chanchi, I have no objection to her reading them.

The people of Phoenix are not completely good, but are relatively good. You need to gain more experience of this. I consider it your duty to go to the press even if you are not enthused by it. If in your view Phoenix stinks, your conduct ought to be such that it spreads fragrance. It is obvious that your aroma would diminish the stench by mixing with the odour of Phoenix.

I am convinced that your views on the school are not correct. I am aware that some of the interests of children are hurt there. The remedy is not any other school. If there were such a good school, we could send them. You may not know, but Jalbhai,[39] despite having passed the examination has been sent letters to return; his conduct has become so bad. There is no school better than the company of good. The poet says, "What can the association with the good not achieve?"

Ram Ram to Chanchidoshi.

Blessings from Mohandas

[P.S.] You will find news about me from newspapers, and letters, if I get to write them. Take good care of Mr. Kallenbach.

Chi. Harilal and Chi. Chanchal,[40]

I received your cable regarding my release. I write to you just for the sake of writing; I have no time at all. This victory has to be recognised as the victory of Truth. The two of you have much to learn from it. Follow Truth and remain steadfast so long as life lasts. Therein lies your welfare. Truth is God and God is Truth. Nurture no doubt about this.

---

39. Son of Gandhiji's associate Parsi Rustomji.
40. Gandhiji was released on 12 December 1908. This letter must have been written soon after that.

Do send the Ramayana pages regularly. Give me exhaustive account of both your lives, your studies, your health and the condition of your minds, and such other things.

I would be displeased to receive short letters.

Blessings from Mohandas

[P.S.] Mohanlal Joshi's wife has died; do write him a letter of consolation.

Chi. Harilal,[41]

Most likely, Sorabji will be sent to jail on Saturday. Think about what you ought to do after his arrest.

I want to come there, but I realise that I may not be able to come. I place the responsibility of the visitors on you. You may not be able to do everything yourself. All will think of you as a child. Do not be perturbed by it. Do your work under the supervision of and in the name of the leader who works. You should meet the visitors and should they face any difficulty meet Mr. Khan. You should ensure that he does the work. Check as to when the steamer is to arrive. Mr. Bernard Gabriel from Delagoa Bay writes that the steamer is to arrive there on the 14th. This information appears to be incorrect; nevertheless, you must check.

We will see what your decision is after Sorabji's arrest. It would be good if you decide to come soon. It would be best if Chanchi also decides to come with Ba. Consider all these carefully.

Do not worry as to what I might think. Your decision will be acceptable to me.

Reach Durban two days before the steamer is to arrive. Keep an account of the expenditure incurred on this trip and take that money from the Satyagrahi Fund.

Blessings from here,

Bapu

---

41. This letter was written on either 24 or 25 June 1909. Sorabji Adajania was arrested on 24 June 1909, and 26 June 1909 was a Saturday, the day on which he was likely to have received his sentence.

2 September 1909

Chi. Harilal,

I read in Sorabji's letter that you will go to J[ohannes]B[urg]. I eagerly await your letter on Saturday. All my letters must have been received.

The settlement is not yet certain. From the signs I see that the settlement will not be total. You will find the details in the letter to Mr. Kallenbach.

The struggle that is to come will be sharp. I see us, father and son, spending time together in jail. I am happy about that. I wish to know your mind. I ask God to give you full strength.

I am tired of this country and its civilisation. I see no goodness in it. We have to learn some things from here and therefore coming here becomes necessary. Otherwise, I see no need for being here. I observe much and think a lot. I constantly feel that it would be good if we were together in prison.

Convey my regards to all. I do not have time to write separate letters to all.

Blessings from Bapu

[P.S.] No definiteness about settlement yet. If a settlement is not reached soon, there is some talk of the English deputation going to India, returning in time for the next session of the English Parliament. Thereafter in October or November, I am proceeding to the Transvaal to be arrested. But nothing definite is yet decided.[42]

14 October 1909[43]

Chi. Harilal,

There is no letter from you. I would not expect one now. I blame that mad little Kamdhuk[44] of a daughter. She must have explained to you that nothing is to be gained by writing now.

---

42. This paragraph is in English in the original.
43. This letter contains the main arguments of *Hind Swaraj*, which Gandhiji was to write aboard *SS Kildonan Castle*, from 13 to 22 November 1909. On the day he wrote this letter to Harilal, Gandhiji also wrote his now well-known letter to his associate H.S.L. Polak, giving an outline of the main arguments of *Hind Swaraj*. (See "Letter to HSL Polak, October 14, 1909", *CWMG*, vol. 9, p. 477–82.)
44. A colloquial expression for the mythical cow Kamadhenu.

My views have altered much by what I have seen here. In a true sense they have not changed, but ideas I felt dimly have been strengthened.

I no longer desire to be a doctor. Hospitals have wreaked desolation. I feel that the profession of doctors is the lowliest of all professions. I see no meaning in that profession. European medicine is sinful. It furthers the evil nature of man. It does so thus: I indulge in vice, I contract syphilis. The doctor cures me, others do likewise. Nature punishes vice. The doctor shows a way other than acceptance of Nature's punishment. This increases vice. The same is true for tuberculosis. I am certain that fewer doctors mean fewer patients. I feel that people should be shown how to remain healthy. But to be cured by medicine is useless. Most of the diseases arise either out of our ignorance or indulgence. The way is clear and simple; we must suffer patiently. Many such arguments come to my mind, but I enumerate only these few.

I clearly see that the country's deliverance is in satyagraha. My mind bears testimony that there is no other way. I clearly see that railway, telegraph and such like have only harmed people, and have done them no good. This idea was plying upon my mind. But now it occupies more ground.

I do not see knowledge of letters as imperative. I see that knowledge of letters devoid of morality is very harmful.

I clearly see that modern civilisation is satanic activity. There is no need for machinery in either India or elsewhere. Machinery has wreaked havoc on people and people have been weakened by them. And they continue to be weakened.

We have only one thing to learn from this civilisation, we must actively propagate *dharma*. Charlatanry must go, if charlatanry goes we are free even today.

There is no harm if those in whom this idea has flowered live by it, till it grows in others. Not just that, it behoves them to alter their lives immediately in accordance with these ideals.

Many such ideas occur to me on this basis. Today I have free time; hence I place my ideas before you, for you to consider them. Do discuss them with me.

I feel that India has very little to learn from others.

I had anticipated that I would be able to leave by the end of this month; but now those hopes are dim. I see that it would be mid-November. There is little hope of an agreement. You would see the details in my public letter.

Your mind must be steady.

Blessings from Mohandas

Chi. Harilal,[45]

Karsandas Kaka's letter is enclosed for your information.

Mr. West writes that the monthly expenditure of our household is between ten and eighteen pounds. If true, it is a torment to know. You must know and reflect as to why our expenditure is so high. You must know how poor I am.

Blessings from Mohandas

26 January 1910
Wednesday Night

Chi. Harilal,

I write this from Mr. Kallenbach's tent. I think we may not be able to meet when you are released. I intend going to Durban to receive other warriors. I think I will be arrested while I return. I have two letters from you. I write my response and share my thoughts with you.

---

45. This letter was probably written after 26 November 1909 and before 29 December 1909. Gandhiji replied to Albert West's letter regarding the increasing expenses in Phoenix on 26 November 1909, and wrote a letter to Maganlal Gandhi on the following day expressing similar concerns. (See "Letter to A.H. West", *CWMG*, vol. 10, p. 79–81; and "Letter to Maganlal Gandhi", *CMWG*, vol. 10, p. 81–82.) On 29 December 1909, Gandhiji wrote to Albert West regarding the changes to be made in Phoenix and in the running of the *Indian Opinion*. (See *CMWG*, vol. 10, p. 106–08.) The size of the *Indian Opinion* was reduced from 1 January 1910.

I have reports of your health from those who have been released from prison. Similarly, I have reports about your conduct. I am satisfied with reports about both. All those who have come out, and especially Mr. Kitchin, Mr. Naidoo and Mr. Nanalal, said many nice things about you, which I was proud to hear.

I have already written about the matter of your going to England. If you insist on going I will send you. Arrangements can be made. I intend to make arrangements that you deem fit. It is not my intention to rule over you or to make you concede that only I am right and the rest are useless. I regard you as a friend and counsel you accordingly.

You will agree that so long as the struggle continues one cannot do anything else but stay in prison. After your release, if you cannot do without it, spend at the most fifteen days in Phoenix. It is desirable not to go there if you can bear with it. If, instead of deporting you, they release you in J[ohannes] B[urg], go to Phoenix with the consent of Mr. Kallenbach and others, and court arrest after fifteen days.

It is worthless to speculate about the struggle. You will see it when released. At this juncture I feel that a settlement would be reached before that.

Your argument about Manilal is correct on the surface. You have not dwelled deep. You are not going to prison for me to secure the trust of the community. Manilal too does not go to the prison for this reason. I do not consider Maniya an ordinary person. In some ways he is an extraordinary boy. For him, the prison is not an immoral place. That it lessens love of luxuries is an insignificant reason for going to prison. It is true that he may not understand the struggle fully. It is a mistake to think of Manilal as a sapling grown in a nursery. Compared to you, Manilal is more careful about looking after himself. You have some mistaken sense of shame, which he does not. The situation in Phoenix is the primary reason for this. Chanchi and he would have got along well. But I saw that Manilal was not very helpful on account of Ba. He could not look after Chanchi well because of Ba's disposition. Ramo and Devo[46]

46. Ramdas and Devdas Gandhi.

were not in the least in his control. Ba's health was not good and Maniyo's heart was restless. He was impatient to be free of Ba's grip. He bore her fire with patience. He was in a hurry to gain education and struggled for it. He wrote to me while I was in England. He had shown readiness to go to prison on your behalf. He wrote to me that he was eager for imprisonment.

I consider prison to be a place of higher learning for those whose morality is formed. Fortunate are those who have gone to prison since childhood. Such a person can give great service in the future and thus attain self-realisation. Those who are trained to bear suffering and to live in simplicity are less likely to be tainted if they were to go to England to seek knowledge of letters. I believe that one learns the great vow of celibacy by bearing the suffering of imprisonment. Swamiji had some bad habits but Maniyo remained untouched by them. He spoke to Swamiji about his own conduct. In some such matters his morality is mature. For a child such as him, jail is a source of great education, have no doubt about it.

I am in search of a good teacher for you. One cannot find teachers by searching. I do not think of sending you back to the country[47] to study under someone. I have benefited by having both of you under me. I believe that I can give you education and not cause harm to morality. But our circumstances are such that I have to be satisfied with the prison.

I had seriously considered all your arguments before sending Manilal to prison. I told him that my views were contrary to yours. I had also discussed it with Chanchi and sought her counsel. Mr. West and others felt that the step was right. Mr. Doke disagreed for other reasons.

It is good that you shared your thoughts with me. It is your duty to do so.

Manilal will be released on Friday. If I change my views subsequent to my meeting him I will inform you. In a way it is good that his first imprisonment is only for ten days. Talking about it and experiencing it are two different things.

Read my chapters on swaraj carefully. Read also what I have written about the benefits of hawking and Tolstoy's "Letter to a Hindoo" as well. It would

47. India.

be good for you to read issues of I[ndian] O[pionion]. My letters from England are worth looking at. You should read both the Gujarati and English sections of the issues that have been published in your absence.

Motichand Odhavji is dead. His son has sent a letter informing me of this. I have kept the letter for you. You must write a letter of consolation to him. It is my impression that Ratilal is your friend.

I am not writing about the changes made in Phoenix. You will know when you go there. We will talk about your doubts, if any, regarding them when we meet. There is much that is new, but I have no time to write about all that.

I have made some changes concerning Chanchi. She was taught composing and is now engaged in that work. I assume that you would like this. She likes the work. She is a girl of good character. She therefore asked what your views would be. She was reassured when I took the responsibility. If your view is contrary to mine, stop her from working as a compositor. I want to give up my practice as a lawyer altogether. In the end I must do with the three pounds that I will receive from Phoenix. I cannot provide for all in this sum. I therefore felt that if Chanchi were to work, she too would receive some payment. We are labourers and peasants. A peasant family does labour and farming. Therefore, even Ramdas is being similarly educated. I cannot say what Ramo would eventually turn out to be. Chanchi does good work even now. Her mind is also filled with joy. She would be of help in case of a crisis in the press. Thus, in every way this seemed a correct decision. If you differ from me, make changes only after serious deliberation. As I gain in experience, I realise that the thoughts expressed in my writings on swaraj are high and mature.

Among the married in Phoenix, you are the only one to have succeeded in observing celibacy. Preserve it like a jewel. It is my desire that till death you retain your essence, remain free from fear and your loved ones remain steadfast to you, even bearing great pain. Such is my blessing as well. I have great hopes for you and Manilal. I constantly wish that you two brothers become capable of nurturing the work begun by me.

What more shall I write? If you go to the prison again and have the opportunity, do study well.

I can only desire to give you a kiss, but cannot give it. I desire to kiss you and to that extent I have the attachment of a father.

Blessings from Bapu

I am preserving the letter regarding Maniyo for you to read.

Chi. Harilal,[48]

Your letter at hand. I am very happy that you have been arrested. After you discharged your duty, I ought to have courted arrest. Act with patience and intelligence. Write to Phoenix regularly. Bear your lot with a smile. The struggle is likely to end soon.

Blessings from Mohandas

21–24 Court Chambers
Corner Rissik
Anderson Street
P O Box: 5588
Johannesburg
14 February[49]

M.K. Gandhi
Attorney

Chi. Harilal,

I am unhappy that there is no letter from you. I am not confident that you stay there for studies. When I sent a cable as asked for, you bring up the excuse of studies. I am unhappy about this. I believe that you act at your own

48. Harilal was arrested six times during the satyagraha in South Africa. This letter was written after his arrest. Gandhiji writes that the struggle is likely to end soon. Based on that, we can infer that the letter was probably written after Harilal's arrest on 23 June 1910.
49. The year is not mentioned. This letter would have been written before 1911 as the Court Chambers were brought over by Gandhiji's former assistant Lewis Ritch in 1911. Gandhiji's last recorded appearance as a lawyer in Johannesburg was on 30 December 1910, where he defended his client Rambhabai Sodha.

pleasure and are not in control...[50] It is not the intention...[51]

Your lifestyle compared to mine...[52] on health I...[53] are good. I believe both of them would be better looked after here. Therefore, if you are not averse to staying with me and if Revashankarbhai consents, both of you at the earliest...[54]

Send me a telegram. I advise you as an elder. Do what pleases you. You have reached an age where I do not want to coerce you into doing anything.
Blessings from Mohandas

Vaisakh Sud 8[55]

Chi. Harilal,

I have sent you a long cable. I shall await a response to it at Lawley. There was no need for you to leave secretly. By doing so, you have set a bad example for your brothers and your friends. I have nothing more to say regarding your conduct. Ba's condition last night was pitiable. She has not stopped crying. Even Devo cried and all others are stunned. But we must forget all this.

When I talked to Joseph[56] about you, he gave me information regarding your movements and also your whereabouts.

It would have been good if you had not gone away in haste. It would have

---

50. As in the source.
51. As in the source.
52. As in the source.
53. As in the source.
54. As in the source.
55. Vikram Samvat 1967 Vaisakh Sud 8 corresponds to 6 May 1911. Gandhiji has clearly erred in giving the date as Vaisakh Sud 8. This letter was written to Harilal after he ran away from home and was identified at Delagoa Bay. Harilal left home on 8 May and after three to four days was spotted at Delagoa Bay. He returned home to Johannesburg on 15 May 1911. This letter was most likely written after 11 May and before 15 May 1911.
56. Joseph Royeppen. A barrister and a satyagrahi, he was the only one aware of Harilal's intention to leave home.

been good if you had left having convinced me. It is not a matter of concern if differences of opinion arise between us. Do what you wish to do. I will advise you as a friend, accept whatever seems appropriate to you. I believe I would be of greater help in making a decision about where to go in the Punjab and such other matters. You ought to consider if you should go there or to any other part of India.

In the letter to Ba your message was that you are going to seek a livelihood. You informed me that you wish to study further. You had promised Sodha[57] and others that you shall meet them. Even then you did not meet them. I felt that your behaviour was no credit to us. You might be able to defend it; if so, do let me know.

If you do not intend to stay back even for a little while, do tell us by which steamer you are going. What about your expenses? Give us all such news. If you do not stay back, Ba's heart will break and there is no reason for that to happen.

I feel like writing more but I know nothing of your condition and therefore do not write.

You have sought monetary help from me. If your endeavour is good I will help you. You must inform me at least where you intend to study and what. I feel that Joseph is uninformed about this matter.

I do not doubt your morality. I know, wherever you may be, you will observe morality.

Blessings from Bapu

57. There were three members of the Sodha family who were associated with the Gandhi family and the satyagraha in South Africa. Sodha Ratanshi Mulji, Sodha Rambhabai Ratanshi and Sodha Revashankar Ratanshi. Probably the reference here is to Revashankar.

Tolstoy Farm
Lawley Station
Transvaal
Kartik Vad 8[58]

Chi. Harilal,

Mr. Kallenbach and I had gone up to Tanga to serve Mr. Gokhale. It has been three days since we were separated from him. We are now returning and at this place...[59] Both of us have purchased deck tickets. We have experienced two nights on the deck...[60]

You complain that I do not write regularly. I have to state just this: letters written to you must have been misplaced. Only this time has it been a month and a half since I last wrote to you. This has never ever happened before...[61]

I did not consider it proper to bind him in conditions. If I had placed conditions they would have been accepted. It was, and continues to be, my belief that it behoves us that a Parsi should benefit from a scholarship instituted by a Hindu. I expect great deeds from Medh.[62] Moreover, I do not see us getting more scholarships.

How can you be sent on the same conditions as Sorabji?[63] If I send you, it would be tantamount to negation of my ideals. I am unable to wish that you become a barrister. I do not desire that you be imprinted with vice. I can have only one desire for you—that you attain the capability to possess all that is truly mine in my character. Use the wealth that is character and increase it. It is my firm belief that this inheritance requires no degrees. I do not say that your needs and aspirations cannot be the same as those with degrees. I wish

58. Gokhaleji left for India on 29 November 1912 from Zanzibar where Gandhiji took leave of him. This letter was most probably written on 2 December 1912 from Darussalam.
59. As in the original.
60. As in the original.
61. As in the original.
62. Surendra Medh.
63. Sorabji Shapurji Adajania.

that all your good desires are fulfilled. May you succeed in your aspirations to attain glory in universities and other such places. I am confident that you will not forsake good conduct. Your desire to study in England is lodged in my mind. I shall help you if I remain alive.

I intend coming there in June–July if the struggle ends in March–April. I believe that my character would become firmer and more useful there. It is constricted here. I constantly feel that there is no country other than India for one who seeks full manifestation of character.

I understand about Chanchal. Ramdas–Devdas were born against my will after I became conscious of the need for celibacy. How then can I blame you? I wish that you and Chanchal continuously strive.

The eleventh discourse of Srimad Bhagvad Gita has many good thoughts, which I read in this book. It has been published by Sastu Sahitya. Make a habit of reading it, if you have already not done so.

Blessings from Bapu

Chi. Harilal,[64]

Your letter at hand. Why did you not write before 12 noon?

I cannot stop worrying about Rama and Deva.[65] I cannot understand how their condition remained so, for so many days. You should have reported about them on the very first day.

Both should be administered earth poultice and given a diet of roti and dry fruits. Do not give them dal-rice, etc. What is the colour of Rama's tongue? What did the doctor say when he examined him? You should write in detail about both of them. There is no report, as usual, about the institution in your first letter. It says nothing about happenings in Charlestown.

---

64. It has not been possible to estimate the date of this letter. It makes a reference to Gulabbehn's father, Haridas Vora. He had met Gandhiji on 4 September 1907, and had spent some time in Phoenix recuperating. The letter should have been written after that meeting.
65. Ramdas and Devdas Gandhi.

I am sorry to read about Haridasbhai.

I have sent Ba's letter for you to read. After reading it you must destroy it. Bear in mind what is underlined. If you cannot make Ba happy, it would be your failing. You should be determined to win her over. You must be playful around her. You need not be grave with her. Even if unreasonable, you must listen to her. You should remember that even now, and forever, you can sleep with your head on her lap. She would be happy even if you talk to her till she tires. I cannot teach you how to please her. That should be within your grasp. You must not think that you could break the norms of love and good conduct in trying to please her.

I point to you your failings and give advice through my letters, do not therefore think that I do not recognise your virtues.

I am not writing a separate letter to Chanchi. I need some time to write...[66]

Blessings from Mohandas

Thursday[67]

Chi. Harilal,

I do not want to write to Ba what you want me to write to her. She would be more angry because of it. It was just as well that you informed me. In case of...[68] you must explain that justice ought to be done. If you do not succeed at first, explain again and again with humility and affection...[69] It is not difficult for you to win Ba over with affection. In many such cases the affection of the husband is not as effective as the love of children for their parents. For, the love of the husband, howsoever honest, entails sensual enjoyment. The love of children for their parents is always free of sensuality. The husband–wife relationship is, to an extent, accidental. Love follows the

66. As in the source.
67. Not dated. It has not been possible to determine the approximate date on which this letter was written.
68. As in the original.
69. As in the original.

relationship, the reasons for which are not very difficult to grasp. Children are born of the body of the parents, and parents bear great hardships during the infancy of the children and give love naturally. Please convey all the news. I had five free minutes during which I wrote this. Someone has come to meet me, hence I stop here.

Mohandas

Chi. Harilal,[70]

You must make a habit of reading the newspaper, at least for a few minutes everyday. If there is a word that you do not know, or do not understand, you must immediately consult a dictionary or ask either me or Mr. Polak. This will increase your power of observation and sharpen your intellect. You must eat banana and such like perforce at lunch. If you feel the need for roti, make the necessary changes. Your constitution is still being formed and therefore you need to eat the foods that I have written about. I see the need for you to eat these foods at least once a day. You should drink one glass of unboiled milk in the morning, if it suits you.

Blessings from Mohandas

Chi. Harilal,[71]

The watch is without the key. Please send me the watch received from Mr. Isaac through Mr. Kallenbach. I will bring yours back. Mr. Kallenbach will come by the morning train on Thursday. We have to get a watch similar to Bapuji's.[72]

I do not see light on your face. I want to see a soft smile and light on your face always. I would like that you ask me many questions. At present, the state

70. Not dated. It has not been possible to determine the approximate date on which this letter was written.
71. Not dated. It has not been possible to determine an approximate date.
72. Gandhiji is probably referring to himself; this becomes clear when the term is used for the second time in the last line of the letter.

of the father is so pure that asking questions and seeking answers would do good. Just as Mr. Polak leads his life by asking me questions, I would like you to do the same. Bapuji can also act, having sought your opinion.

Blessings from Mohandas

Chi. Harilal,[73]

Your telegram makes me anxious. How did you miss the train? What will you do now? Do what you deem proper. Come if your courage is with you. I think your coming would be in order. If it is your fate you will get imprisoned immediately. I feel that they will not arrest you. My heart is in turmoil. A father's heart is on fire, leaving you behind. I must go for the sake of the struggle. I leave everything to your will. You will learn more from Mr. Polak.

Blessings from Bapu

[P.S.] Please read the letter to Ba.

Chi. Chanchal,[74]

You must give up any false sense of shame. Make attempts to forsake the fondness for jewellery. I want nothing from you by force. I wish to counsel you.

Be very careful about food and drink. Make sure that you take nothing but milk and milk-rice.

Understand and read the Gita*ji* and the Ramayana, later participate in it.

Blessings from Mohandas

73. Not dated. It has not been possible to determine the approximate date either.
74. Not dated. It has not been possible to determine the approximate date on which the letter was written.

Translator's Appendix 5

12 February 1908
Phoenix
Natal

Dear Mr. & Mrs. Doke,

Yesterday I sent a short telegraphic message thanking you for your great kindness to my father. I would now like to express more fully the thanks my mother and we all feel. When the sad news reached us my mother wished to proceed to Johannesburg at once, so great was the anxiety she felt. So it was with great relief that we heard of your kindness in taking my father to your home and giving to him the comforts of nursing and sympathy.

We can never forget your Christian and brotherly sympathy with our countrymen during the crisis and I feel sure that you would receive the highest reward possible.

I remain

Yours faithfully

Harilal M. Gandhi

per C.K. Gandhi

14 February 1908
Phoenix
Natal

Dear & Rev. Sir,

My father writes to us that you and Mrs. Doke have been treating him so well as to make him forget home in the midst of suffering. He says that you do not give yourself any rest and that even during night you often go to his room to see if he need[s] any assistance.

My mother asks me to thank you and Mrs. Doke very heartfully and for all your doing for my father.[1] She hopes that you may in the near future be able to visit the settlement at Phoenix and give us the privilege of making your personal acquaintance.

My mother is sorry that owing to her not knowing English she is unable to write to you herself.

With regards from my mother and with respects from my brothers and myself,

I remain

Yours faithfully

Harilal Gandhi

1. See Letter no. 6, Translator's Appendix 4, from Gandhiji to Harilal, probably written on 20 January 1908, referring to his use of the word 'heartfully'.

Translator's Appendix 6

Solapur
6 August 1915
Shravan Vad 12

C/o
The Solapur Spinning and Weaving Company
Station Road
Solapur

My Beloved,

I have your letter. Last time I could not write a letter to you, while I wrote to Nanabhai. Do not think that I did not write because I am angry with you. I did not write because I had no time. Moreover, you were to leave from there, and I also had to move from here. With these thoughts, and believing and hoping that we would soon meet, I did not write. It was my hope that not only would we meet soon, but also stay together. God willing, meet we shall. But, staying together just as yet appears difficult. I am required to travel to Nagpur and its surrounding areas. That would take at least a month. After which, if the mill shop is not opened in this area, I will return to Solapur. Soon after my return, I will have to travel again for cotton procurement. The procurement of cotton is my responsibility; that was also the condition of my employment. I had asked to be given this work. There are prospects for moving up in this line of work. In this situation, I have to consider what I wish to do. There is no choice, but to perform one's duty. Unhappiness is followed by happiness. But what would be your situation during this period? The season for cotton procurement lasts for about six months. What would you do during this period? I am concerned about that. How can you travel with me carrying an infant? Or else we could have travelled together. I get, and will continue to get, second-class fare for travel. It would not have been unaffordable for me to have you travel with me. But, how can we travel with

Shanti, is the question. At the same time, how long can I keep you at Rajkot, your natal home? It is natural that you experience boredom. You are forlorn living in Ahmedabad. There are hardships in living there, that I understand. (But they are not so many as you imagine.) Both you and I need to think, given the circumstances. You think over it. I have thought about it and my thoughts are as under.

Before going to Nagpur, I will go to Ahmedabad for two days. If I am satisfied and if facilities exist, I will call you over and you should come. I will speak with Bapu and have the possible hardships removed. But if I am not satisfied and if difficulties persist, I shall not ask you to come. If this is acceptable to you for now, I shall ask you to come once I am in Ahmedabad. You should be ready and leave for Ahmedabad as soon as I send you a cable. I will be there and we shall meet. If you are late, I may have left. And after some time, while returning by the same route, I will come to Ahmedabad to meet you. I will come often to Ahmedabad to meet you, have no doubt regarding that. Ba would like that. You would be able to stay for a longer time with Ba. She would be happy at heart and others would stop criticising. You will face no misery staying with Ba, I am certain of that.

Write to me after having thought this over.

Nanabhai would allow you to leave only after pajjushana.[1] One cannot leave home during pajjushana, that is also a fact. We should take Kanti along with us as of now. We shall deal with problems, if any, later. I see no difficulty in leaving Kanti with your mother after a while.

I think it will take me another eight days before I can leave Solapur.

If you are unhappy in Ahmedabad, if you are not treated well, and if I am convinced of it, I will take you away from there immediately. This is my word to you. You know that nobody would come in my way if I do not want you to stay there. I am miserable in your pain and joyous in your happiness. How will I remain a spectator if you are unhappy in Ahmedabad—I am your

1. Prakrit term for Paryushana, an annual Jain ritual for self-purification observed in the auspicious month of Bhadrapad of the Hindu calendar. The ritual extends from the fifth day to the fourteenth day of the bright fortnight.

beloved. "Come and fetch me"—I would rush to you on hearing these words. I would remove your misery if it were in my power to do so. Sri Ram is omnipotent. Hence do not be afraid. Be courageous and decide to live in Ahmedabad; write to me about it.

You write nothing regarding Shanti's health. How is Rami's tooth? How is my Rasyo?[2] Kanti's maternal grandmother would not tolerate him being deprived of anything. Kisses to you. Your health must be fine. I am well by the grace of God. My regards to all. How is Kumibai?[3]

Yours only,

Hari

2. Rasik Gandhi
3. Gulabbehn's sister

Translator's Appendix 7

Tele Address: Assiduity
4, Pollock Street
Calcutta

31 December 1918

R.K. Desai
Merchants & Agents

Affectionate Balibehn,

I received your [long] letter. Letters are unlikely to be misplaced. I will be careful.

I understand your fears about the children. Therein I see your affection for them. Have no fears. I have not given them away to the ashram. Please understand that they are with parents. They will visit you as well. It would not be wrong for you to visit them [in Ahmedabad]. Do not have anxiety regarding me. Regard me as your brother-in-law, as before. What can I write regarding another marriage? Do you not know my feelings for your sister? How can I put a blot on those feelings! In discussions about my possible remarriage, allow me my silence. Time will do its work and all will know when the time comes. But for your solace, I give you my promise that I will inform you if I enter into another relationship. I used to tease your sister: "Porbandar women are better." But that was joyful banter. Therein lies my unprecedented feeling for her. You may not know, but towards the end of her life your sister had developed great affection for our servant Jhilu. He was a good, honest and religious servant. He was mild and hardworking. Your sister liked these qualities, because they are rarely to be found in servants. She, therefore, liked him. I used to tease her: "You show great love for Jhilu." Your sister would get angry, I would laugh and then we would reconcile joyously. You may not know but I am ready to give anything that he asks to the servant, for the sake of your sister. I like him as he was beloved to your sister. But the poor man's wife has also died and he has gone to his native place. If giving my life brought me any merit, I would have given my life for your sister. But suicide is considered a sin. If not death, I have pledged her my life.

Just as you have not been able to say much with regard to this subject, I too have not been able to say much to you. We will talk when we meet.

Just at present I am concerned about acquiring money, hence I lead a merchant's life. We will consider other matters once Rami's health improves.

Consider Bapu as you would your father. Please ask after the children, but do not be worried about them. What can be better than their being with him? Though an aunt, you are like a mother to the children. My mother is a mother to you. You would get your way with such sentiments. I have no doubt that Kanti is a son to you.

For the time being I shall stay in this region. From time to time I will come and visit you. You and Manibhabhi should live in harmony. Carry Damarbhai along with you.

Rami's health improves day by day. Be on the lookout for a good husband for her. Be on the lookout discreetly. No one should get a sense that we are looking around for Rami. Keep that in mind. We shall do the needful later. Do not ask anyone. If you consider the Modh families, you would get an idea as to who belongs to which family. If the family is good, the boy will be good as well. We should look for a good family. We can concern ourselves about the boy later. Keep writing to me. I do not hold a good opinion of Kathiawadis (except the coastal people) with regard to their straightforwardness. Therefore set your sights on the coastal people.

I do not think that any aspect of your letter remains unanswered. I ask of you only this—if you accept my advice and act accordingly, I would belong to you.

I hope your health is good. Ask for things that you need. I am fine. My dandvat to Manibhabhi.

I met Kamu in Mumbai at her in-laws' place for about five minutes. I left soon, as I had to set off to Calcutta. There was not much time for conversation at her in-laws' place. I am ever happy to care for her welfare. I still consider her a child. Please write to her that it would make me happy if she were to write to me.

Shubh,[1]

Harilal

[P.S.] Even if Nanabhai does not come to your house, you should go to his. Consider him as you would think of me. I have written to him.

Calcutta

16 February 1919

Affectionate Balibehn,

Received your letter, a postcard and yet another letter. My laziness is the only reason for my delayed response. You might therefore ask how do I conduct my business if I am so lazy in responding to letters. Laziness in business means difficulty in finding food; hence lethargy in business is unaffordable.

What can I possibly write in response? You are made from the same blood that I worship. My feelings for you therefore increase day by day. I want you to be free from worry. Do consider my children to be yours. Their staying in the ashram for the present is good for them and for me. If you consider what is good for us good for you, then this arrangement is good for you too.

I want you to write to my Ba regarding Rami. She will do what is appropriate. I cannot bring up that matter at present. Moreover, given Rami's health, it is not a matter for me to broach. But you can bring it up anytime. And just by writing to Ba. If I bring up the issue, it could only be with the assurance of success. At present, a direct approach from me is unlikely to succeed. If you write to Ba, Bapu's attention will be drawn. He will pay attention to any truthful and good issue. I believe that he is more concerned about Rami than I am. Not just that, these are also his words. Therefore, I am free of worry. Do keep writing letters to the children.

1. Literally, 'auspicious'.

Convey my dandvat to Manibhabhi.

Gangakaki would have performed the year ending rituals after your sister. I had sent a telegram to Nanabhai asking him to request Gangakaki to perform the rituals, as he did not have the time. You must have given clothes to Brahmins from among the clothes of your sister. My health is good. Do not be worried.

Shubh,
Regards,
Harilal

Calcutta
9 June 1919

Affectionate Balibehn,

Received your letter. I was thinking of writing to you, meanwhile I received your letter.

Did you go to the ashram on your way back from Mumbai? How are the children doing at the ashram? I also wanted to know your experiences of the ashram. Do write about them the next time.

My laxity in writing to you is not due to absence of feelings for you. I cannot but feel that with the passing away of your sister I am uncared for. I not only loved her, I worshipped her, I was afraid of her. She guided me and I was guided by her. Such was my disposition towards her. You would understand that my sorrow is limitless. I no longer feel that there is anyone I can call my own on this earth. I have many hopes with regard to you. If a time were to come to hand over the responsibility and the guardianship of the children completely to you—you have still not been able to assure me if you would be capable of caring for them with the same feelings of heart as your sister. The assurance cannot be given by mere words or letters. Just as the light of a lamp is never hidden, similarly this too would come to light.

I write to you with pure feelings and an open heart. I write to you as a friend would. I wish to say nothing by claiming to be your superior or one concerned about your welfare. I might be late in writing, but will continue to write to you. Do not stop writing because I do not write.

Ask for anything that you might need without hesitation. I need not say this. Dandvat to Manibhabhi. How is Tulsidas? How is Kumi? Where does she live? Write all such news. I am well. My health is good.

Regards,
Harilal

Calcutta
13 August 1920

Affectionate Balibehn,

Received your letter. I could not reply by the return post, as I remain very busy with my work and business. Moreover, doing business without money causes many anxieties and requires hard work.

My health has improved considerably. There was an injury to my teeth. I am better now. One tooth remains bad, it will improve gradually. There is no cause for concern. Earlier there was a fear of losing three to four teeth, it is no longer so.

You give me no news from your side; do write about it. Even if I do not write, why should you not write?

Where is Kamu? Does she know? When did you last see the children? What have you decided about Rami? How is her health? I want your consideration on all such issues, but I fear that you do not think about them.

My Ba and Bapu lead a life of asceticism. It is not so for us. Therefore, such burdens should be borne by us. I bear my share of the burden. I need a woman's help. I look towards you. I keep feeling that you are unable to give me the assurance that you will bear that burden. I need from you the same absolute confidence that your sister had for me. It is for you to obtain similar confidence from me. I write all this, as I am worried about Rami. Write to me having thought about all these issues, I want you to have the same concerns as I do.

Pranam to Manibhabhi.

Regards,
Harilal

Calcutta
20 April 1921

Affectionate Balibehn,

I received your letter. Do keep writing. Do not think that I do not read your letters or feel bored reading them. I feel freed from anxiety when your letter brings me news of that side; it gives me assurance and hence your letters make me happy. Do not hesitate to write often and about all issues.

I am sorry that a death took place in the family of your in-laws. I am sorry too about the death in Manibhabhi's family. We have to live as God wills for us. You have borne the clouds of sorrow with equanimity; bear with this also and leave the rest to the will of God.

Stay as long as possible with the children. Gradually secure a separate room. Do not think that I am not worried about them. Unable to find any other way for the present, I am pained. But I have faith that all will be well. I cannot get leave for the next few months. We will decide once I come there. In the absence of Ba...[illegible] I am free of worry.

My work is all right. Damarbhai's boy Liladhar works for me. At present he works for Rs. 5 in our shop. We needed a person and he came. He eats his food separately. He sleeps in our office. Thus, we do not have to bear much of the burden. If he learns some work he can work in other places too. A cook has been retained for my kitchen. There are two of us, my partner and me. Sometimes there is a guest. I stay in my old room. My partner is married. His wife was here for two to four months. She has been in their native place for the past seven to eight months, as she is pregnant. I slept in the office while she was here. My health is good. Do not worry. Give my regards to Behn Kamu whenever you write to her. I hope she keeps good health. Does Tulsidas earn these days?

I hope you are keeping good health. Write to me about things that you need or want. Nanabhai must be meeting you. Please ask him to write a letter.

Regards,

Harilal

No. 22
Amratala Street
Calcutta
23 November 1922

Affectionate Balibehn,

It has been long since I wrote to you.

Ba and Ramdas are here. The children are well. Rasik has typhoid; the fever has subsided after fifteen days. Due to weakness, he is still in bed. Manu has come with Ba. After a few days, once the Congress meetings are over, Ba will travel to the Punjab. She will return in fifteen days. She will be back here on December 7 or 8. The children will go back with her. As I wrote to you earlier and you agreed, the children should stay with you. I have told Ba that she should hand the children over to you. Manu can stay with Ba if she wants. Rasik, Rami and Kanti will stay with you. Please admit Kanti and Rasik to a school and teach household work to Rami. I will come there when possible and settle matters for her. It is natural for motherless children to be flung from hither to thither. Yet, I am firm in my resolve not to place them in the care of a stepmother. You, though an aunt, could be a mother to them and I am confident that you will be their mother. I have fought a lot with Kamu but I am confident that her feelings for me will remain the same over time.

I will send you money for the monthly expenses for the children. I believe that you will care for them even if I do not want to send the money for the expenses. But I will send it. You will not face hardship.

Your leg must be improving. If it is not getting any better you should come here for treatment; I am certain that you will get better. If so, come soon. You can come with Damarbhai's son Liladhar. You will get other companions, if you were to ask Nanabhai. One of our men, Manshankar, is in Rajkot. He will come here once his leave is over. You can come with him. You come here, you can get your leg treated and travel back with the children. Do whatever you feel up to. Dandvat to Manibhabhi. Do write from time to time.

Regards,
Harilal

H. M. Gandhi & Co.[2]
Coal Merchants & Commission Agents
22, Amratala Street
Calcutta
Telephone: 4514
Telegram: Agrahi

Affectionate Balibehn,

I received your letter. I keep feeling that I should come there and settle matters for Rami, but I am not able to come. The work here requires my presence. Since I cannot come, I do not even feel like writing letters. I keep thinking of you. I pass my days pining to come there. The desire becomes sharper when I write a letter and in order to prevent that pain I do not sit down to write. After your last letter, I should have sent you money. Even that I did not do. I have sent Rs. 100 with this letter, do please send a receipt for it. Along with Rs. 100 for you, I have sent Rs. 200 for Kaku so that he can come here with Kanti. Kaku owes us about Rs. 2000; we still have to recover the money. Despite that, I have to spend money on him. He said that his wife was ill and that he had to spend Rs. 300. He asked us for Rs. 300 to come here. I do not have trees that grow money. So I did not send the money. Now I have sent the money for Kanti's sake. Kaku has spread false rumours that he has to sit there because I have not sent him the money. Ba wrote that Kamu told her so in Mumbai. Even my mama wrote. Anyway, this was for your information.

Do not feel anxious if you need or want anything. Ask for it without hesitation. I will send money often. I will try and come [there] as early as possible. Do what you deem fit for Rami and Rasik's education. It would be good for Kanti to come here. He will grow clever here, and what he learns now will be useful in times to come.

---

2. This letter was most probably written in 1923. Harilal established this company in 1923, and in January 1924 he travelled to Rajkot where Ramibehn's marriage was fixed.

Do write to me about your health. Your leg must be getting better. See if you can come this side sometime. You can get your leg treated here.

Moreover, the documents relating to our house are with you. Send them to me by register. There is a possibility of securing a large order from a government department. I will send the documents back after having produced it before the department. Do not harbour any doubts. Send them by return post, registered. I hope you will trust me now. Rest all right, love to the children.

Regards,
Harilal

Delhi
11 March 1929

Affectionate Balibehn,

There has been no letter from anyone after you left Delhi. What is the reason? I hope that you will get either Kunvarji or Rami to write a letter.

How is everyone? Behn Kamu, Tulsidas and Bachu must be well. Has Tulsidas gone to Ahmedabad? Meanwhile, I went to Kanpur and returned to Delhi, where I am resting. I deeply mourn Rasik. The passions of the mind and the heart have receded. I feel like just lazing around. Do I have a choice but to make my mind stronger? I will stay here for another two or three days, after which I will go to Lahore. Nanabhai must have been informed. Tell him, what can I write! Nevertheless, I will write after my mind is somewhat steady. Do tell me if I could do anything for you. And do stay happy. Rest all right.

Regards,
Harilal

[P.S.] Write a letter addressed to me c/o Devdas Gandhi, Karol Bagh, Delhi.

Nizamiah Hotel
Frere Road
Opp. GPO
Mumbai
17 April 1933
Monday

Affectionate Balibehn,

I have no option but to write to you. How can our quarrels be for life? You are like a mother to my children. You care for them, how can I forget your benevolence? I wrote to Behn Kamu before writing to you. That letter must have come to your hands. Kamubehn has come here. When I learnt of it, I went to meet her at Ghatkopar yesterday. It is natural for me to be concerned about Manu.

Quite by accident, some days ago I met a Modh Bania Bhai Shri Bhagwandas Harjivandas Parekh and learnt that he wants to get his son Dhirajlal re-married. This I have learnt for a fact. Dhirajlal is married to your Narmada (Nabhi), daughter of Kalidas Kanji. It is said that Nabhi suffers from tuberculosis and that two of her brothers have died of tuberculosis; hence her in-laws want her husband to divorce her. She has not been called to her in-laws for a few years. I find Dhirajlal – Nabhi's husband – and his father good-natured. Dhirajlal appears to have a mature disposition. Can't we think of getting our Manu married to him? Manu may possibly decline [to marry] but I feel that we must be concerned about a sixteen-year-old daughter. The family I write about is good and wealthy. Even the shastras permit divorce from a consumptive woman. They are not the type who would ever decline to send Manu back to you, if she were to be married into their family. You could discreetly find out the complaints that Nabhi has regarding her in-laws. We can also take it in writing that Manu and Nabhi would not be made to live together. Don't dismiss this outright. Moreover, Prabhakunvar is no well-wisher of yours. Prabhakunvar is Nabhi's sister.

More specifically, I am tired of leading a lonely life. I need a life companion. I am considering marriage—that is, re-marriage. I say this with pain—if all of you become obstinate I will arrange for my own marriage, and absolve myself of responsibility for Manu. Then, the world will laugh at Bapu and all of you.

We should, to the extent possible, act harmoniously. Quieten your mind and write your response in peace. I hope that you will let bygones be bygones and not allow the passions of the past to brim over in your response. You must be well. Do write to me about Nanabhai.

Harilal

C/o M. Abbas Ali
Old Lakdi Mandi
House No. 5832
Nampally
Hyderabad (Deccan)
5 May 1934

Affectionate Balibehn,

Possibly Bapu wrote to you that I am in Hydrabad. I met him when he was here. Chi. Bhai Ramdas wrote that Kusum has died. Rami and Manu must be in good health. Chi. Kunvarji, Tulsidas and Kamubehn must be well. After meeting Bapu this time, my rage about you has receded. I do not write this to flatter you, but it is a true statement.

I write this out of my own need. My health no longer holds. I have had fever for the past eight odd days. I work, having settled here, for Sun-Life-Of Canada, an insurance firm. But fate does not favour me. I have no money. I have no clothes or cover. It would be an act of great kindness if you were to send by telegraphic transfer Rs. 50, upon receipt of this letter. I will return it in two months. I understand that you spend money over Rami and other children. To care for each other is a human obligation. Do care for me now. I eat at an eatery on credit promising to pay with the money that you would send.

Please remember me to Nanabhai and send through him Rs. 50 by telegram to the above address. Convey my regards to Anandlalbhai, Harishankarbhai and all others. I hope your health is good.

Regards,

Harilal

C/o Seth Tulsiram
Opp. Custom House
Nampally
Hyderabad
25 June 1934

Affectionate Balibehn,

After long I have received your letter. I accept that you have incurred expenditure. I accept too, Manu's rebuke. I am still in Hydrabad. Every four to six days I get high fever. I cannot eat anything. There is no one to give me succour or even to hand me a glass of water. I stretch my limits even in illness and look after myself. I have no money for medicines. If I could pay for a servant I would get one. But even that I do not have. I have no money for either milk or fruits. I feed myself with difficulty, how am I to nurture my addictions? Do forgive me now, but if you wish to save my life, send telegraphically Rs. 50 to the above address. I plead to you to even incur debt for my sake. The address has changed. Write the address in English. My hands tremble. I cannot write any more. I have a strong desire to come that side once I am better. I eat by selling my clothes and belongings. My condition is pitiable.

Regards,
Harilal

C/o Shri Ishvarlal Amrutlal Gandhi
Bhojeshwar Plot
Porbandar
21 September 1934

Affectionate Balibehn and Chi. Behn Manu,

I received your letter. Kamubehn must have reached. Convey my regards to her and it would be best if she were to get her eyes treated immediately. Do call the children. If Bhai Tulsidas has come, convey my regards to him as well. All of you must be keeping good health.

Manubehn, why this anxiety about studies? You should study slowly in a way that does not induce boredom. To give it up altogether is cowardice. Do not study by exerting yourself. If you cannot read much, or do not feel up to going to school, read less and go to school less. It is not a problem if you are absent. Your health is weak, and therefore Manubai, do what you feel like. Masi will not put pressure on you. Correspondence with Pujya Bapuji is going on. Most likely, I would as per his wish join khadi work. Bapu will either give me a salary or have a salary given to me. Therefore Manubehn need not worry. Your desire will be fulfilled. I am not sitting idle. I will inform you as to what happens. I wanted to go see a friend in Limbdi. I will not go now. Bapuji has drawn me towards him.

I will know about my movements after Bapuji's letter comes. I might have to come there to meet Narayandasbhai.

Blessings,

Bhai

Shraddhanand Shuddhi Sabha
Naya Bazar
Delhi
4 April 1937

Affectionate Balibehn,

Manubehn...[3] a child can refuse to be a child, but parents cannot refuse to be parents. Manu is your child. I am also there for them. I am bound to provide for them. God has granted me strength and will continue to do so. But, you still occupy the place of a mother. You should not take out your anger towards me on a motherless, powerless girl. You are intelligent enough to understand this. I have no doubt about that...[4]Abandon even the anger that you feel towards me. The acts of the theatre that is life are strange. To err is human. No one who inhabits a body is complete. Our atonement...[5]to abandon ill feelings and act with God as our witness. I never forget your acts of kindness.

If possible, do your duty towards Manu. For long, not a day passes when

3. As in the source.
4. As in the source.
5. As in the source.

I do not remember Kamubai. Blessings to her and her children. If she feels like writing to me, give her this letter to read. Look after Kanti's education. Allow him privacy so that he passes the examination. Do let me know if I could do anything.

Rest all right.

Regards,

Harilal

Translator's Appendix 8

Friday

Respected Behnshri,

I received your letter yesterday. Do forward the letter to Ba. We will spend all of Sunday with Kamu and leave for Calcutta on Monday 12 noon by train. I am leaving Rasik with Ba. You will be displeased, but we must make our minds stronger. Your brother-in-law has written that even Kanti should be left behind. But I have not left Kanti behind. How would he pass his days if he is left at someplace! Rasik has mingled well with the others. He will not take my going away very hard. Bapu did not say either yes or no. He left it to my will. I will not be exhausted and Rasik will be happier, hence I asked that he stay. After sometime, if he no longer likes it, I will call him over or will go and fetch him. It is not a binding decision. Whenever we want it, he can be brought to us. He is not being given to the ashram. He lives with Ba–Bapu. He will not be unhappy at all. Bapu feels that Kanti cannot be made to stay without me for even one or two months, as he would be spoilt there. Such are the ways of the world. It is futile for us to be attached, believing something to be only ours. Recite the name of God, therein lies fulfilment. Wherever the place He keeps us, may God keep us happy. I believe that Rasik is fortunate that he will live with Bapu from now on. Bapu would serve him so long as he stays there. These days Bapu carries Rasik and Kanti on his shoulders like a horse and takes them for their bath; and they follow him everywhere. He also plays with Shanti. Ba has conveyed her blessings. My regards to Bhabhi, Damarbhai and others. Do not write anything about the children to your brother-in-law. If you write, he turns recalcitrant. Tear the letter after reading it. I will write with more explanations once I reach there. If a decision is made to keep Rami here, I will stay at the ashram. More later.

Dandvat,

Gulab

Sunday

Respected Behnshri,

I received your letter yesterday and acquainted myself with the details. I wrote a letter to Kamu yesterday. My health is improving. I have no fever. My eye is also improving. I put drops three times and also wash it. Nanabhai's letter, asking for the money to be sent, has arrived. We will send you fifteen rupees shortly. Be careful about the expenditure. It appears as if we will stay here permanently. We need to save gradually for the sake of Rami. She has given up her studies. We will see about Shanti once he grows up. Rami's Bhai[1] will also observe the fast by eating one meal on Saturday. I will make ritual offering of water to the pitru during the month of Shravan. I had resolved to perform a Satyanarayan katha if I could leave before the second day of the lunar calendar. Meanwhile, I had to go to the ashram, therefore I no longer had to perform the katha. I have resolved not to eat udad.[2] We will go to Sarangpur when I come, till then I will not have udad. He is passing through a phase ruled by the malign influence of Saturn and has to wear a Saturn stone. Please write to me as to from where can I get one and of what type it should be. Rami's Bhai is convinced that he is passing through a phase controlled by Saturn's influence; please ask as to how many more years remain. Kanti received your letters in the morning and kept them with him throughout the day. He serves his Bhai well. He brings his Bhai whatever he needs. He carries complaints about me, Rami and Rasik to his Bhai. He has become a favourite of his Bhai. These days he does not teach. I teach instead. Rami too works well. Now I look after the children. I have made a preparation with edible gum, iron, sugar and ghee for my eyes. It is very beneficial for the eyes, the brain and the back. So I eat that every morning. The woman who cooks for us gave the recipe. The doctor will soon give me a tonic to improve my blood and strength. I will eat the preparation regularly. Do not worry about me. It would be good for Tulsidas to get a job paying Rs. 50 while we are here. If we stay together, the expenditure would also be less. That is also a benefit. But we think of you and feel that it would be good for you to

1. Refers to Harilal.
2. Split blackgram.

have Kamu in Mumbai. Someone should stay closer to you. One cannot come from here often. Kamu can travel up and down in sixty rupees. We can come when we have two hundred rupees to spare. This place is also very expensive. What we earn, we spend. Five hundred grams of milk costs four annas. Fifty rupees in Calcutta would be less for Tulsidas. It is sufficient for two people. I have written about it to Kamu. She has sent her views. It would be good if we can stay here permanently. Rami's Bhai too feels the same. It is too difficult to move from place to place. If the Sheth asks him to move someplace else, he will get relieved from the Sheth and start some business here. We are not thinking of leaving Calcutta. Sheth needs us, so we get to stay here. Please tell mother not to worry about me. My dandvat to her and Bhabhi. Do give me news from that side. Bapu is no longer angry with us. He writes to us regularly. Manilal lied and therefore he has to learn weaving in Madras with Bapu's help. Until such time he will not return to the ashram. He has been left to fend on his own. Bapu helps him from far. Untruth does not hold before Bapu. No harm ever comes if truth is spoken. Manilal has received your letter. He wrote that he has yet to reply to you. We have got utensils and other things. Only the dhoko[3] has not reached. Rajkot has become irreligious. So why should it rain? Rami's Bhai feels that if you had not bought the house you too could have come to live here.

We are all happy here. How much money did you pay to Lallubhai towards the bill? It would be good if a job for Tulsidas is found in Rajkot. Someone should stay near you.

I cannot forget Bapuji and Bhai. I remember them so very often. There is no one left in the natal home. Such is our fate! Popatkaka met Rami's Bhai twice. First time he asked about me. Rami's Bhai said that I had reached Calcutta. They met for the second time, but nothing was said. Our address was also given to him. People are so selfish. So long as the mother is alive the masi's sons and mama's daughter retain feelings...[4]

Dandvat,

Gulab

---

3. A long-headed wooden mallet used for washing clothes.
4. As in the source.

Translator's Appendix 9

Shraddhanand
Naya Bazar
Delhi
7 April 1937

Chi. Manu,

Kishorlalbhai informs me that your marriage will take place between the 14th and the 20th at Hubli. Be brave, take the name of God and be happy. If you have taken a vow of not writing to me, I would then not insist that you do so. What more would you need but the blessings of Ba and Bapu? If I have hurt your feelings, do find it in your heart to forgive me. That would be good for us both. Do ask for anything that you might need. If you write about your joys and sorrows, they can be redressed. I know that Ba will satisfy you in every respect.

Blessings,
Bhai

~

Hiralal Gandhi
Vedic Missionary
Bhartiya Shraddhanand Shuddhi Sabha
Naya Bazar
Delhi
24 April 1937

Chi. Surendra and Aa. Sau.[1] Behn Manu,

Received your letters. Did you receive mine and Devdaskaka's telegrams on the day of the marriage or earlier?

---

1. Aakhand Saubhagyavati.

I am glad that you are happy. It is my duty to be happy in your joys and unhappy in your sorrows. You may not feel that I further your joys, but you would not find me contributing to your sorrows. I desire not to be the cause of your pain. It is not your duty to view my personal character with disdain. Though evil, I am yours. No one would feel for you with the same intensity as me. Even the Gods surrender to love. Do not forget worship, recitation, daily rituals and prayer. Ask for things that you might need. Look after your health with care. If you write often, I would give you advice from my experience. It would be only advantageous and not harmful. For all things take advice from all, but do what you consider appropriate.

Today I leave for the Amritsar conclave. I will return on either the 4th or the 5th of next month and I will await your letter upon arrival. Please convey my regards to all. Please meet Ramibehn, Nirmalakaki and Ramdaskaka. Meet mama and mami as well. It speaks of humility.

Rest all right.

Blessings,

Bhai

Translator's Appendix 10

7 February 1944

Chi. Harilal,

I received your letter. I was happy to read it. I have been lax in sending a reply.

My health is as before. You should not worry. How long will you stay there?

My blessings to Manu, Rami, Kunvarji and the children.

Ba's blessings to all

Translator's Appendix 11

Gandhi Family in Prison during the Satyagraha in South Africa[1]

Table 1: Gandhiji

Date	Duration	Release	Remarks
10 January 1908	2 months	30 January 1908	Released early due to the agreement
14 October 1908	2 months	12 December 1908	
25 February 1909	3 months	24 May 1909	
11 November 1913	9 months	18 December 1913	Released on the recommendations of the commission of enquiry
14 November 1913	3 months	18 December 1913	-do-

Table 2: Kasturba Gandhi

Date	Duration	Release
23 September 1913	3 months	22 December 1913

Table 3: Harilal Gandhi

Date	Duration	Release
28 July 1908	7 days	3 August 1908
18 August 1908	1 month	17 September 1908
10 February 1908	6 months	9 August 1909
1 November 1909	6 months	30 April 1910
23 June 1910	3 months	22 September 1910
10 October 1910	3 months	January 1911

1. These tables have been derived from Chandulal Bhagubhai Dalal, *Gandhiji ni Dakshin Africa ni Ladat,* parts IV and V.

Table 4: Manilal Gandhi

Date	Duration	Release
19 January 1910	10 days	28 January 1910
7 February 1910	10 days	16 February 1910
24 February 1910	3 months	23 May 1910
30 September 1913	7 days	7 October 1913
9 October 1913	10 days	18 October 1913
27 October 1913	3 months	26 January 1914

Translator's Appendix 12

Family tree: Mohandas Gandhi

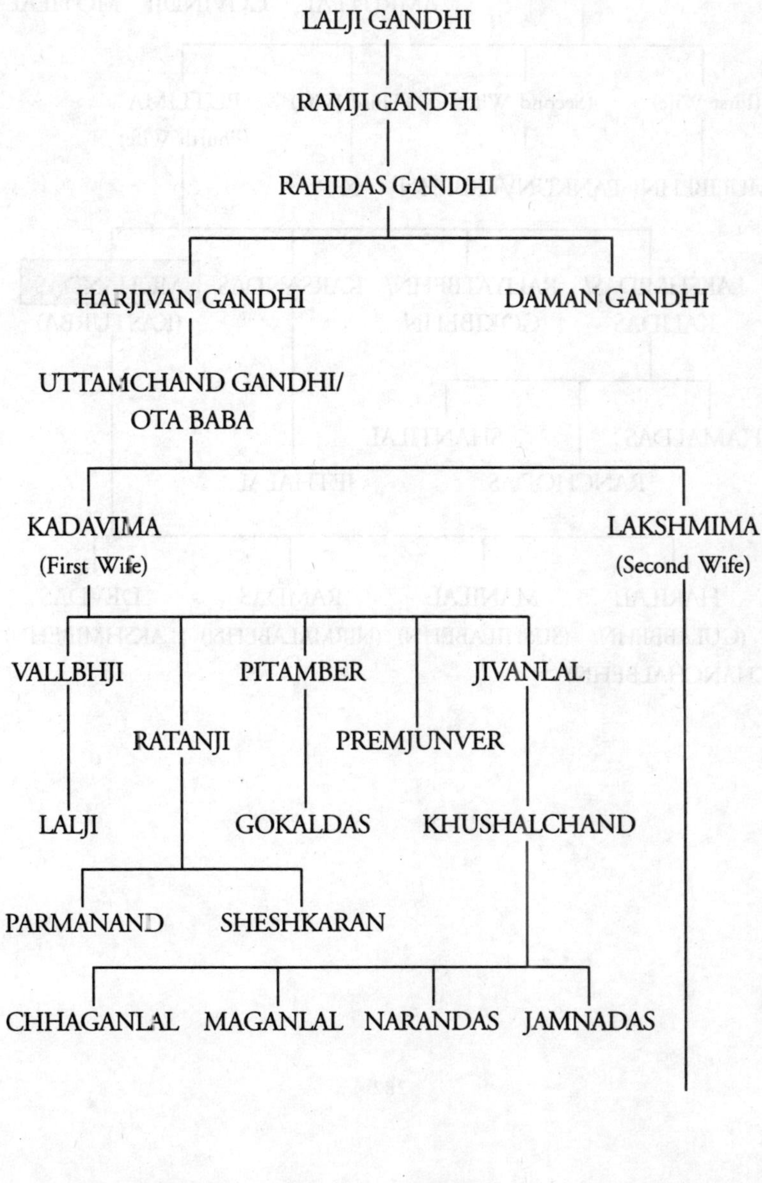

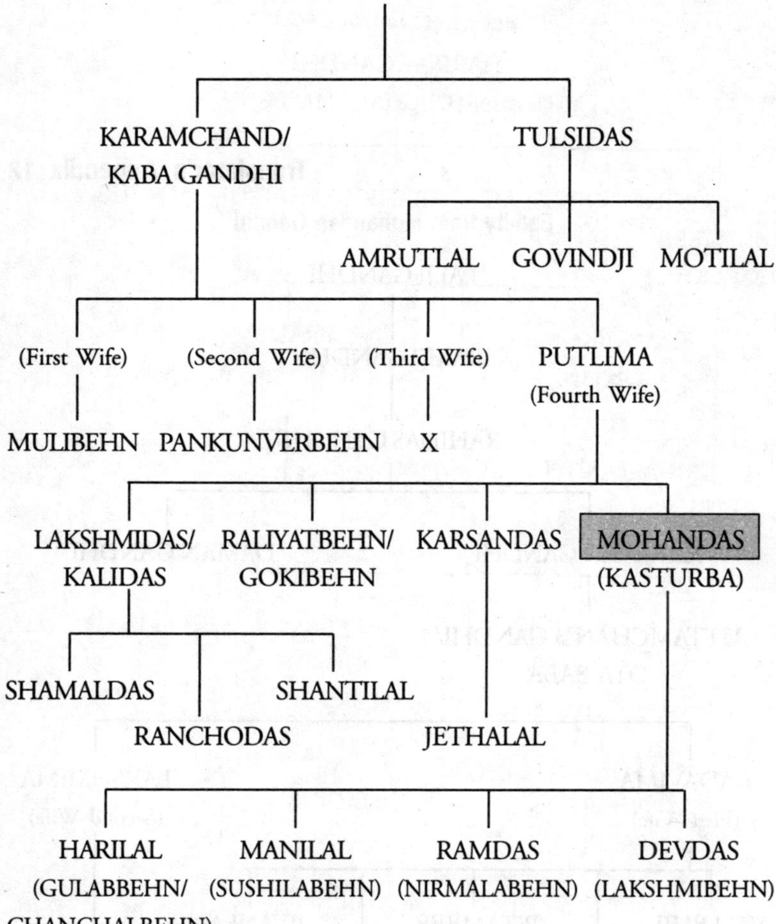
KARAMCHAND/
KABA GANDHI
TULSIDAS
AMRUTLAL
GOVINDJI
MOTILAL
(First Wife)
(Second Wife)
(Third Wife)
PUTLIMA
(Fourth Wife)
MULIBEHN
PANKUNVERBEHN
X
LAKSHMIDAS/
KALIDAS
RALIYATBEHN/
GOKIBEHN
KARSANDAS
MOHANDAS
(KASTURBA)
SHAMALDAS
SHANTILAL
RANCHODAS
JETHALAL
HARILAL
(GULABBEHN/
CHANCHALBEHN)
MANILAL
(SUSHILABEHN)
RAMDAS
(NIRMALABEHN)
DEVDAS
(LAKSHMIBEHN)

Family tree: Harilal Gandhi

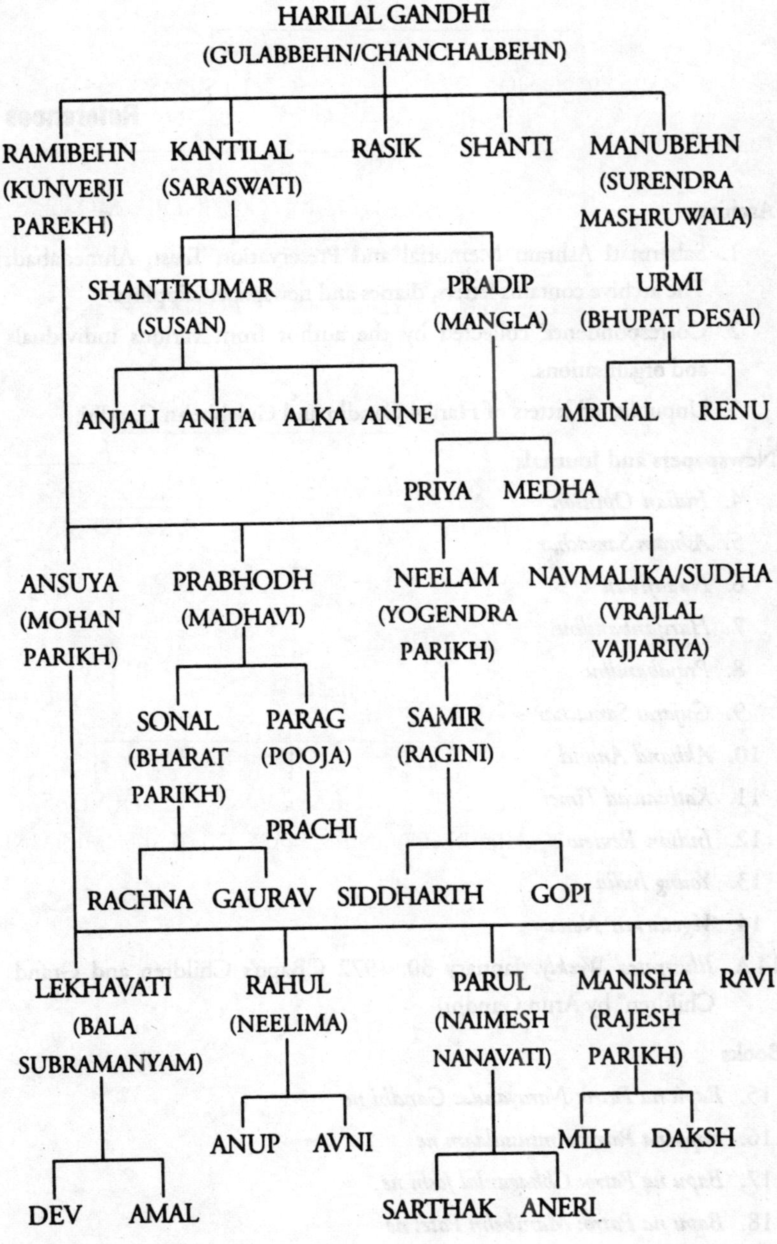

References

Archives

1. Sabarmati Ashram Memorial and Preservation Trust, Ahmedabad. The archive contains letters, diaries and newspaper clippings.
2. Correspondence collected by the author from various individuals and organisations.
3. Unpublished letters of Harilal Gandhi and Gulabbehn Gandhi.

Newspapers and Journals

4. *Indian Opinion*
5. *Ashram Samachar*
6. *Navajivan*
7. *Harijanbandhu*
8. *Prajabandhu*
9. *Gujarat Samachar*
10. *Akhand Anand*
11. *Kathiawad Times*
12. *Indian Review*
13. *Young India*
14. *Vegetarian News*

14 A. *Illustrated Weekly*, January 30, 1972 ("Bapu's Children and Grand Children" by Arun Gandhi)

Books

15. *Bapu na Patro: Narayandas Gandhi ne*
16. *Bapu na Patro: Amtussalaam ne*
17. *Bapu na Patro: Chhaganlal Joshi ne*
18. *Bapu na Patro: Manibehn Patel ne*
19. *Bapu na Patro: Jamnalal Bajaj ne*

20. *Bapu's Letters to Mira*
21. *Gandhiji ni Diary,* 1915
22. *Bapu Smaran,* Jamnalal Bajaj
23. *Collected Works of Mahatma Gandhi* and *Gandhiji no Akshardeh*
24. *Mahadevbhai ni Diary* (published and unpublished)
25. *Reminiscences of Gandhi,* ed. Chandrashankar Shukla
26. *Samsmrano,* Ramdas Gandhi
27. *Gandhiji na Samsmrano,* Shantikumar
28. *Jivan nu Parodh,* Prabhudas Gandhi
29. *Jivan Prabhat,* Prabhudas Gandhi
30. *Amara Ba,* Vanmala Parikh
31. *Shreyarthi ni Sadhana,* Narhari Parikh
32. *Gandhiji ni Sadhana,* Ravjibhai M. Patel
33. *Bapu ni Prasadi,* Mathurdas Trikamji
34. *Bapu ni Chayyama,* Balwant Singh
35. *An Autobiography or The Story of My Experiments with Truth*
36. *Life of Mahatma Gandhi,* Louis Fischer
37. *Gandhi,* Geoffrey Ashe
38. *Gandhi,* Robert Payne
39. *Status of Indians Abroad: Fiji—A Colony For India,* East India Association
40. *Gandhiji ni Dakshin Africa ni Ladat,* Chandulal Bhagubhai Dalal
41. *Rajkot State Directory*
42. *Gandhiji ni Dinwari 1915–1948,* Chandulal Bhagubhai Dalal
43. *Gandhiji ni Dinwari 1869–1915,* Chandulal Bhagubhai Dalal
44. *Otabapa no Vadlo,* Prabhudas Gandhi

INDEX